1971
A Year in the Life of Color

Darby English

The University of Chicago Press — Chicago and London

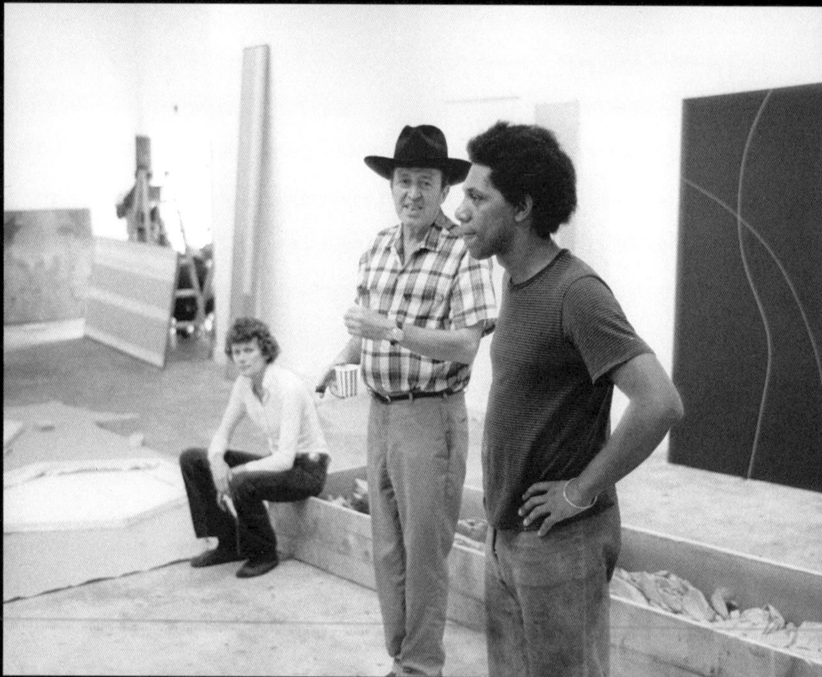

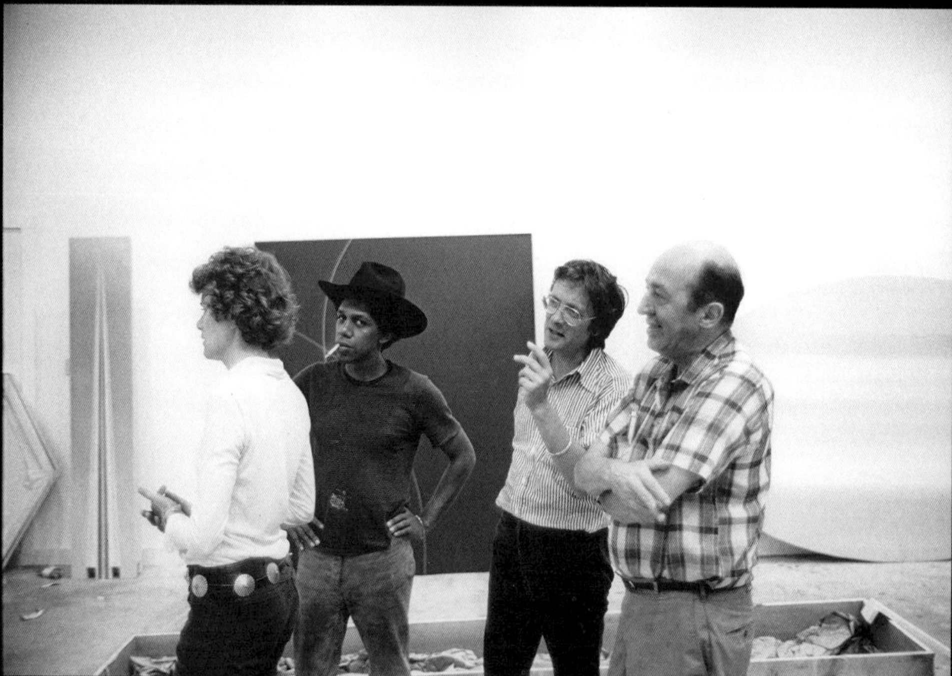

Introduction

Social Experiments with Modernism

Two photographs document an intriguing episode in late modernism that, late in the summer of 1971, moved quickly from conception to execution to the deepest reserves of historical memory (fig. I.1). The photographs were taken on August 21, 1971, in Houston. The first shows the critic Clement Greenberg standing between Helen Winkler, then a curatorial assistant to the art patrons Dominique and John de Menil, and the painter Peter Bradley. In the second, Greenberg is pictured with Winkler, Bradley, and Kenneth Noland. Residents of Manhattan at the time, Bradley, Greenberg, and Noland were in Houston to install *The DeLuxe Show*, which Bradley curated at John de Menil's invitation. *The DeLuxe Show* presented a group of modernist paintings and sculptures in a converted movie theater located in what people sometimes call the black part of town. The first racially integrated exhibition of modern art in the United States of its scale, the exhibition was, above all else, a social experiment undertaken in the belief that the best color painting of the moment had important work[1] to do in a southern black ghetto.

Figure I.1. Helen Winkler, Clement Greenberg, and Peter Bradley installing *The DeLuxe Show*, 1971. Menil Archives, The Menil Collection, Houston. Photo: Hickey-Robertson, Houston.

Figure I.2. Helen Winkler, Peter Bradley, Kenneth Noland, and Clement Greenberg installing *The DeLuxe Show*, 1971. Menil Archives, The Menil Collection, Houston. Photo: Hickey-Robertson, Houston.

1. In this study, the sense of "work" rhymes historically and conceptually with the guiding problematic of Julia Bryan-Wilson, *Art Workers: Radical Practice in the Vietnam Era* (Berkeley: University of California Press, 2009), a study its author describes as tracking "the unprecedented formation in the US of an advanced, leftist art not committed to populism, that is, not primarily concerned with making its images accessible to the very people with whom these artists [centrally Carl Andre, Hans Haacke, Lucy Lippard, and Robert Morris] asserted a fragile solidarity. At the same time, it attends to these artists' commitment to political change and their belief that art matters" (3). However, rather than artists, my own ascriptions concern exhibitions, their organizers, and the intentions and effects of each. In this way an alternative formulation of "work" may be

Color painting is a loosely arranged formalism that accommodated many painters' fervent exploration of hue, depth, density, texture, shape, and color relations' capacity to mutually inform pictorial structures. Greenberg was a cautious commentator. However, the grinning figure in the cowboy hat at the center of the first photograph suggests that he really got into the spirit of things.[2] The hat brings a welcome displacement of the old familiar Greenberg. It locates him in a foreign situation: somehow we know this isn't New York. One *wonders* what Greenberg is up to. The West that the Stetson evokes is more literal, differently mythical than the one Greenberg's criticism annexed as a stage for modernist triumphs. In a way it echoes a sentiment buried deep within Greenberg's singular criticism: his tremendous capacity for surprise.

Considerable reflection on this Greenberg triggered in me a reluctant acknowledgment that I belonged to a near-systemic culture of what Eve Sedgwick called paranoid reading and characterized as "a distinctly rigid relation to temporality, at once anticipatory and retroactive, averse above all to surprise."[3] The reader will recognize in paranoid reading a common disciplinary attitude toward Greenberg, one that places the critic off limits and often disparages modernism as a whole. But without renouncing this knowingness, one is powerless to understand the enterprise these photographs record. Surprise also triggered my intransigent fascination with that hat, and especially the event of its exchange.

The second photo (fig. I.2) finds the Stetson on the head of Peter Bradley, a Yale-trained color painter who, following Jules Olitski's lead, worked almost exclusively with a spray gun from 1965 to 1971. Greenberg and Bradley were familiar with each other through Perls Gallery, where the painter worked as associate director. Bradley

---

more apposite: "that which is susceptible of introducing a significant difference in the field of knowledge, at the cost of a certain difficulty for the author and the reader, with, however, the eventual recompense of *a certain pleasure, that is to say, of access to another figure of truth.*" Michel Foucault, "Des travaux," in *Dits et Écrits* (Paris: Éditions Gallimard, 1994), 4:367, emphasis added.

2. Someone in the cohort picked up the hat at Stelzig's, a (now-defunct) western apparel store in Houston to which Helen Winkler frequently took guests of her employers, the de Menils. Helen Fosdick, conversation with author, June 2011.

3. Eve Kosofsky Sedgwick, "Paranoid Reading and Reparative Reading, or You're So Paranoid, You Probably Think This Essay Is about You," in her *Touching Feeling: Affect, Performativity, Pedagogy* (Durham, NC: Duke University Press, 2003), 146.

enjoyed none of the commercial success of the artists popularly identified with Greenberg at the time, artists such as his friend and neighbor Kenneth Noland, or Olitski. Bradley was in it for the love of painting, an ambition Greenberg supported in him and in many other artists scantily represented in the literature on modernist practices.[4] Lively advocacy was crucial for tastemakers and career artists alike: modernism was embattled, and its cultural project remained unfulfilled. However confident they were in their idiom's rightness and power, those with modernist proclivities were quickly becoming (art) history. They were united in being marginalized, and this amidst widespread interest in Conceptual art, which then had little need for painting, sculpture, or galleries designed to flatter it. Indeed artists increasingly saw these as fetishes at best and obstructions at worst.[5]

On some level, *The DeLuxe Show* must have looked to Greenberg like a way to stay in the game. But there was a great deal more to the project, for everyone involved. The surviving principals recall neither who gave the hat to whom nor any particulars about its exchange, but its movement captures the animating spirit of the exhibition project: a casual statement of affinity between the races, expressed through a shared commitment to the ongoing relevance of abstract art, cheerfully staged in a site (the black urban ghetto) that we might otherwise write off as encapsulating the pitched racial crisis in which "post–civil rights America" then found itself. Circumstances made modernism available to cultural politics in ways it had not been in a long while.

4. Greenberg's meticulous personal schedule records an acquaintance with Bradley dating from April 1968, when Bradley wrote the critic to thank him for attending an exhibition of Bradley's work at Andre Emmerich's gallery, and continuing to at least January 1974, when Greenberg expected to help the painter hang another show, now of Bradley's own pictures. The two appear to have seen each other regularly during the intervening period, either in Greenberg's apartment or in Bradley's studio. Clement Greenberg Papers, Getty Research Institute, Los Angeles.

5. Greenberg had just months before given the Bennington Seminars, nine marathon sessions held between April 6 and April 22 and made up of talks and extended question-answer periods with faculty and students of Bennington College and observers. As Charles Harrison points out, these "furnished a kind of public apogee to Greenberg's long and influential career as an observer of modern art, and as such they coincided with the widespread interest in the Conceptual Art movement, perhaps the first global manifestation of an artistic Postmodernism," or a consolidation in artistic practice of the increasingly vehement backlash against the felt limitations of modernist institutions. Charles Harrison, "Introduction: The Judgment of Art," in Clement Greenberg, *Homemade Esthetics: Observations on Art and Taste* (New York: Oxford University Press, 1999), xviii.

But perhaps we ought not to be so surprised.

Together, the photographs—specifically, the warmly experimental scene they document—remind us that two main endorsements of the more notorious elements of Greenberg's practice were a protracted empathy with certain efforts to *do things with abstract art*, and an unfathomably deep concern for the conditions that permit modernism to thrive or to fail. For Greenberg, criticism was a forum not merely for the display of analytic acumen and erudition but for the public exercise of thought about the conditions of art's necessity.[6] His broad project teaches us to consider what things are in themselves: where they come from,[7] how they help us to construe the discrete ambitions they subtly realize, and how our experience of them might first frustrate but then expand our conceptions of the possible.[8] A rarely noted dialectical relationship between artistic practice and critical judgment discloses the empathic core of Greenberg's criticism: a work is literally unimaginable apart from efforts to understand it. Criticism at once sheltered and projected one of modernism's determining fantasies: that through a dedicated practice, the principal parties to art—the maker, the made thing, and its viewer—briefly attained a clarity and intensity no other kind of experience could offer.

Greenberg is as good a figure as any to help us recover the aspirational dimension of modernism, but my principal subject is the modernist sensibility that animated an unprecedented brief swell of

6. In this sense, he presumed to offer up "his" modernism as a safeguard for the health not just of the cultural but also of the psychological ecologies needed for art to thrive on its own terms, which was to say not as an instrument of the general society.

7. In Greenberg's 1971 view, for instance, "the tastes of artists themselves [have] kept high art going." "Night Six, April 15, 1971," in *Homemade Esthetics*, 145.

8. The lone entry in Greenberg's datebook for June 3, 1963, reads, "Major ingredient of successful art: *permanent surprise*." Clement Greenberg Papers, Getty Research Institute, Los Angeles, emphasis in original. And on night two of the Bennington Seminars, the critic had this to say: "Also you don't walk into a show of paintings and recognize certain things all of the paintings have in common and say, well, I know this kind of painting and I know it's usually bad. You have to give yourself and the art a better break than that. You look at every painting one by one; don't ever let a work of art get swallowed up in its category. And then you have to be ready. Because you can't choose to like something you don't want to like, you'll find yourself liking works of art that you don't want to like for whatever reason. And there you are, you like it. Now you've got to admit that to yourself. Most people I know in art life don't allow enough of that. . . . You get shaken up in an edifying way that I can't describe here, it's beyond me, when you are forced to like something you don't want to like." "Night Two, April 7, 1971," in *Homemade Esthetics*, 102.

dissent within black political culture that bore deep affinities with intercultural politics (another leftist formation that would become maligned, if not eclipsed, by 1971) and progressive individualism. This book looks specifically at an agenda of cultural work undertaken through recourse to late-modernist abstraction—or color painting, as it is more commonly known. Here color painting operates as a vehicle for the pedagogy I ascribe to Greenberg. Of the book's questions, the largest are simply, what did these exhibitions do to color, actually and conceptually? And how did this doing both reflect and affect the ways the larger culture was metabolizing color? The activities I study occurred at the fringes of modernist culture, in the late 1960s and early 1970s, and revived a social dimension from which modernism had been almost fully decoupled. As a result they *mattered* in ways that will have to be reconstructed.

On this Texan horizon, a modernist formation took shape that will be at least as unfamiliar to us as the image of Greenberg in a Stetson. It revealed a politics long buried within the modernism we have come to know largely through countermodernist art histories. For the first time since the postwar advent of the "great age" of American art, modernists, now on the defensive, were forced to work against the grain.[9] Their forms had to be explosive, and they even got a little queer. The exhibitions at the heart of this study exemplify this development.

At the same time, a profound change in the timbre of modernist criticism echoed this productive deformation of canonical modernism. Relationality entered the space of modernist criticism, leading to strenuous formulations of the interactive element of the aesthetic experience invited by the new painting and sculpture. The writers exploring this experience now found that it depended as utterly on a viewer's embodied presence and active questioning of an object's terms as it had on the mere presence of an object to behold. The phenomenological thrust of these new positions restored a body to optical experience (Krauss on Olitski—in many ways the star of

9. I am deeply grateful to Julian Myers for his suggestion, at an early stage of my research, that I conceptualize 1971 as a moment of possibility, rather than failure, for a late modernist imagination thrown into the shadow of advanced practices that now took a certain theatricality, or inclination toward performance, as a salutary starting point rather than a condition to be avoided.

The DeLuxe Show—in 1968), and the ethical project that comprised their observations forcefully asserted that body's contingency, how it was embedded in a sociopolitical medium (Cavell, "Some Modernist Painting," 1971). Though always there, this intimacy had not until this moment been seen as salutary in critical accounts of modernist art, and indeed some exemplary texts of the era had militated against the unapologetic *hereness* of new art.

An art object's need for intimate relation was, for Michael Fried in 1967, cause to banish it from the realm of art to take seriously. Probably it had been no coincidence that he explicated artists' widespread adoption of staining, monolithic construction, and optical color in a vocabulary of "opticality," "conviction," and finally "presentness," to convey the critic's efforts to prevent the loss of art that would seem to follow him collapsing into his object. For the very means of that object's construction—say, with paints that sink into a canvas's texture rather than massing atop it, or with color whose intensity actually blurs one's perception of the boundaries separating not only the elements of a composition but indeed oneself from one's object—now severely contracted the beholder's sense of distance from what he beheld. In Fried's criticism, art begat art with the unique forcefulness of genuine formal invention; it can seem as though viewer participation in the production of art was nearly perfunctory. But for our purposes, it is instructive that Fried had resisted still more emphatic minimalist efforts to underline participation in art's *reception*. Perhaps chief among the many unintended avowals of "Art and Objecthood," then, was that viewer and object no longer shared the same idea of distance as a structural necessity in the art situation.

Not every critic worked so vigorously to contain this development. Some, such as Stanley Cavell (himself a confidant and close, if differing, reader of Fried at this moment), welcomed it as a new way to understand the the fullness of a worldly encounter with art, and even used the same art that Fried believed would save art from objecthood. This criticism found a way to do modernism without abstracting away the sociality and the politics that made it matter. The avowal of one's intimacy with the work of art; the mutual cultivation of that attachment as its visual intensity affected the whole body; the suggestion that an ethics applicable to nonart situations was already contained in this structure—these were cryptic appeals to recognize late modernist art's immediate social relevance. Importantly, however, they were less cryptic than the criticism they revised. For them, intimacy was immanent to reception, involving what Cavell called "the courage of sensuality—to marry one's desire";[10] the experience of modernist art was pedagogical, and possibly even reparative, a proving ground for compassionate participation in the public sphere, when high-stakes encounters with strong difference were the norm.

As we have seen, modernist criticism in the mid- to late 1960s worked to mask its preoccupation with the relational-ethical questions foreclosed in formalist analysis. But as we will now see, late modernist criticism, which reached an apogee in 1971, actually declared color painting to be *about* being with the other, in the sense that its abstractness not only spoke to but *generated* the necessary difficulty of living with contingency. It announced the end of a modernist project dedicated to using this art to deny the centrality of contingency to contemporary life.[11] It did this by shifting critical emphasis to the theme of openness (Bradley: "this art is all light and open") and by privileging the inescapably relational question form (Krauss: "Olitski changes the syntax of the question 'Where?'"). The paranoid variant survives. The reparative one attempts rebirth in the following pages.

The many caricatures of "high modernism" thrust upon generations of students by its most ardent critics permit us to think of it only as a self-indulgent elitism epitomized by Greenberg, his followers (few of whom followed him very far), and their famously closed canons.[12]

10. Stanley Cavell, *The World Viewed: Reflections on the Ontology of Film* (New York: Vintage, 1971), 121.

11. Fried's seminal but largely forgotten "Modernist Painting and Formal Criticism" (1964) foretells the systematic denial of art's contingency that would characterize this art's most powerful criticism. At one dramatic moment, form swallows politics whole: "While modernist painting . . . has increasingly divorced itself from the concerns of the society in which it precariously flourishes, the actual dialectic by which it is made has taken on more and more of the denseness, structure, and complexity of . . . life itself." Michael Fried, "Modernist Painting and Formal Criticism," *American Scholar* 33 (1964): 642–48.

12. Reflecting on this trend in his sensitive introduction to a posthumous collection of Greenberg's writings, Charles Harrison writes, "In the journalism of the art world, Greenberg often appears as one who enforced a form of critical doctrine through his power as a maker and breaker of movements and reputations, and through his influence upon acolytes and upon the market. Prevalent as though this image has become, it is difficult to reconcile with the actual published writings, or to support with any but the most selective quotations from them." Harrison, "Introduction: The Judgment of Art," in Clement Greenberg, *Homemade Esthetics: Observations on Art and Taste* (New York: Oxford University Press, 1999), xiv.

the dominant criterion of political art—explicit coding—diminishes object-sense in favor of reading-for-"relevance," as though objects can't be relevant to anything that really matters. For within the contemporary constrictions of black art shows, the presence of a color painter would be seen to mitigate any curatorial ambition to exhibit blackness.

This book experiments with a way of historicizing modernist practitioners and their efforts in direct relation to both black political culture and late American modernism—for these individuals belong to both formations. I suggest a way to think of Black Art as something greater than a set of attitudes and motifs thrust by pervasive structures of racism into the disciplinary isolation it shares with its master discourse, African American art history. First, let us recognize that this isolation was elected and cultivated. While certainly a historical effect of exclusion from disciplinary mainstreams addled by prejudice and apathy, the edifice that Black Art and African American art history coconstitute was elaborated through cultural practices: theory and ideology combined with real apparatuses of authority and power. A frank perspective will allow us to see how little yet another history of Black Art can relate about these social experiments with modernism around 1971. Abstraction's role (or lack of one) in African American art history tells how thoroughly the subdiscipline constitutes an ideology of representation.

Discourses such as African American art history need to be examined historically in at least two ways: genealogically, in order to demonstrate their provenance, kinship, and affiliation with other ideas and with social and political institutions; and as practical systems for accumulation (of power, of ideological legitimacy) and displacement (of other ideas and other legitimacies).[19] This isn't an easy task: Black Art—and specifically the ideology of representation that underwrites it—enjoys an unchallenged hegemony in the liberal academy, even though its elaboration has often been destructive of the very individuals it would represent to history. What particularly need to be understood are the costs that African American art history has exacted from nonconforming elements and its strikingly effectual

19. In this characterization I follow the lead Edward Said established in "Zionism from the Standpoint of Its Victims," *Social Text* 1 (Winter 1979): 7–58.

discriminations between relevant and irrelevant black people. Recent years have seen a number of efforts to restore attention to the likes of Bradley, Frank Bowling, Barbara Chase-Riboud, Ed Clark, Melvin Edwards, Frederick Eversley, Sam Gilliam, Marvin Harden, Felrath Hines, Sue Irons / Senga Nengudi, Tom Lloyd, Loving, Joe Overstreet, Saunders, Alvin Smith, Alma Thomas, Stanley Whitney, Jack Whitten, and William T. Williams. Yet none of these efforts actually historicizes the intervening forty-year silence around these artists, or the fact that that silence is the result of a specific force and specific strategies, many of which still operate through the methods of the recovery agents themselves.

Bringing out the history of these artists and their early advocates, as I seek to do here, is part of a larger effort to resist the techniques of exclusion that continue to structure historical studies of difference.[20] The exhibitions I study evince that, in the context of "black art," modernism responded to the travail and expense of separation imposed by the essentialist vogue and carried forward in subsequent historical, critical, curatorial, and institutional practice. For these artists, taking up a position within modernism also meant taking some distance from the black community that articulated itself by insistently representational means. As it was framed publicly (and one sees this framing reflected throughout the literature), the resulting schism set the pleading, "relevant" images of a Benny Andrews, say, over and against the deductive structures of Frederick Eversley or Alma Thomas (fig. I.6, fig. I.7, fig. I.8). Modernist affiliations were dangerous: they signified that a so-called art front was, in fact, fragmented and that the black art world was anything but unified. Modernism was a connective space: it answered the need to nurture interracial relations in a situation marked—as chapter 1 demonstrates—by the forcible separation of things *for the sake of separation itself.* Abstraction answered an existential need for modes of knowledge, coexistence, and culture not separated out from the actuality of mixing, of stepping beyond boundaries—all decidedly more creative activities than drawing boundaries and calling this cultural production. With results far more culturally complex than the label *black abstraction* can even begin to suggest.

20. Cf. ibid., 11.

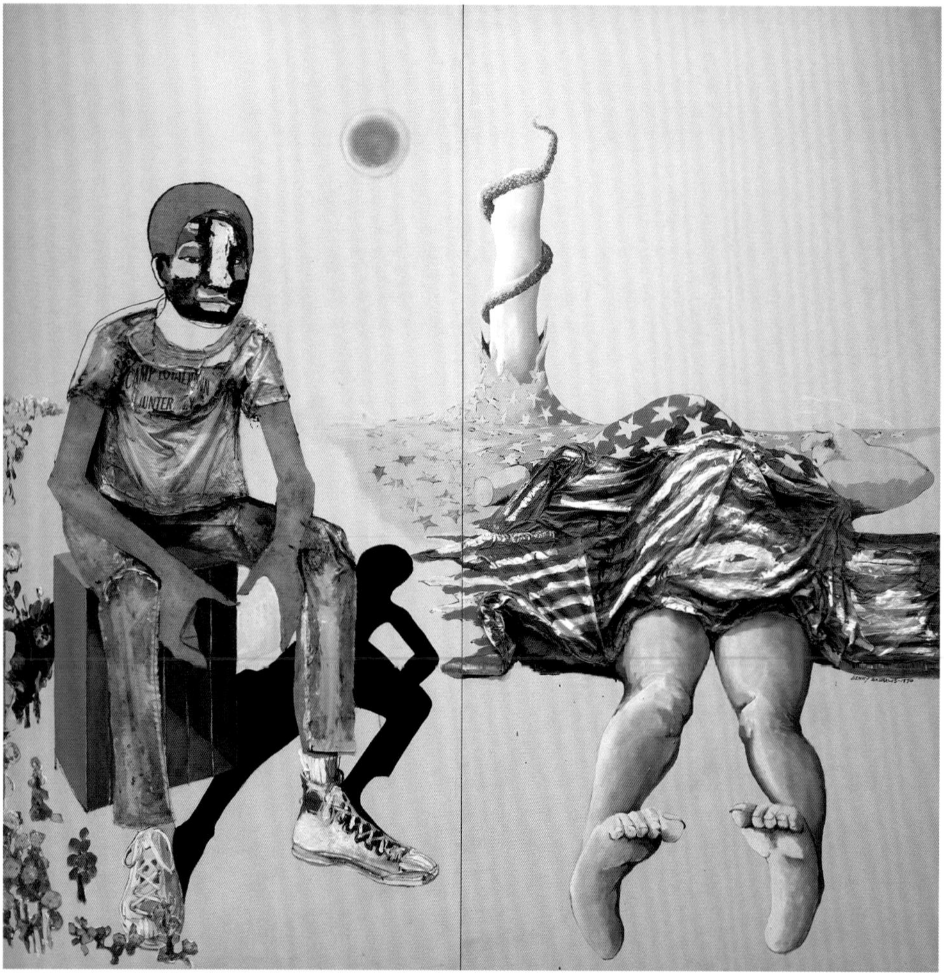

Figure I.6. Benny Andrews (1930–2006), *No More Games*, 1970. Oil on canvas with collage of cloth and canvas, diptych, 100⅞ × 49⅞ in. (256.2 × 126.7 cm) and 100⅞ × 51 in. (256.2 × 129.3 cm). The Museum of Modern Art, New York. Blanchette Hooker Rockefeller Fund. Art © Estate of Benny Andrews/Licensed by VAGA, New York, NY. Digital image © The Museum of Modern Art/Licensed by SCALA/Art Resource, NY.

Figure I.7. Fred Eversley (b. 1941), *Untitled*, 1970. Polyester resin, 20¾ × 7⅝ × 7⅜ in. (52.7 × 19.4 × 18.7 cm). Whitney Musum of American Art, New York; purchase (70.55). Digital image © Whitney Museum, New York. Courtesy of the artist.

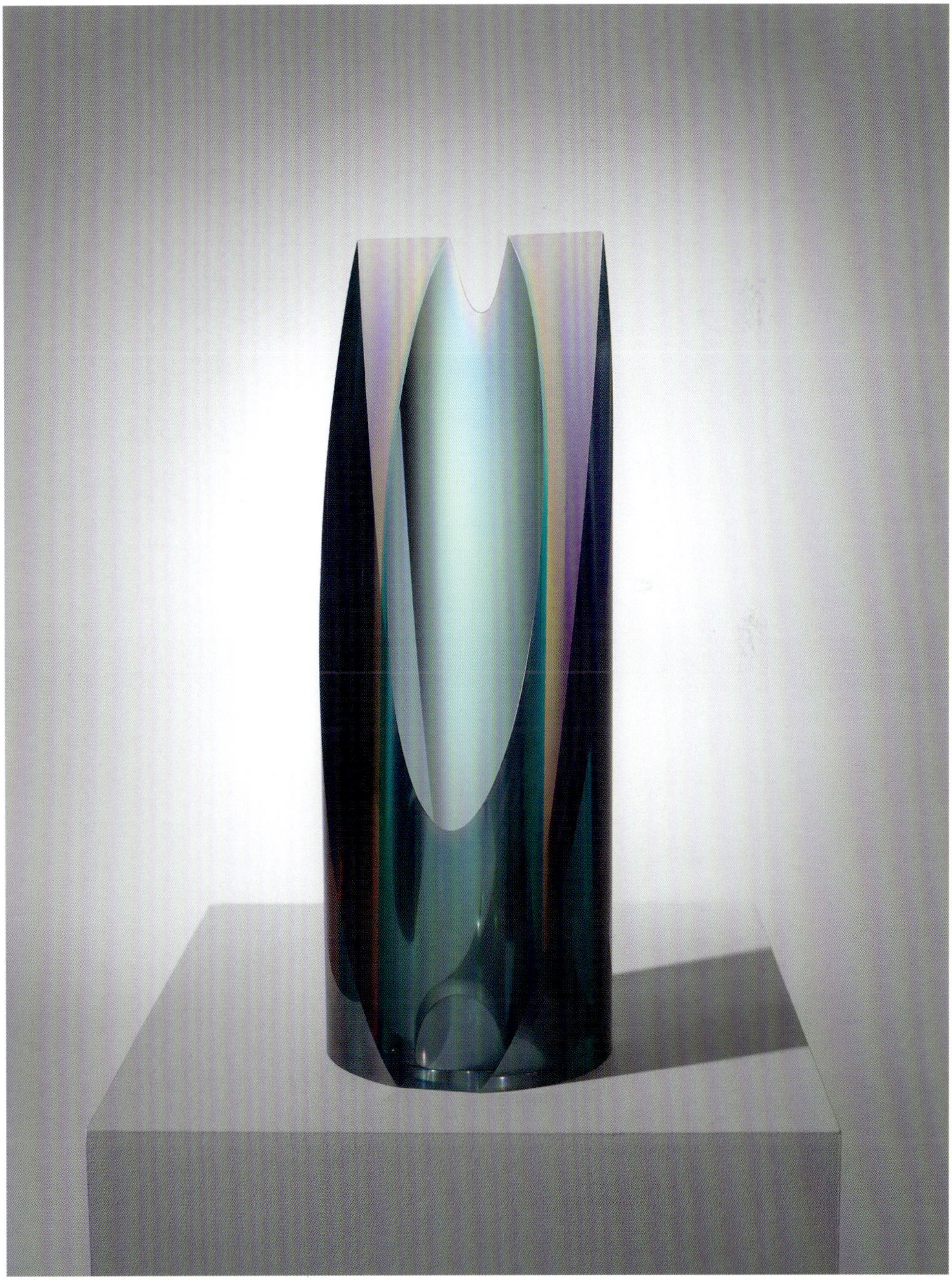

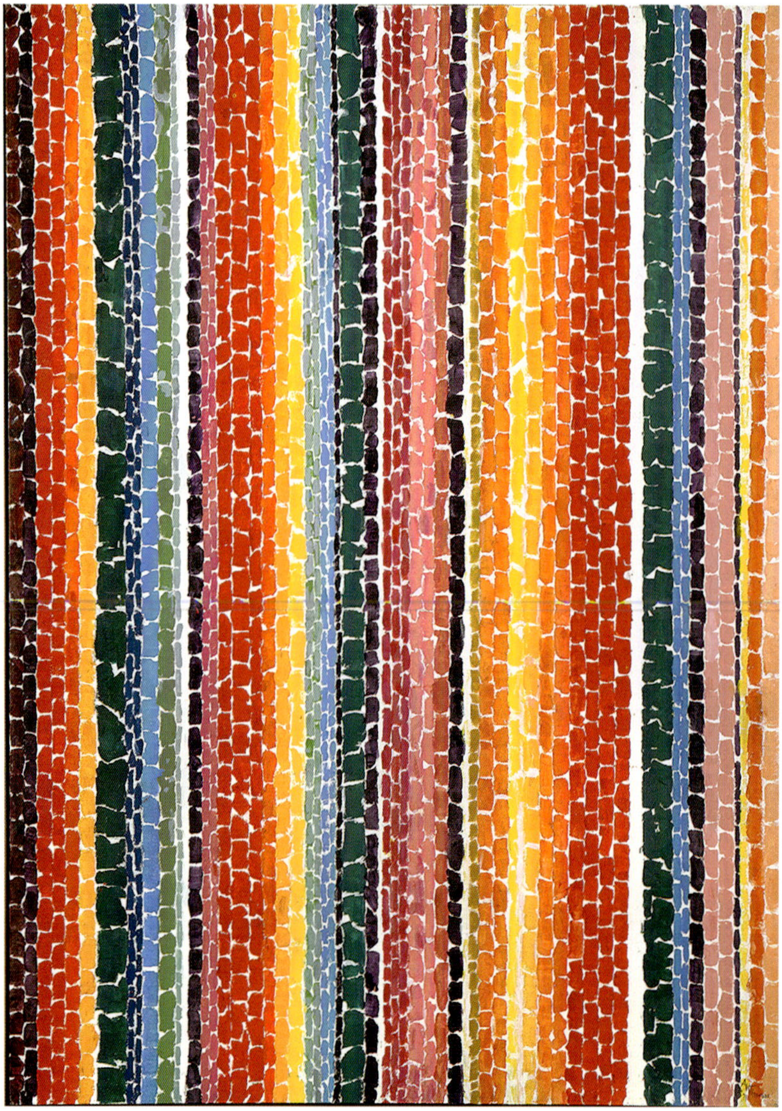

Figure I.8. Alma Thomas (1891–1978), *Earth Sermon—Beauty, Love and Peace*, 1971. Acrylic on canvas, 72 × 52⅛ in. (182.9 × 132.2 cm). Hirshhorn Museum and Sculpture Garden, Smithsonian Institution. The Martha Jackson Memorial Collection: Gift of Mr. and Mrs. David K. Anderson, 1980. Photography by Lee Stalsworth.

In 1971 modernism was briefly annexed to a specific but not yet broadly achieved mode of sociality. The ambition and intensity of the social experiments undertaken that year compel us to seriously consider what modernism made it possible to think and do that was positive in affect and how it helped repair conditions of alienation within and between racial communities.

That modernism had an integrationist appeal seems to have originated in a peculiar idea of community specific to late modernist art and its criticism (rather than in some "lost" politics). Bradley and his fellow black modernists belonged to a moment when modernist criticism first took pains to conceptualize artistic consciousness and practice in terms of an artist's field of references, which it always regarded as *a relational set*. Fried's critical representation of Morris Louis in 1970 serves as a paradigmatic case.

> Louis's paintings do more than underline or point to aspects of Pollock's canvases which otherwise one might not have noticed; there is an important sense in which Louis's paintings create the aspects in question. . . . At the same time, the fact that Pollock's paintings, and not those of some other painter, are the ones which Louis's paintings invest with meaning in this way testifies to the fecundating power of Pollock's achievement and makes that investment seem, or be, a revelation of what was, in some sense, already there. The paintings of Noland and Olitski stand in an analogous relation to Louis's work; and in general the unprecedented depth of relationships of this kind is one of the characteristic, even defining, features of modernist painting.[21]

Fried's text doesn't merely bring some "canvases" into a categorical affinity. It discloses a whole field of "relationships" bearing a special charge for the modernist. Such relationships may be writable (that is, explicable through critique) only when they occur between paintings. But undeniably they also provide the fixative that binds modernist practitioners themselves in community. *On this scene, painting engenders relations.* Modernism now established its cultural density by bringing individuals together across notable spans of time and historical experience. And for certain black modernists and their advocates, it was precisely this easy relationality that made art an unfussy way of doing integration: working as an artist by definition involved

21. Michael Fried, *Morris Louis* (New York: Abrams, 1970), 213–14 n7.

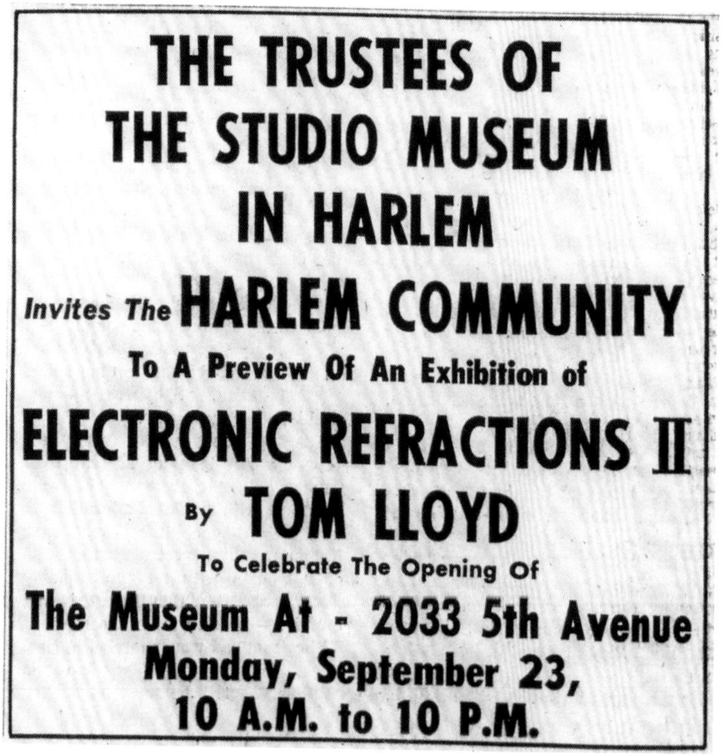

Figure I.10. Advertisement for Tom Lloyd's *Electronic Refractions II* exhibition, *Amsterdam News*, September 14, 1968, 16. General Research & Reference Division, Schomburg Center for Research in Black Culture, The New York Public Library, Astor, Lenox and Tilden Foundations. Courtesy of The Studio Museum in Harlem.

Figure I.11. Tom Lloyd (second from left) and assistants assembling works for *Electronic Refractions II*, an opening-season exhibition at The Studio Museum in Harlem. September, 1968. Courtesy of The Studio Museum in Harlem.

representative emphasis should be a kind of color insistence[43] that would manage the local complexities of exhibited works so as to keep blackness at the fore. Given that the priority of the museum was to avow a certain insistence on color, under its optic the larger place(s) "reflected" in the work—the sociality—literally connotes "impurity." Too much them, there, and I; not here, not we enough. The presentation of art as cultural material would contract rather than diffuse the pertinent cultural territory. Historians seldom acknowledge that the community reaction to Lloyd's exhibition was hostile. In fact one of Lloyd's sculptures "was mysteriously broken and the episode was explained by some as an indication of the failure of such

43. I borrow this fabulously elastic term from Adrian Stokes, who used it in a very different sense that I nevertheless find apposite: "By the insistence of a colour we usually understand the strength with which it bores itself into consciousness." Adrian Stokes, "Colour and Form" [1937], in *The Critical Writings of Adrian Stokes*, vol. 2, *1937–1958* (London: Thames and Hudson, 1978), 18.

'mainstream' art to relate to the black experience."[44] The episode wasn't reported until the Studio Museum's fifth anniversary, even though one month after the opening the founding director, Charles Inniss, resigned. Edward Spriggs, a poet and the editor of *Black Dialogue* magazine, succeeded him. Reflecting in 1973 on the museum's launch, Spriggs observed, "It was *unnatural* to separate the art work from the background of the people."[45] Between the person and "the people" lay all the difference: this was the principle that

44. Jean Bergantino Grillo, "The Studio Museum in Harlem, a Home for the Evolving Black Esthetic," *Art News* 72, no. 8 (October 1973): 48.
45. Ibid.

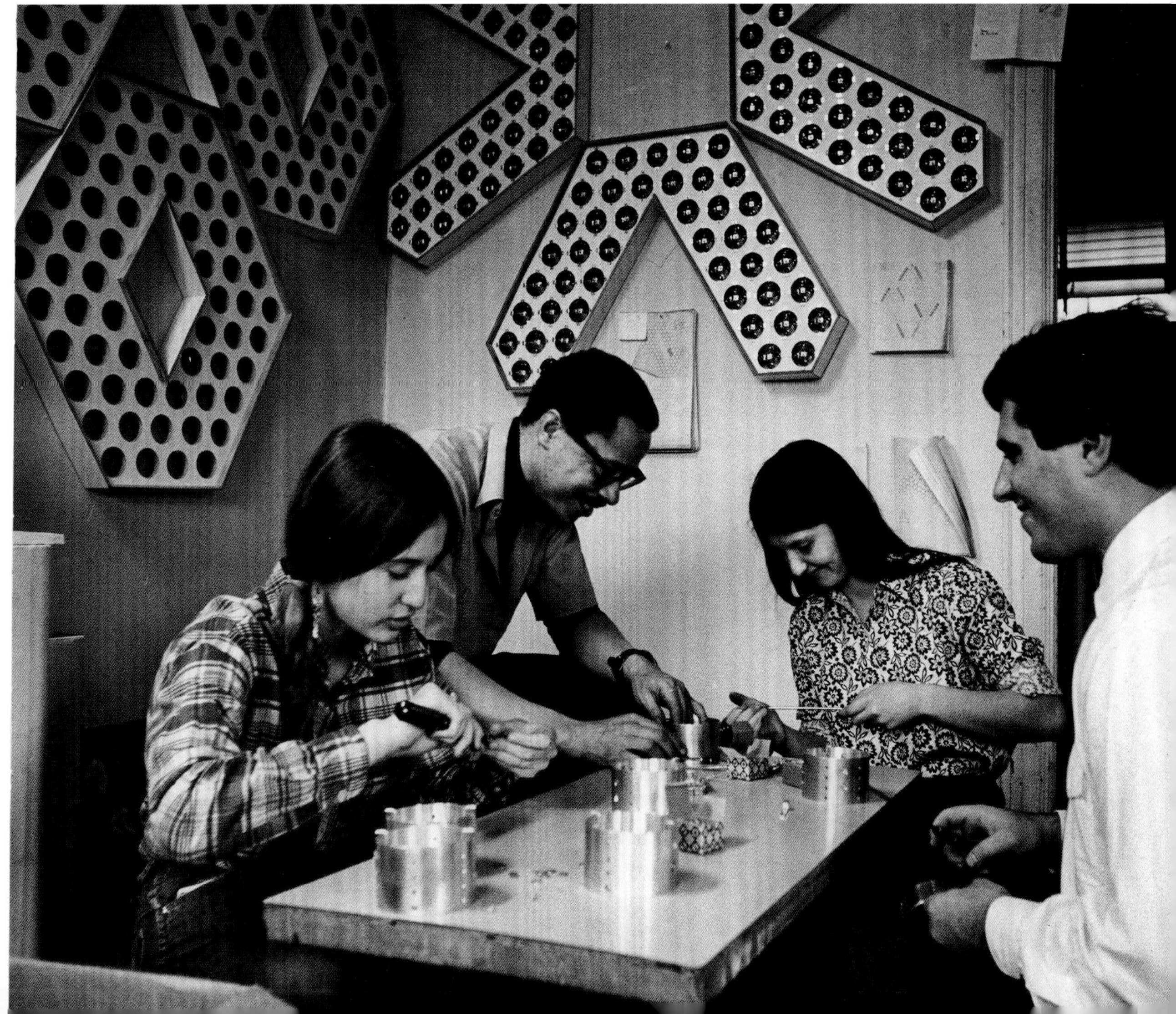

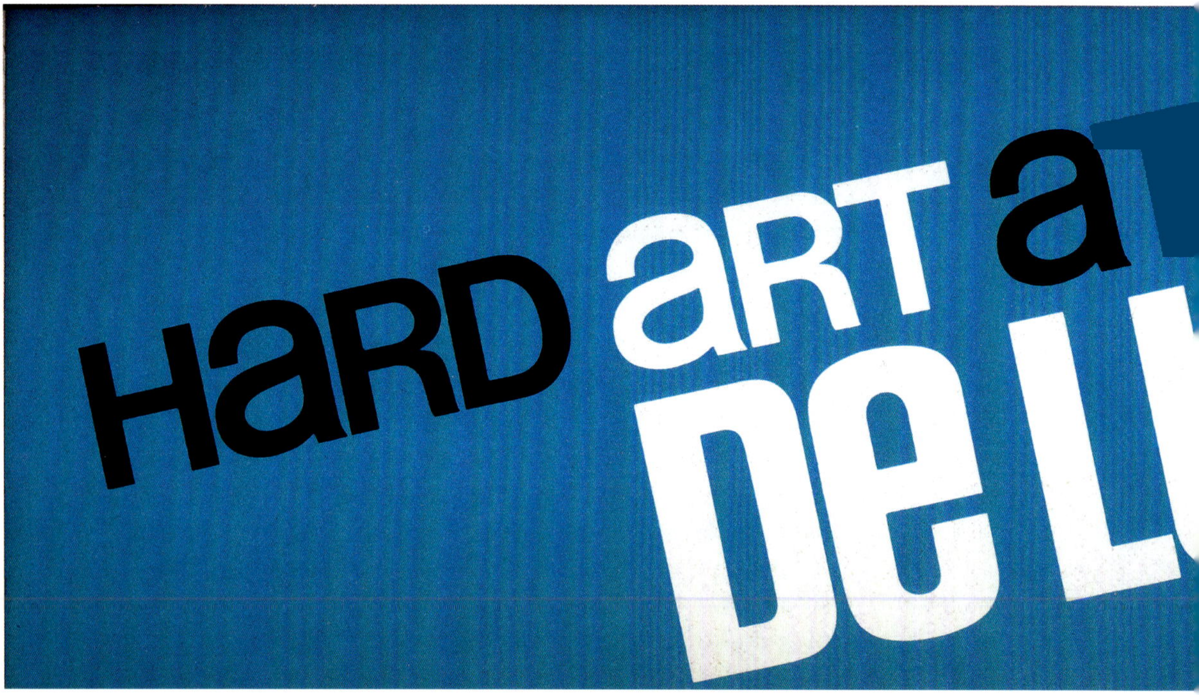

extended to do:[60] here it showed that color could be pushed beyond the limits of both its formalist functions and the rhetoric of emergent cultural formations, and could reexamine a defining problem of American life—color and color relations—in an exhilaratingly open-ended way. Ludwig Wittgenstein, Ed Clark, Frederick Eversley, Alma Thomas, and Peter Bradley: these individuals shared a passion for the opening articulations of color. And why not, given its proven capacity for what Greenberg called "permanent surprise"? Color, in this mode, was a consummately accommodating habitat for change.

By 1971 critics such as Amiri Baraka, Jeff Donaldson, Ray Elkins, and others had launched determined efforts to construe modernism as damaging to the efficacy of black experience. Chapter 1 assesses the peculiar fate of the black modernist in the writing of African American art history. Asking what kind of real conceptual work happens when the racialist position worries about abstraction in the ways that it does,

60. See T. J. Clark, "Clement Greenberg's Theory of Art," in *Pollock and After: The Critical Debate*, ed. Francis Frascina (New York: Routledge, 1985), 83.

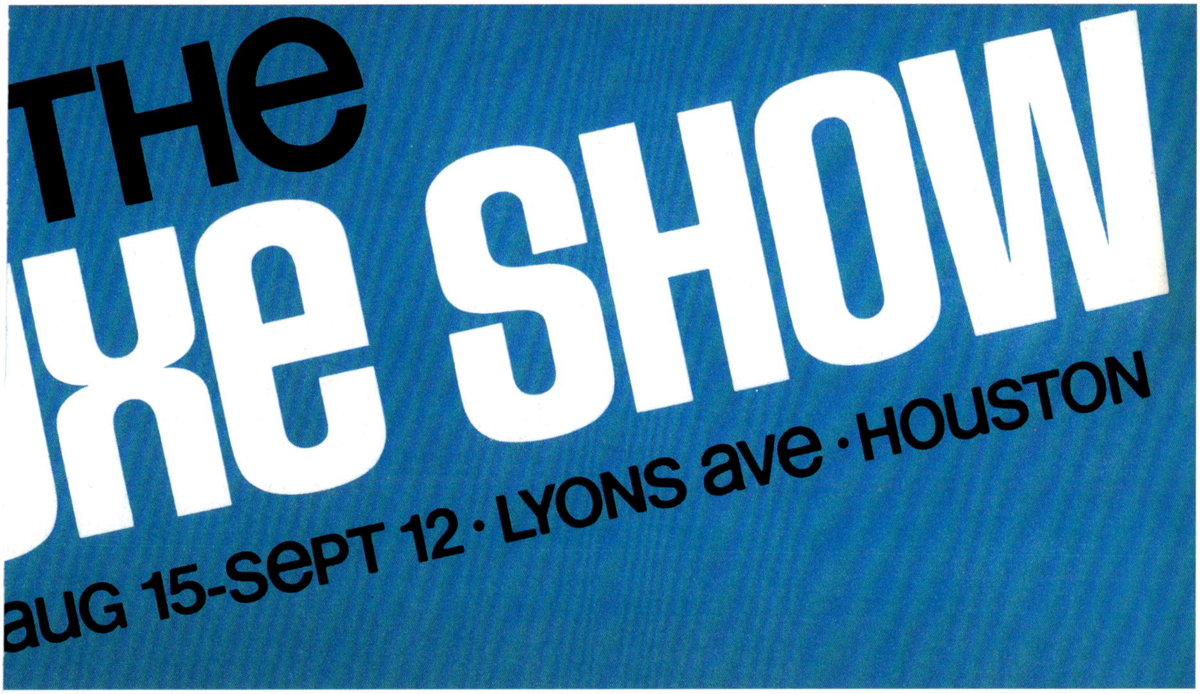

Figure I.12. Bumper sticker created to promote *The DeLuxe Show*. Menil Archives, The Menil Collection, Houston.

I share with Sedgwick a concern for the "local, contingent relations between any given piece of knowledge and its narrative/epistemological entailments for the seeker/knower/teller."[61] When a writer effaces the explicit nonrepresentativeness of the modernist object before her, what work does the resulting knowledge perform?

I will look at the form and method of a foundational text for modern African American art history, Cedric Dover's 1960 survey *American Negro Art*, before turning to more recent accounts. Dover's text inscribes more deeply than any other of the time the localist orientation that would increasingly shape accounts of black political culture. Because in Dover's analysis Negro culture is an antidote to the alienations of systematic racism, it constitutes a totalizing unity. Regardless of their cultural orientations, black artists serve Dover as numbers with which to populate a unique territory, one that consolidates a vast, interlocking set of relationships. In this context, localism also meant that the network encompassing individual artists'

61. Sedgwick, "Paranoid Reading," 124.

What Doty did for black modernist sensibility *DeLuxe* did for autonomous personhood. If *Contemporary Black Artists in America* made room for a different kind of idiom from that of representation, *The DeLuxe Show* sought to cultivate that agency. It was abstract work's "openness" and "freedom" that Bradley chose to showcase. *DeLuxe* challenged one of the strongest conventions of black cultural discourse, which held that blacks aren't capable of abstraction—though we are supremely capable of disavowing it as "the white man's art."[67] But to speak of abstraction in this way is to forgo the question of art. Instead it makes the art situation disclose for the umpteenth time that subtle forms of white entrapment are everywhere, and that representation is the paradigmatic site for affirming blackness (even in its absence). In averring that children were the ideal audience for *The DeLuxe Show*, Bradley was proposing that they lacked the mechanisms of disavowal that would conjure whiteness from abstraction. Exposing children to modernist work would, he fantasized, prevent their consciousness from being colonized by nationalist pedagogy and its "localisms of the mind." Black children were capable of abstraction. "They haven't been indoctrinated by ethnic art," he said. Specifically this art's emphatic openness and the resonance of color with countless features of daily life would show that the condition of being in the ghetto and experience do not necessarily correlate. The art in the show availed a mode of subjectivity not synchronized with the objective world. To confront abstract art is to confront the world as it exists for another person, as it is refracted by subjectivity itself. Between viewer and viewed there arises an orientation to the other that brings out one's own contingency. Hence Cavell's invocation of "abstracts of intimacy." The formulation is surprisingly apt in describing the exhibition as an array laid before viewers: it imagines a way of being with others without sacrificing one's privacy.

From a certain perspective, *The DeLuxe Show* looks like an

Sue Irons, Alvin Smith, Bob Thompson, and Ruth Tunstall. At the time of the exhibition Ghent held the position of director of the Community Gallery of the Brooklyn Museum, but Doty also knew him both as an associate of the Black Emergency Cultural Coalition, at whose demand the Whitney's exhibition was initially planned, and as a former consultant to Doty's own office at the Whitney, as well as that of John I. H. Baur, then the museum's director.

67. Vivian Ayers, quoted in D. J. Hobdy, "DeLuxe Art Show in Ghetto Met with Mixture of Reactions," *Houston Chronicle*, October 1, 1971, unpaginated.

exploitative public relations gambit perpetrated by rich whites on the black poor, or perhaps like a civilizing mission. My arguments engage such cynicisms as little as possible, though I recognize that some will think that I overindulge Bradley and his cohort's optimism. Let me be emphatic, then: unearthing optimism is a project of overriding concern for me. Modernist art may seem like anything but an easy path to an optimistic sensibility—"Come See Hard Art at the DeLuxe Theater" read the exhibition's promotional bumper sticker, which neighborhood children distributed all over Houston (fig. I.12). In fact that hardness, that difficulty, suffuses the scenes of this book: we find it in the nonpolemical articulations of most of the black modernists themselves; in Black Art discourse's strained reactions to them; in the futility of Doty's and Bradley's projects; and in the historical near-illegibility of their aspirations. Difficulty will accompany any optimism that arises in a situation which proscribes it so vigorously.

Shows like these are funny historical objects. Irrecoverable, they rhyme formally with that world of hopes, affects, and intentions that modernism made available to this coterie of artists. The exhibitions experimented with black cultural politics and with modernist art in ways that skewed both. In a crucial sense they were *creations*, but as specifically public events they also gave relevance to other, related attempts at creation: by breaking with the given state of affairs, they lent form to the hope that modernism appeared to offer and suggested other shapes that optimism could take. They invited the possibility that abstract painting and sculpture weren't the only ways to actualize black cultural work without resorting to racial positivism, which is just color insistence by another name.

By compelling this lost world, which only *might have been*, to function as an object, I want to suggest another direction that black cultural history might have taken or might still take: a way oriented not to restitutions for damage incurred by exclusion and difference but toward specific, even failed, reparative strategies emphasizing livable, creative potentials. What would it mean to historicize interracial sociality apart from violence, pathology, or escapism? I think it will leave us in a vastly better position to do justice to a wealth of culturally central practices that become invisible under an optic exclusively trained on suffering and its resistance.[68] Considering what didn't happen but might have—say, a future for modernism or black cultural politics that looked more like *Contemporary Black Artists in America* and *The DeLuxe Show* than the present does—is already a way radically to adjust one's outlook. In different ways these exhibitions affirm the discomfiting realization that the normative order opposed by black modernists was not white but black. They support a larger claim that the mutual inscription of black thought with the topic of racism may be less necessary than its practitioners usually assume.[69] The exhibitions anticipated a cultural politics that remains to be elaborated.

As experiments, they show with a clarity heightened by the exhibition form that often *what art is* is people inserting into cultural space something that differs in intention from that space. Self-consciously critical or not, such actions direct attention to the protocols governing cultural space. Attempting to register profound historical and social change with shockingly subtle means, the experiments I discuss targeted conventionally "white" and "black" spaces alike. Description, interpretation, and analysis of the exhibitions alone would not even begin to reveal how complex their briefs were. Coming to terms with the vast scope of the work these interventions allowed their participants to do means facing down the particular formations that work courageously sought to shatter.

68. See Sedgwick, "Paranoid Reading," 147.
69. Part of this sentence interpolates ibid., 146.

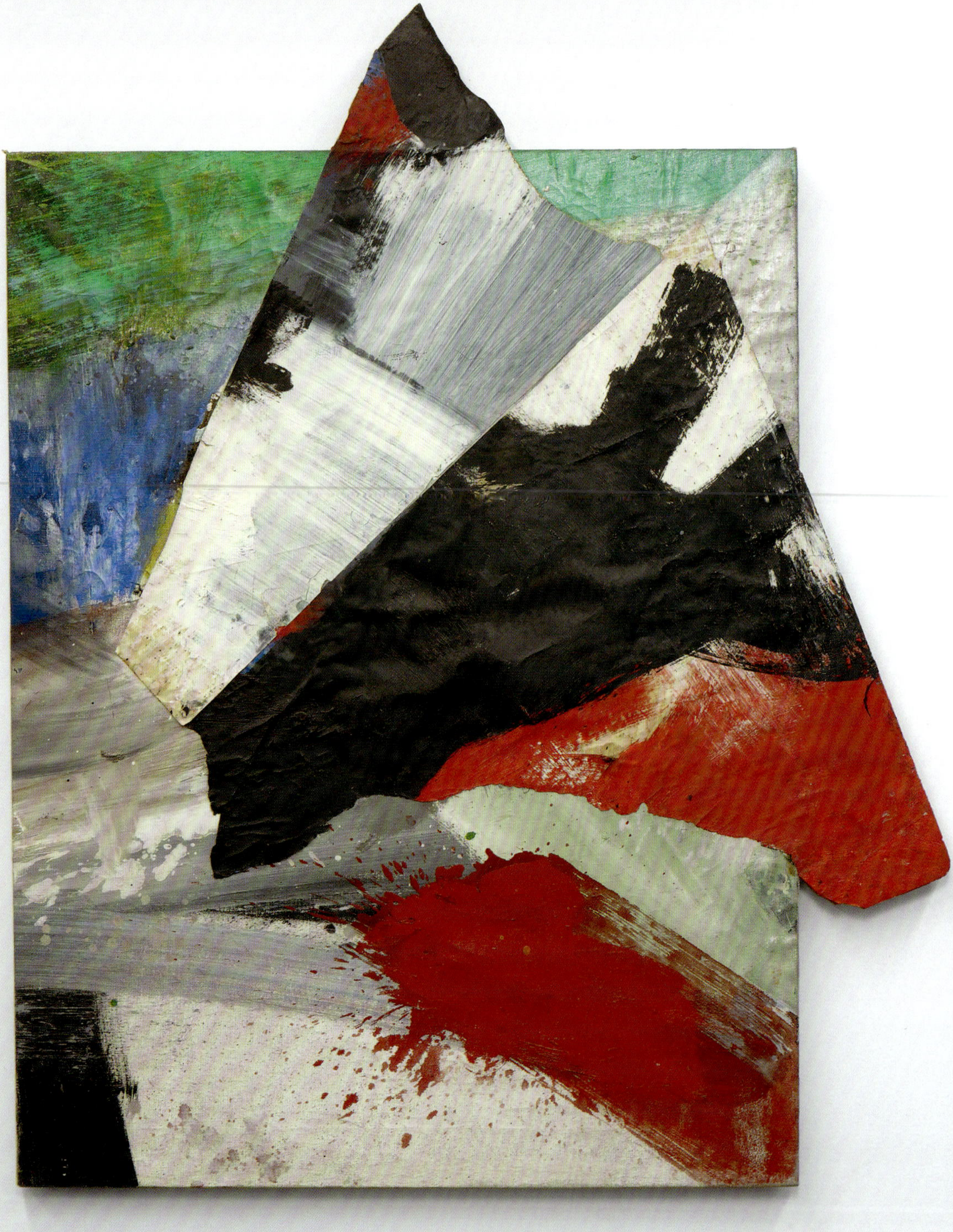

Chapter 1

How It Looks to Be a Problem

Each category has its own history. If we wish to present a partial framework in which to describe such events, we might think of two vectors. One is the vector of labeling from above, from a community of experts who create a "reality" that some people make their own. Different from this is the vector of the autonomous behavior of the person so labeled, which presses from below, creating a reality every expert must face.

Ian Hacking, "Making Up People"[1]

It was among modernism's best affordances that through it individual persons could become autonomous of the label "black artist." But what happens when abstraction arrives in black representational space? The art-historical fortunes of Ed Clark, an American painter born in 1926, suggest some answers.

Clark was probably the first modernist to prepare a canvas by shaping it. He presented his earliest effort—titled *Untitled*—in 1957 with the Tenth Street–based Brata collective,[2] of which Clark was a

Figure 1.1. Ed Clark (b. 1926), *Untitled*, 1957. Oil on canvas and paper, on wood, 46 × 55 in. (116.84 × 139.7 cm). The Art Institute of Chicago. Restricted gift of an anonymous donor; Samuel A. Marx Endowment, 1999.243. Courtesy of the artist.

1. Ian Hacking, "Making Up People," in *Reconstructing Individualism*, ed. T. L. Heller, M. Sosna, and D. Wellbery (Palo Alto, CA: Stanford University Press, 1985), 168.

2. Among the more reliable and astute contemporary observers of the Tenth Street scene's significance was Harold Rosenberg, who lived but a stone's throw west of St. Mark's Church. In 1959 Rosenberg praised the scene's catholicity as "hospitable to anything, except what might denote a norm." Continuing, Rosenberg ventured that everything on 10th Street is one of a kind: a liquor store with a large 'wino' clientele; up a flight of iron steps, a foreign-language club restaurant; up another flight, a hotel-workers' employment agency; in a basement, a poolroom. . . . The modernism of 10th Street has passed beyond the dogma of 'aesthetic space,' as its ethnic openness has transcended the bellicose verbal internationalism of the thirties. Its studios and its canvases have room for the given and for the haphazard." Rosenberg, "10th Street: A Geography of Modern Art," *Art News Annual* 28 (1959): 120–43.

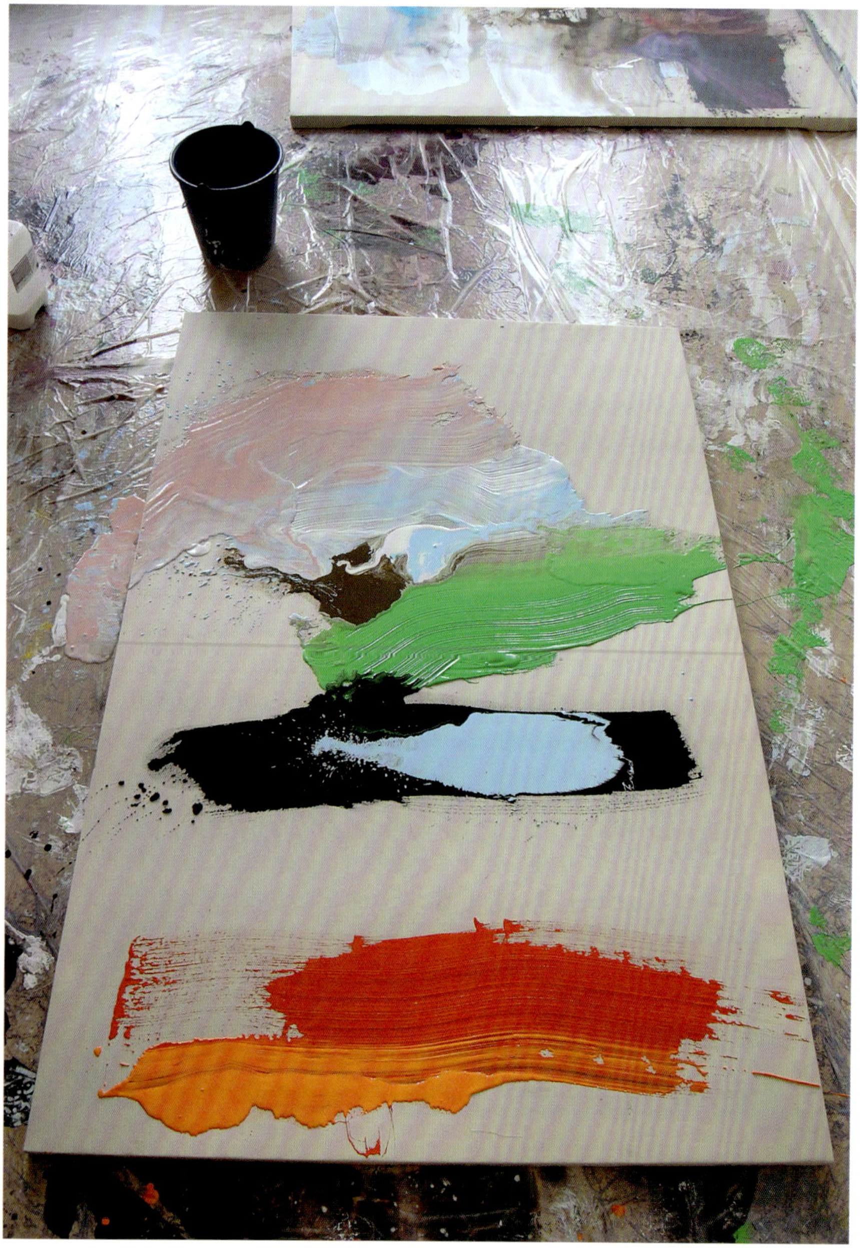

Figure 1.2. Ed Clark work in progress, 2009. Photo by Lauren Goldenberg. Courtesy of the artist.

modulation of colors distributed across the push-broom's path. They reconcile the painted picture to the protean independence of the stroke, which declares the colored canvas to be a thing while underscoring the turbulence within its wholeness.

Clark thus evolved the stroke into a subject that was neither an image nor a cipher for the impassioned human content of abstract painting. The migrations of strokes across the canvas signal the strident integrity of the *activity* of abstract marking. The stroke is for sure a trademark of Clark's work and has been its principal subject since the early 1960s. But it is by no means the signature of an autonomous personality; a given canvas always contains a multiplicity of such marks in an interaction that takes precedence over Clark's own signatory authority. Clark's stroke, developed from the far end of a push-broom's span and shaped in the intermixture of paint between the bristles running along its bar, empties from the stroke-as-device any content born of clichéd, showy abstract expressionist interpositions of the self.

The disinhabited character of Clark's mark allowed him to insert a real distance—of time as well as space—between his creative decisions, the actions of his hands, arms, and body, and his painting's record of these gesticulations. Compared with the spontaneity and implied speed of painterly gesture, everything slows and quiets down. Clark's stroke is better comprehended in terms of modernist art's move away from statements of a personal nature and toward inquiries into a medium's natures and its component parts. Clark's stroke, in the prominence and opacity of its traces, and more precisely in its reluctance to be seen as an image,[9] confines its declarations to statements about color. The physical and conceptual work in the art is color's: independent and local to color, not to Clark.

With this, the paintings' evocation of palette work becomes the more intensive. By *palette work* I mean two things: the making of color that must precede the making of paintings, as well as the painted figure's reminder that a playful and purposive blending—creation, really—of color took place before the paint arrived at the picture

9. Cf. Roy Lichtenstein's (always cursive) brush-stroke paintings, which declare their historical and ideological distance from abstract expressionist gesture by ironizing its iconicity—a tack that is profoundly different from Clark's.

surface. (Relatedly, Thomas Hess described "the moving flesh of pigment" in de Kooning.)[10] Traditionally, palette work comes before mark-making and is for the viewer a negligible stage in the fabrication of objects for presentation in a painted scene. Now it follows color all the way to the canvas, where outsized, overconspicuous brushstrokes become subject matter. Suspending color in just this liminal zone identified with the "before" of painting forces the viewer to apprehend both the collaborative nature of color relations and the decisions impelling them. Curiously, with Clark this never feels like a triumph or declaration of identity. Rather, palette work suspends the coalescence of color into image: deployed as a specific intensity, abstraction keeps image at bay. Clark's mark thus communicates itself to be an indefinite protraction of the preliminary, underscoring what Meyer Schapiro would call the "drama of decision" entailed by creative process.

In this way the broom allowed Clark's color to take a reflective turn that appears the more decisive in light of two shifts in his method. Both occurred around 1961.[11] First, he abandoned the lurid, ponderous color chords he had favored since 1957 for more high-keyed shades, many approaching pastel, that had a concentrated spectrum with more subtle and numerous transitions of hue.

Second, Clark adopted a different shape of canvas to support his monumental images of blended color, a buoyant oval ranging in width from 11 to 21 feet, which he used from 1968 to the late 1970s (figs. 1.3 and 1.4). The implicit reference was to the sun, the source of all light (and thus all color). With the sun Clark was declaring his unequivocal interest both in the notion of color suspended between preparation and use, conceptualization and actualization, and in how colors influence each other.

By now the most salient idea in his practice involved the creation of paintings as spaces for the refraction of light effects, the light in color, in an interminable modulation. He would tell a reviewer in 1973, "I'm interested in the expanding image, and the best way to expand an image is an ellipse,"[12] a format with explicit origins in stress, gravity, and a positive disposition toward horizontal relations.

10. Thomas B. Hess, untitled essay in Sidney Janis Gallery, *De Kooning*, unpaginated.
11. See Garrett Holg, "Ed Alert," *Chicago Sun Times*, September 28, 1997.
12. See Robins, "Edward Clark: Push-Broom and Canvas."

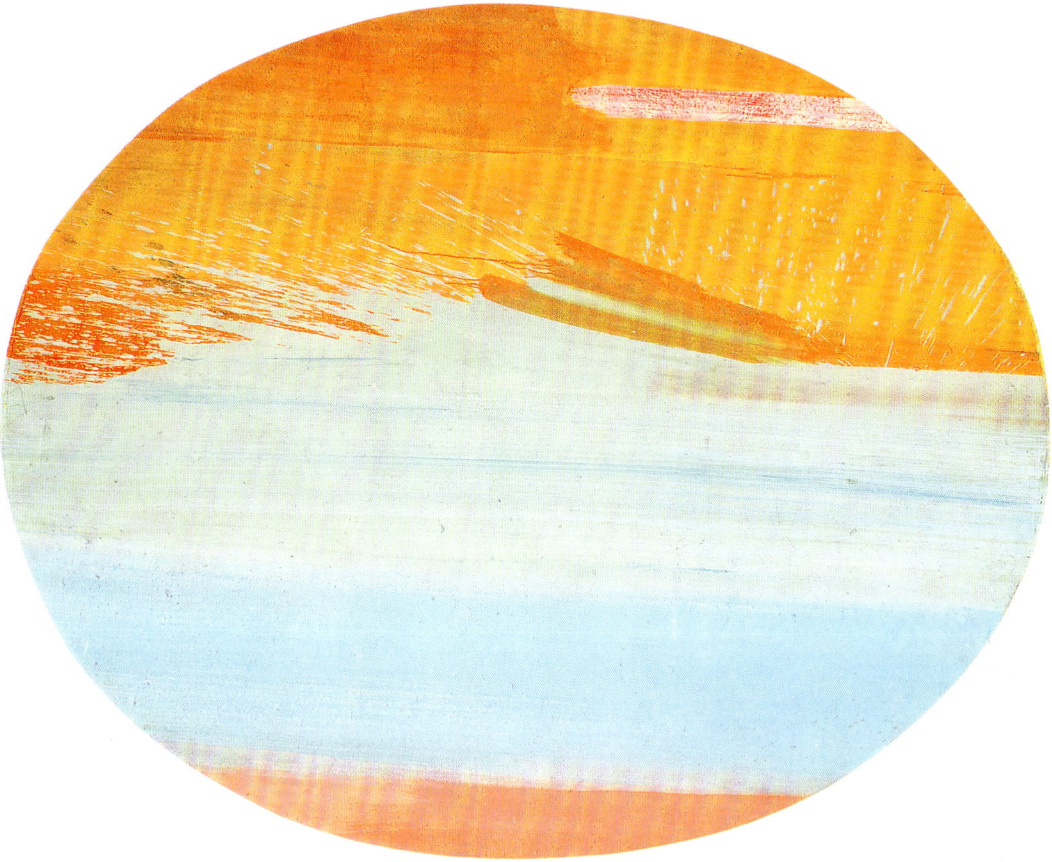

Figure 1.3. Ed Clark, *The First Oval (Vetheuil)*, 1968. Acrylic on canvas, 64½ × 83 in. (163.8 × 210.8 cm). Courtesy of the artist.

Clark's conception of expansion bears an important affinity to the antiformal tendency in much postwar American art, which was influenced by Gestalt psychology and later theorized by Yve-Alain Bois. In Bois's account, antiform understands that "gravity vectors the phenomenological field, separating experience into two domains: the optical one and the kinesthetic, bodily one."[13] Gestaltists such as Wolfgang Köhler and Erwin Straus conceived of vision as a vertically structured field not beholden to gravitational forces; they described the "visual subject's relation to its image-world as 'fronto-parallel' to it, a function of its standing erect, independent of the

13. Rosalind Krauss et al., *Art since 1900: Modernism, Antimodernism, Postmodernism* (London: Thames and Hudson, 2005), 359. For a fuller account, see Yve-Alain Bois and Rosalind Krauss, *Formless: A User's Guide* (New York: Zone, 1997), 88–92, 134–35, 242.

Figure 1.4. Ed Clark, *Yenom (#9)*, 1970. Acrylic on canvas, 72 × 113½ in. (182.9 × 288.3 cm). Courtesy of the artist.

ground." We experience the image, therefore, as a vertical: "its very coherence as a form . . . is based on this uprightness, this rise into verticality which is how the imagination constitutes its images."[14]

In the thinking of another psychology of the postwar era, now informed by Georges Bataille as well as Freud, the reorientation of painting to the horizontal field—most famously in the characteristic painting of Jackson Pollock, "a horizontal antiform as an abstractness uncolonized by the vertical 'one'"[15]—involved a direct attack on the obligation that artworks offer immediate visual pleasure. The ellipse, then, also allowed Clark's paintings to retain the energized horizontality of the process in which they originated even after they

14. Krauss et al., *Art since 1900*, 359.

15. Bois and Krauss, *Formless: A User's Guide*, 92. See also Krauss et al., *Art since 1900*, 359.

were hung vertically on the wall of the studio or museum. The dimensionality of color Clark explores through his painting and indeed his larger project to "expand the image" are, in this pointed horizontality, completely out of synch with color ways identified with head-on representations of the world.

What distinguishes Clark's work of this period, then, is not only the exhilarating openness of its color but also the intensity with which he was devising ingenious ways to achieve it. The combinations of colors, color areas, and shearing strokes, the indications of direction, elision, and decision, operate in a density significantly greater than play. It is a menagerie of technical problems, none existing in isolation and all arising from the shifting magma of the painter's accumulated experience.[16] There is no predetermined formal goal; it's about seeking more than finding. Clark elected to investigate the stroke as a discipline, an inquiry into the work that goes into a work.

Because the work so contains the matter of the intellectual activity and physical conditions that eventuated it, it must be understood to reflect its immediate engagement with the specific life of its maker. But especially when met on its own terms, Clark's work has crucial but unexplored implications for the thriving discursive formation known as African American art, into which Clark was formally inserted in 1980, the year of his retrospective at the Studio Museum in Harlem.

It is not enough simply to say that Clark's rigorous destructuration of color demonstrates his distance from that formation; it demands we seriously consider the effects of his rigorously open color work (his defining contribution to modernist art history) on the putative blackness of his art. Prevailing histories of so-called Black Art generally adopt an antimaterialist, homogenizing approach to problems of color, structure, and meaning—problems of the very sort Clark's open color work and artifactual color produce in massive volume. To understand what black modernists' practices have to teach us about the functions of art in public life, we should address the challenges some of them pose to our assumptions about the public life of color.

The first serious review of Clark's work appeared in 1954, when he was twenty-nine, on the GI Bill, and studying painting in Paris,

16. This formulation is inspired by Harold Rosenberg, *De Kooning* (New York: Abrams, 1973), 31.

basking in the colored light of Monet and Nicolas de Staël and marveling at the solar intake of Paris studios, whose plentiful skylights meant "you can paint out-of-this-world colors."[17] Since then his work has been the subject of a fair, though hardly generous, amount of art writing. And that literature overlooks the subject and problems of color that pervade Clark's art. It turns away from the implications of his painting's insistently antiessentialist, antirepresentational chromaticism. Consider, for example, the lead essay in the catalogue accompanying the 1980 exhibition *Afro-American Abstraction*, curated by April Kingsley. Even the exhibition's title, *Afro-American Abstraction*, encodes Kingsley's ambition to assimilate the work of black modernists such as Clark to a spectral historical formation and, moreover, to apologize for their deviance from the more localized visual arts of the American black community.[18] Kingsley claims that Clark, venturing forth from that racial enclave, brought to abstract expressionism a "bold physicality" identified with "the great African tradition." Elsewhere she sees that quality in the "straight path of the push-broom," making the implement "the perfect tool for expressing the aggressive sexuality of [Clark's] personal style."[19]

Needless to say, this is hardly an "expanding image" of Clark's practice. Rather it reflects a desire to institute something by way of Clark—an Afro-American *version* of chromatic abstraction. Our view of Clark's practice is thus made to contract. In the catalogue for the artist's retrospective that same year at the Studio Museum, curator Anita Feldman displaces Clark's practice from the context in which it finds its motive force, upon which it builds, and away from which it decisively and intelligently moves (Louis Rittman, de Kooning, de Staël, Motherwell). Further, she restitutes the whole of Clark's practice to the "author identity" position evaded in his most significant work.

17. Review by Michel Conil-Lecoste, *Le Monde*, March 12, 1954, n.p.

18. April Kingsley, *Afro-American Abstraction* (New York: PS 1, 1980). See also Studio Museum in Harlem, *Edward Clark: A Complex Identity* (New York: Studio Museum in Harlem, 1980). Another 1980 essay, by Anita Feldman, guest curator of Clark's retrospective at the Studio Museum in Harlem, remains the most substantive account of his work and represents the limited and limiting nature of art-historical interest in this artist. See Feldman, "A Complex Identity: Edward Clark, 'Noir de Grand Talent,'" in *Edward Clark: A Complex Identity*, n.p.

19. See Kingsley, "Edward Clark's Luminous Expanses," 38.

That was in 1980. After two decades of relative dormancy, interest in Clark has recently resurged. In 2002 David Hammons included Clark in *Quiet as It's Kept*, a small exhibition of abstract painting that Hammons organized for the Galerie Christine König in Vienna. Then Kellie Jones included Clark in *Energy/Experimentation: Black Artists and Abstraction, 1964–1980*, which had a celebrated run at the Studio Museum in Harlem in 2005.[20] Though invaluable for showing grossly underviewed art, these exhibitions extend the arguments established in the literature on Clark. They fix on an idea of the artist's mystical transmission of black culture into his paintings, which allows us to think of blackness as an "alien" (sufficiently different) but manifest (sufficiently buried) presence within modernism. This has become a subtext the critic may repeatedly disclose in reading after reading of the race embedded in the work.

This plays out in funny ways.[21] In surveying the black artists in *Energy/Experimentation*, Kellie Jones repurposes *maximalism*, a term

20. Clark's work also appeared in *High Times, Hard Times: New York Painting, 1967–75*, an exhibition whose argument makes the crucial, if counterintuitive. point that in a late-sixties/early-seventies context wherein many Americans were pursuing politics, and specifically rights gains, with unprecedented ardency and fervor, many of them were transforming abstraction from an icon of political exemption into a progressive political instrument. The exhibition had the worthy goal of shrinking the gap that has long separated formalist art from the social forms it has sometimes sought to advance, and with which it always coexisted. Such a show makes a badly needed contribution to a counter-history of late modernism in which a critical mass of artists, many of them cultural minorities, persisted with abstraction at a really inopportune time: when its currency was sharply devalued and the most visible/viable political art practices were employing far more demonstrative means to manifest difference and dissent in the spaces of art. But in fact it ends up serving a progressive narrative in art history that delights in demoting abstraction in favor of work seen to be more politically crucial, more evidently exigent in mood. Thus today, to utter the names of figures as varied as Judy Chicago, Philip Guston, Miriam Schapiro, and Robert Smithson, is to invoke a litany of turnings away from modernism toward those intermedial, performative, and discursive modalities of creation and commentary that would suffuse the art associated with the postmodern turn announced later in the same decade. If 1971—the year of the two exhibitions that anchor this study—didn't see the death of the modernist project, it did see its hegemony destroyed. It marks a point by which performance and body art had cornered the marketplace of ideas on aesthetic politicality. It's to a year like 1971 that one turns to illustrate the downturn of high modernism and its presumptive cause—an acute ascendancy of identity politics as a style or anti-institution within advanced art. Steady appraisal of progressive experiments involving modernist art is an important project indeed but tends to foreclose the idea that they can be seen as effective without being drawn into elaborate conceptual affinities with very divergent methodologies.

21. Take, for example, the following exposition, which ostensibly concerns the

coined by Barbara Chase-Riboud, to show how the forms of abstract art produced by black artists in the 1960s–1970s literally "incorporated something that 'functioned' in life, in the larger social world, even (or perhaps especially) on a metaphysical level." How this incorporation actually worked goes unanalyzed. Instead the mere mention cues us to be on the lookout for the vaunted signs of "other experiences, thoughts and notions of blackness, Diaspora, labor, culture and emotions,"[22] anything that might secure the abstraction's standing as an image.

This passion for the code (the term is Baudrillard's) is stronger at some moments than others, but each manifestation reveals that "maximalism," in the hands of these authors, exploits the historical prerogative; it is a critical operation, a way to create the work one needs in order to beget the signification one desires. Above all, the work must *mean*. In the *Quiet as It's Kept* catalogue essay, Geoffrey Jacques at first seems to dismiss the notion of reading Clark's paintings racially: "You may ask if any of this work has . . . to do with the experience of being African-American. It's a fair question, but in a studio visit, it doesn't come up." But just a few lines later, Jacques turns searchingly to Ed Clark's broom:

> One could . . . make something of . . . the push broom as a symbol . . . of the kind of labor available to African-Americans . . . arriving from the [South] to the cities. . . . Clark lives in a loft in an old office building, where the maintenance crews during the building's heyday . . . were probably African-American. . . . That Clark uses this instrument that signifies . . . exploitation [to make] such unusual abstract paintings is an act of symbolism that is . . . inescapable. But that's only at the level of symbolism.[23]

---

paintings Joe Overstreet produced after a 1992 vacation to the Senegalese coast. Thomas McEvilley knowingly writes: "These paintings show a sensibility that has been thoroughly initiated into European-derived artistic practices and seems affirmatively at home with them, yet at the same time they cloak beneath their sumptuous colorism the dark secret of Euro-American history—the rape of Africa through slave trade, colonialism, and imperialism." Biography and race converge here, too, to transform the formal exercise of colorism into a ground for the belief that, in addition to their profoundly racial "character," these works somehow harbor, as a kind of buried treasure, a general narrative of race and racism. McEvilley and Overstreet with Piche, *Joe Overstreet: (Re)Call and Response*, 31.

22. Jones, "To the Max: Energy and Experimentation," 31.

23. Jacques, "Quiet as It's Kept," 35.

Jacques's disavowal of the symbolism he introduces is difficult to take seriously: he takes such pains to construct it into the pictures before him and then pretends to cast it aside. (He knows enough not to bring it up with the artist, yet back at the typewriter, there it is . . .) Such interpretation wants nothing more than to bring Clark's pictures into view as a kind of figuration. In Jacques's account the pictures are a material for the production of an art—or the idea of an art—in which social content is so immanent that it doesn't have to be seen in order to be evident. Like the other textual maneuvers I have cited, and many others that one could, Jacques's reading at once annexes Clark's practice to Black Art and tries to overwhelm its abstraction. It dismisses the work's invitations to both vision and thought.

Plainly, Clark's work asks to be seen in a different light from this. The work before us (on the wall and in the mind) is infinitely harder than these texts suggest. But the peregrinations of logic at the heart of Jacques's account actually help us understand the revisionist logic at the heart of recent historical encounters with black modernist artists, encounters framed by the assumption that their work must be *made* political, as if the local circumstances of its emergence didn't politicize it right from the start. Another reason to nullify the abstract character of this art is that it permits one to sidestep the contradiction it produces: namely, that this critical mass of black modernists meant a rupture between the type "black American artist" and the practice of representative figuration.

These aggressive domestications of emphatically noncompliant paintings derive from commentators' beholdenness to the idea of their subjects' difference and from the assumption that modernism has no place for us. At the end of the day, there is nothing persuasive about their claims to restitute these artists to modernism, for those claims are not sincere. It seems more like something they feel they must do, which is not to reimagine modernism—as a legitimate resource for black artists who found unexpectedly reciprocal and giving relations there—but rather to cast a black light on it so that both formations can retain their customary difference-in-separateness. In other words, this project widens the canon of black art to include modernists, using symbolism to compensate for their strangeness, rather than considering how these figures' rigorous engagement with modernism endangers the possibility of a canon in the first place.

If anything, their project restores the vitality of modernism itself, inviting reconsideration of its profound, though always differently experienced, freedom-giving aspect, alongside its well-known efficacy as a site of formal experiment.

This trend points to a troubling methodological conclusion: because modernism and black artists' activities must remain in separate and opposed domains despite the evidence of figures such as Clark, scholars necessarily represent the black differend as infiltrator, stain, or alien presence—anything that preserves a contrastive separation between figure and ground. The black alien thus "influences" the terrain of modernism only in ways that allow her to persist in her essential alterity. Within these terms, whatever it is that Ed Clark's untitled construction of 1957 is thinking about, whatever it may be doing with or to painting, is literally beside the point of analysis. The urge for symmetry between biography and picture-effects is so strong in black art history that the turbulent color work in the art is impotent next to the sureness that it, or *something* in the picture, reflects back all the unassailable epistemological stability of Clark's racial blackness. (And notably more so next to the claim that these pictures draw out the story of countless faceless broom-laden janitors.) In other words, it is through a suspension of interest in how Clark's painting actually works and develops as art, how it asks to be related to its varying social and historical contexts, that this discourse makes him make a difference to modernism in the name of an "Afro-American" or "discrepant" or "political" abstraction. The fact is, abstraction has always been political precisely in its *opposition* to the fetish that the figure becomes in circumstances of unremitting spectatorial narcissism.

However well such methods may answer the desire to enrich the cultural history of black Americans, their imprecision only deepens the historian's responsibility to critically assess distortions that bracket or bury inconvenient, and therefore crucial, detail in representations of culture. Though far from unified, most of the work on this art posits easy relationships between it and canonical modernism or Black Art when, in fact, linking it to either is anything but easy. In one variation, writers, supposedly seeking to counter a decades-long trend in which "race and representation theory" has held art captive, celebrate black modernists' apparent disinterest in such themes as well as their works' capacity to promote "a complex conceptual vision of black humanity"[24] by the special communicative power of *pure black form.* The two texts we've seen typify how this framework despecifies the practice of abstraction in order to rehabilitate its forms as a general cultural practice. Thus we are told in Jacques's essay about the three artists in *Quiet as It's Kept* that their abstractness is a kind of black vernacular. "Suppression of narrative . . . discourse in the valorization of the image [and] of color have all been common . . . among African-American artists throughout our era."[25]

Jacques uses the grid at the heart of Stanley Whitney's paintings to work up a theoretical racial content against the materiality of the objects before us as well as against the grid's historicity as a device in modernist art. Jacques invokes the quilt designs that were popular "as an art form" among African American slaves. "Their designs were not only founded on the grid," Jacques writes, directing our attention away from the surfaces of Whitney's paintings. "The colors . . . contain[ed] a narrative component that was known to the slaves but *kept secret from white people.* The designs contained messages . . . pointing the way to freedom. All this should draw our attention to the life, the rhythm . . . of Whitney as a colorist."[26]

Another strategy in black art history advances a specific conflict precisely in order to resolve it. This unfolds around two seemingly contradictory moves: one claiming to restitute the work to an expanded field of canonical abstraction, and another installing a racial difference in an abstract work to compel it to function figuratively. This practice restricts interpretation to engaging those extra-aesthetic details imagined to ground origin narratives waiting to be summoned. It dwells on the most explicitly nonnormative component of an aesthetic project. Such sleights-of-hand epitomize how art-historical attention to literal politics can erase the nonliteral politicality of a project.

Here's an example: an essay in which Ann Gibson seeks to come to grips with the hermetic work of Joe Overstreet.[27] Gibson describes

24. Bey, "Ironies of Diversity."

25. Jacques, "Quiet as It's Kept," 45.

26. Ibid., 39–40. Emphases in original and added.

27. Ann Gibson, "Strange Fruit: Texture and Text in the Work of Joe Overstreet," *International Review of African-American Art* 13, no. 3 (1996): 24–31. As often will be the case here, the cited texts represent the most thorough monographic treatment yet given the artist's work. The consistency with which this applies signals one of the direst consequences of these artists' neglect by scholars of modernism and "black art" alike.

Overstreet's peripatetic movement among sources and forms of abstraction with terms such as *polyglot* and *heterogeneous*. She even describes Overstreet as "a person in *between* languages," an artist "whose purpose is to undo the illusory [notion of] stability."[28] Yet in assessing the complexity of Overstreet's assimilation her account succumbs to the clarity of social documentary. Such "layered associations," we are told, "run though Overstreet's paintings like the strands of hair, those attached to the scalp and those incorporated from elsewhere, [which] his mother . . . wove together in her hair weaving salon in Oakland [when Overstreet was a child]."[29] This passage, which renders the artist's origins in scenic detail, earnestly wants to find the same legibility in Overstreet's paintings. Even though the actual practice of hair weaving strives for unity that hides the heterogeneous origins of its strands, Gibson asks us to regard his mother's beauty salon as giving Overstreet not only a personal experience for absorbing the differences he saw in the world but also a culturally specific way to register it. Obviously the vernacular valence of this image does a great deal of work for the historian. Yet what could be less illuminating than tracking a practice to such a deep root? I know of no statement by Overstreet—visual or verbal—that could support this interpretation. The interpretation exists to fulfill the need to locate Overstreet's practice; it serves an end both devised and satisfied in a conceptual space that exists apart from any serious engagement with his production.

Impatient to close meaning by sweeping every materialization under the sign of race, both kinds of writing sampled here exhibit the uneasiness, the category anxiety that encounters with the political personage of the black modernist routinely produce. To the extent that both want for something like "black abstraction"—a self-contradictory label that would split the difference between the black modernist's defining formations but leaves each order intact—they indicate their fealty to representation. Amazingly, abstraction is just another way of representing blackness (as though such were all a black painter ever wanted to do). They disdain these artists' principal occupation *not* to represent, or more precisely, for the intellectual difficulties it poses.

28. Ibid., 34. Emphasis added.
29. Ibid.

In sorting out this scholarship and its objects, one quickly feels the accumulation of implausible content scholars use to overwhelm their targets. In fact this violates the moral right of the artist, contravenes her practical claim to inconsistency, opacity, and voluntary disclosure in her work—and to have some say in the construction of its consequence. Within such a practice of cultural or social explanation, it is as if these objects exist minimally, or *purely* abstractly. When such a practice proceeds unimpeded over decades, it becomes all but impossible to interrupt it.

When we raise such an aesthetics to the level of a moral system, as proponents of "black abstraction" do, it warrants notice. This discourse holds out for an aesthetic experience that seems to me insufficiently distinct from the kind of absolute self-knowledge—and correspondingly, absolute knowledge of strangers—we are over-encouraged to have in our everyday world. What we miss in an experience so saturated with meaning is the concentrated, open-ended intimacy that comes from not knowing, from being left unsure—discomposed, as the case may be—by the things and beings of the world.[30]

This study recalls a couple of moments in 1971 when racially mixed corps of modernists, recognizing that risk, or discomposure, as a source of value, made their commitments public. In order to historicize that recognition as a core component of their experiments, I will in remaining pages of this chapter review some of the prodigious efforts undertaken, over the past four decades, to invalidate the very impulses on which those individuals acted. I have adopted the cumbersome term *representationalism* to refer to the formalist and rigorist nature of the foreclosures that militate against any practice not dedicated to figuration. I want particularly to explore two suggestions of representationalism's extreme reduction of art to black universals. First, that this famously "affirmative" activity has typically functioned negatively, through prohibition, as will be demonstrated in its treatment of abstraction and those who practiced it. Second, given the historical fact that this standpoint was hastened into being by the proliferating cross-cultural intimacies reorganizing the social in the wake of official desegregation, it can be understood as a kind of last-ditch

30. See Gumbrecht, *Production of Presence*, 105.

stand against the possibility that black and nonblack Americans would find their ways forward together. That is, it was an attempt to keep a grip on something like a moral-racial minimum that could be protected from the most radical effects of integration, which in the visual arts were most strongly registered in the culture of modernism.

In the system I'm describing, freedom can exist only in negativity: my own freedom is reduced to an absolute minimum where the only thinkable freedoms must be consistent with the reigning values. Thus a typical black artist sacrifices herself as a model individual over whom racial rationality exercises unchecked dominion. Among the lessons to be learned from the (supposed) rarity and denigration of deviance is something about the degree to which racial morality has made a necessity of renunciation of the self. The reward for this renunciation never arrives; thus renunciation turns into something that is a good in itself.[31] Making the black modernist an impossible figure in affirmative history: unthinkable, because unwanted, in the black world.

At the same time, seen in the light of political optimism, this figure illustrates how the domination of the general over the specific has conquered the languages of black culture, calling our attention to the difference between what is called for and what simply is. Unpacking the difficulties masked by the two critical gambits described here will show that black practitioners of modernist art were radical, inassimilable elements—deviants—in both spheres they occupied, black culture and modernism. To their black peers they were *less expected*, and so more dangerous, than their lighter-skinned counterparts in modernism.

A major claim of this study is that the language of African American art history has been sadly indifferent to the effects of this deviant work and to the complex representational ambitions of its creators.

31. See Adorno, *PMP*, 139: "The situation seems to be that civilization in general demands that we exercise rational control over ourselves and over external nature in the world in which we live, but that it is not able to discover any appropriate reward, while the demand is sustained so that civilization should be preserved. But if that is the case, because civilization cannot prove that such control has benefits for others or is rational in a prudential sense, there is nothing for it but for this demand to become an absolute and to be inflated into something existing in its own right. . . . This applies with particular force in situations where people tend to regard renunciation as a good even though non-renunciation does not involve anything wicked or evil or destructive."

I write from a conviction that their activities should enter history with their ambivalence preserved rather than resolved away.

My point is not to defend abstraction tout court but rather to suggest that the relentless representational thrust of the art history so far elaborated for these figures poses huge obstacles to reckoning the importance of their independent decisions *not* to represent. This was a hugely unfashionable way to occupy political space around 1971, so in our historical representations of that political landscape, we have failed to imagine what many progressive artists felt the prevailing bias toward the figure, bodies, liveness, and polemics *prevented.* With respect to Clark—and to Frank Bowling, Peter Bradley, Chase-Riboud, Melvin Edwards, Frederick Eversley, Alvin Loving, Sue Irons / Senga Nengudi, Joe Overstreet, Raymond Saunders, Alma Thomas, Whitney, Jack Whitten, William T. Williams, and others—we have failed to recognize that what these artists "represent" is the degree to which the institution of Black Art undertook acts of exclusion at least as merciless as those it sought to overturn. We have failed to confront the implications of these figures' determinate negation of the representational(ist) imperative imposed on them by popular opinion and institutional practice and extended even today in certain histories of art. In fact, as we will see, historical representations of racial experience were never as symmetrical with the public life of color as we have been led to believe.

Confining this subject to art-historical projects may be part of the problem. Our frameworks for making sense of the sixties tend to pit a baldly political, antiformalist art against a retrograde aftermath of high modernist abstraction, when in fact the actual material embarrasses both caricatures. For instance, between the tantalizing detail of Clark's biography—his racial identity as a black man—and the decentering energy animating his colorism, an important vibration arises. We're forced to hold in mind two supposedly incompatible conceptual-historical structures: modernism and postwar black cultural politics. The examples we have seen so far of representivist history show how nimbly it dampens this vibration by reducing things to one term or the other, or to an inarticulate hybrid of the two, rather than exploring the effects they create together. Everywhere Clark's abstraction meets with distortion or apology, making one wonder: Where were the attempts to imagine the culturally queer, historically necessary place from whence Clark's project came? Who was there to imagine what it might do for Clark, or anyone else black, not to paint like a black person? What means existed to deal generously with individuals who dared in public to feel the burden of their art more heavily than that of race?

Clark exhibited *Untitled* the same year that Meyer Schapiro published an essay in *Art News* presenting a spirited defense of the embattled avant-garde (fig. 1.5). Schapiro adopted as his focus the cultural work in abstract art. For him, this began with the artist's decision to follow a course of her own. To really *see* avant-garde art, Schapiro suggested, one had to apprehend what it—and its creator—were *not* doing as much as what it, and she, *were*: "If the painter cannot celebrate many current values, it may be that these values are not worth celebrating. In the absence of ideal values stimulating to his imagination, the artist must cultivate his own garden as the only secure field in the violence and uncertainties of our time."[32]

Schapiro's avant-gardist is an emblem of social tension. The work of such an artist not only frustrates the representational tradition to which it responds; it leads an audience to confront its own reluctance to endorse an art suffused with uncertainty. This of course is the very difficulty that traditional picture-viewing was meant to relieve. What viewers might experience as antagonism in an avant-garde work, Schapiro interpreted in a more generous light, as a salutary recognition of alternative impulses.

> Abstraction implies then a criticism of the accepted contents of the preceding representations as ideal values or life interests. This does not mean that painters, in giving up landscape, no longer enjoy nature; but they do not believe, as did the poets, the philosophers, and the painters of the nineteenth century, that nature can serve as a model of harmony for man, nor do they feel that the experience of nature's moods is an exalting one on which to found an adequate philosophy of life. New problems, situations and experiences of greater import have emerged: the challenge of social conflict and development, the exploration of the self, the discovery of its hidden

32. Meyer Schapiro, "The Liberating Quality of Avant-Garde Art," *Art News* 56, no. 4 (Summer 1957): 42.

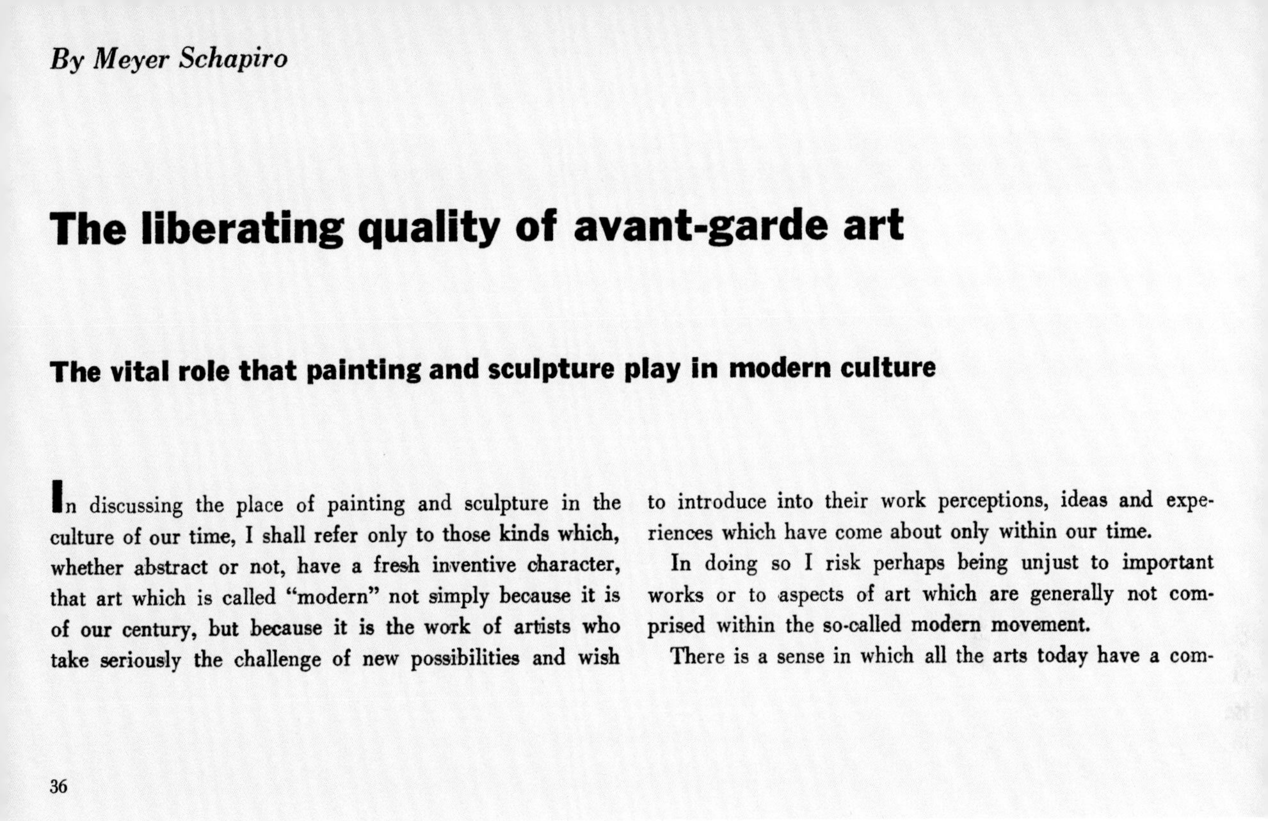

By Meyer Schapiro

The liberating quality of avant-garde art

The vital role that painting and sculpture play in modern culture

In discussing the place of painting and sculpture in the culture of our time, I shall refer only to those kinds which, whether abstract or not, have a fresh inventive character, that art which is called "modern" not simply because it is of our century, but because it is the work of artists who take seriously the challenge of new possibilities and wish to introduce into their work perceptions, ideas and experiences which have come about only within our time.

In doing so I risk perhaps being unjust to important works or to aspects of art which are generally not comprised within the so-called modern movement.

There is a sense in which all the arts today have a com-

36

Figure 1.5. Meyer Schapiro, "The Liberating Quality of Avant-Garde Art," *Art News* 56, no. 4 (Summer 1957): 36. Courtesy of The Meyer Schapiro Estate.

> motivations and processes, the advance of human creativeness in science and technology.[33]

As Schapiro saw it, "the significance of the change in painting and sculpture" originated in a broad retreat on a social scale from the rationalization of all activity, and through it, being. Though his language is generalizing, the pivotal movement it describes is from the general to the specific. As possibly "the last handmade, personal objects within our culture,"[34] works of avant-garde art stood for (Schapiro does not say "represent") contemporary efforts to preserve the domain of personality amidst increasingly standardized notions of work that conscripted individuals into collective forms of service. To Schapiro, avant-garde activity offered the individual a kind of space that was rapidly dwindling in the general culture: some space, however circumscribed, where the distinction between "our" work and "my" work counted for everything.

33. Ibid., 38.
34. Ibid.

Schapiro's richest articulations stop well short of the romantic individualism sometimes attributed to him. His *Art News* article simply said that something *could* be done and *was* being done about the fact that perfectly rational persons harbored desires that were unanticipated by collective aims and divergent from expert imperatives. In this way, Schapiro's account radiates compassion for the human need that the inward turn toward total abstraction sometimes announced.

At the same time, Schapiro's paean to avant-garde art strenuously avoids solipsism, placing front and center the need to view it dialectically at every level and never detached from the conditions in which it appears. In his articulations Schapiro is equally forceful about the place into which avant-garde art thrusts the viewer. This art achieves its social density facilitating an encounter between individualities, but without guarantees: "The painting symbolizes an individual who realizes freedom and deep engagement of the self within his work. It is addressed to others who will cherish it, if it gives them joy, and will attend to every mark of the painter's imagination and feeling."[35]

With his "self-involved lines which impress us as possessing the qualities not so much of things as of impulses, of excited movements emerging and changing before our eyes," wrote Schapiro, "the artist places himself in the focus of *your* space."[36] These marks and lines are anything but perfunctory references to the "indescribable" stuff of abstract art. Rather, they allow Schapiro to invoke that stuff without annexing it to a logical category or the expressionism of a particular social type. The essay's richest descriptive passages are lax in a way that suggests an interpretive openness, arising from an actively appreciative but not-precisely-comprehending regard. One of them describes a kind of "characteristic" avant-garde art as nothing more precise than a move away from "object character" and toward forms "which are open, fluid, or mobile."[37] Yet Schapiro's argument is animated by a spirit of deference to concrete instances of creative activity:

> The consciousness of the personal and spontaneous in the painting and sculpture stimulates the artist to invent devices of handling, processing,

35. Ibid.
36. Ibid., 39. Emphasis added.
37. Ibid.

> surfacing, which confer to the utmost degree the aspect of the freely made. Hence the great importance of the mark, the stroke, the brush, the drip, the quality of the substance of the paint itself, and the surface of the canvas as a texture and field of operation—all signs of the artist's active presence.[38]

All guarantors, moreover, of a work's right to be treated in its specifics. Though Schapiro elides the artist with her creation, he never presumes to describe the character or content of a work, only the node from which it arises. This in no way diminishes the artwork's materiality but offers a way to figure an open-endedness that must not be seen as a threat to be neutralized or a chaos to be organized. The essay understands that individual constructions display irreducible differences from other ones, making them impossible to generalize.

Here is an inescapable component of abstraction's difficulty. Avant-garde art was the shared property of a remaindered subclass of individuals linked by nothing more than a conviction that "the practical activity by which we live" didn't merit their "full loyalty." If it said "there is other work to do," what that work entailed was specific works of art. For Schapiro it was better to leave it at that than to consign abstract work wholesale to a category that would suppress its variance. Access required nothing so much as a *different practical relationship* to the work of vision, one unencumbered by the need to draw practical or metaphorical inferences from everything one sees.

> Only a mind open to the qualities of things, with a habit of discrimination, sensitized by experience and responsive to new forms and ideas, will be prepared for the enjoyment of this art. The experience of the work of art, like the creation of the work of art itself, is a process ultimately opposed to communication as it is understood now. What has appeared as noise in the first encounter becomes in the end message or necessity, though never message in a perfectly reproducible sense. You cannot translate it into words or make a copy of it which will be quite the same thing.
>
> But if painting and sculpture do not communicate they induce an attitude of communion and contemplation. . . . It is primarily in modern painting and sculpture that such contemplativeness and communion with the work of another human being, the sensing of another's perfected feeling and imagination, becomes possible.[39]

38. Ibid.
39. Ibid., 41.

Schapiro's appeal turns on the political performativity of abstraction: its ability to open a situation where closure reigned, and to promote surprise and generosity and closeness, rather than suspicion, in confronting individuality. "This art is deeply rooted, I believe, in the self and its relation to the surrounding world. And the pathos of the reduction or fragility of the self within a culture that becomes increasingly organized . . . intensifies the desire of the artist to create forms that will manifest his liberty in this striking way."[40] The scene of that desire's realization is neither the studio nor the canvas plane, but the vastly more public scene of viewing, when the artwork can become "the possession of everyone and is related to everyday experience."[41] Abstraction suggested the practicability of an "objective changeable world" (Paul Goodman) because it gave freedom the form of a practical exercise undertaken in collaboration. The work of avant-garde art is a medium of connection precisely because it neither invites an immediate orientation to its subject nor limits its conception of contact to a transmission of preexistent knowledge. Abstraction makes a conception of universality possible to the extent that through it one realizes affinity.

More than any other observer I know, Schapiro, in his palpably empathic language, imagines abstraction at its most generous: he wrote about it in connection to circumstances that gave it something beyond itself to do, something importantly distinct from the arts of communication and the enfeebling modes of knowledge they naturalize, as well as from the romance of monumental individuality. "The artist does not wish to create a work in which he transmits an already prepared and complete message."[42] The artist seeks instead an occasion to explore creation among varieties of human being, even and especially within the confines of an individual life, in direct reflection of the principle actually governing social reality.

This study reflects Schapiro's positive account of the avant-garde artist's negativity. Rather than "Why were black practitioners of abstract art cast aside?" we ask, "What forms of cultural work further proliferated by their diminishment?" Simply put, black modernists figured *loosening* in the imagined social order of black life that it has

40. Ibid., 40.
41. Ibid.
42. Ibid., 41.

been the duty of the black artist to bind together the more firmly. The very existence of these deviants proved there was an unaccounted-for element, a floating remainder, in a zone of the culture that was being conceived as a totality, a positivity without exceptions, which, as we have seen, was a self-enclosed moral system. The black artist, seen as a good in itself, embodied conviction in the idea of black culture, its coherence and continuity, even if many black people regarded this nearly spontaneous generation of reified blackness with considered pause. Because many (though not all) of the new cultural practices instated in the civil rights era sought to reestablish a closed culture that had ceased to exist—and promised to collapse the distance between really existing beings and a weakening idea of race—black artists could be said to make black art by default, regardless of its character. Thus "their abstract work . . . can be seen as a product . . . of ideas about color, structure and content that were gleaned from their own heritage and reality." In such a condition, the deviant can be domesticated with remarkable ease.

As we will see, the managaement of black modernists is itself proof that the late career of the black American artist was founded on a denigration as total as the larger, older exclusionary system to which Black Art is meant to provide both censure and relief. To treat these deviants with any historical precision, we need analyses of the instrumentalization to which they have been subjected. For they played a role in the near-spontaneous generation of black culture in the 1960s. Looking at their situation, we see how the empowerment of persons was functionally prohibited by contemporary formations of community. Because they articulated community as the source and goal of the universal subjectivity implied by black morality, virtually no room remained for vigorously individual persons such as the black modernist exemplified for the individual. Helping this exclusionary politics of black culture to thrive were the accepted models of public morality of the postwar period, especially its freedom movements. With "harmony between the public customs [and] ethically correct behavior, the moral life of the individual" so enthusiastically sought, the community enjoyed an overwhelming power in its relations with the individual.[43]

43. See Adorno, *PMP*, 12.

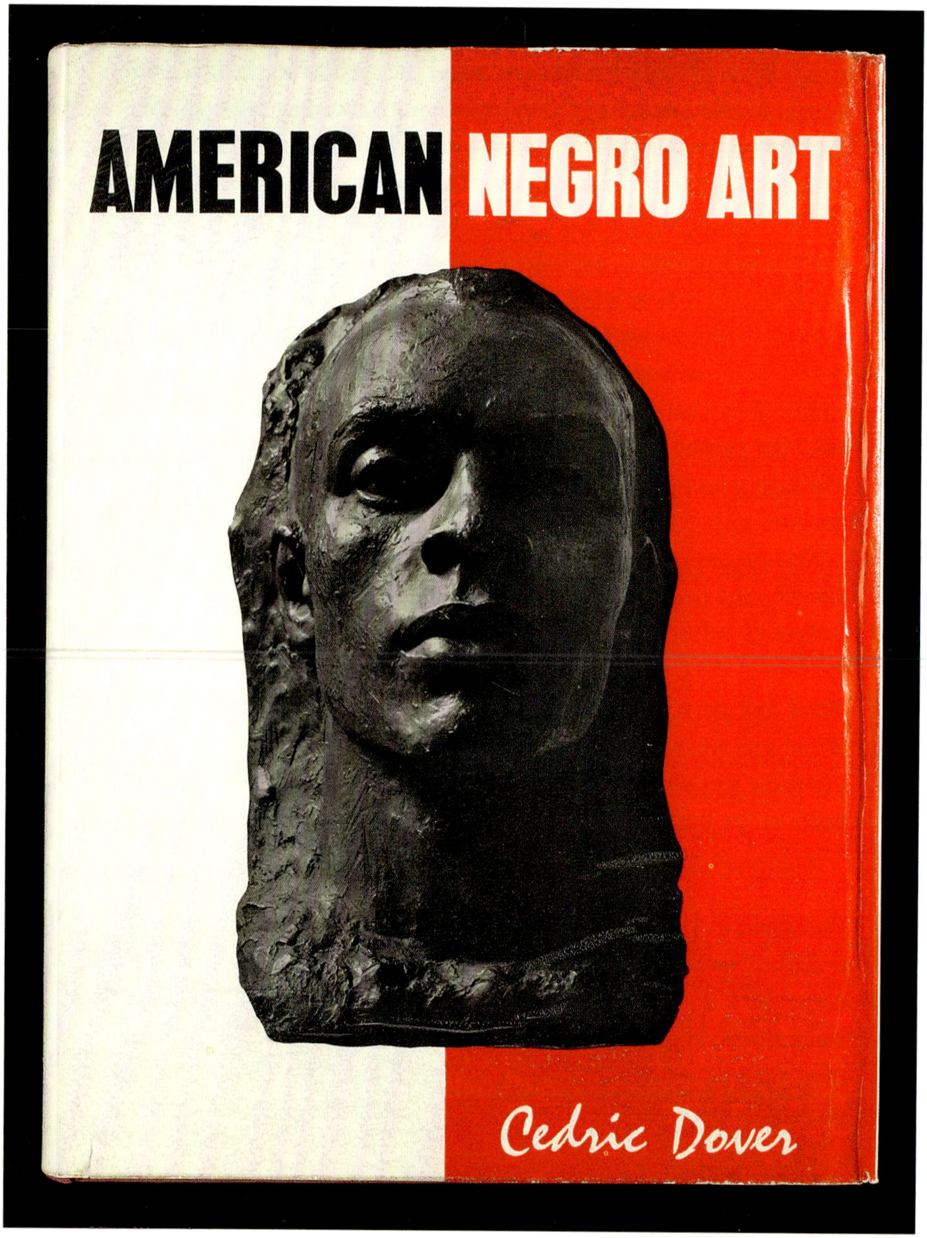

Figure 1.6.
Cedric Dover,
American Negro Art
(Greenwich, CT:
New York Graphic
Society, 1960).

the very moment that a number of artists were turning to the practices that would come to full flower in 1971, *American Negro Art* registers the withering impact of modernist sensibility on the central tenet of cultural leadership—selflessness, fealty to one's "proper function." The critical stance of *American Negro Art* thus equates artistic success with adherence to a narrow, ascetic ideal to which black artists are bound by identity. Because Dover's paradigm for American Negro Art doesn't merely presuppose but enforces an inviolable symmetry between the interests of the individual creator and those of the people she serves, a main agenda of the text is to indict artists who sought inspiration beyond the clan. To this end, Dover's depictions include flagrant acts of decredentialing alongside more openly debatable citations and exclusions. By keeping this unpersuaded remainder in view, Dover commends "[the] large number of Negro artists [who] have revealed the everyday living, the rich personalities, the joys and sorrows, the courage, faith and successes, of their own people. This is their greatest achievement and, [as long as] there is a separate Negro minority in America, it will remain their proper function to enlarge it."[50]

Even as Dover aims for his "picturebook of responses to needs, situations, surroundings, and ideas" to "enlarge [the] appreciation of the Negro minority in America," he also claims to believe that, owing to their unity, "the impact of the pictures as a collection will not . . . be very differently felt" by readers of different origins.[51] Dover's motivation is documentary and descriptive, to account a self-reinforcing whole. Thus he is not sympathetic to any form that cannot be reconciled with this methodology. He does, however, retain a place for it precisely as a site upon which to stage the triumph of community over the individual. Mainly a balance sheet of successes and failures, his book is also a lesson in attention. Dover implores the reader to look carefully upon the works in the volume: "What they communicate individually must depend on the eyes with which we see as well as their own artistic appeal. We can look, for example, at Archibald Motley's *Mending Socks*, purely in pictorial terms (what that means I do not exactly know), or we can seek the poetic images that transform

50. Ibid., 122.
51. Ibid., 11.

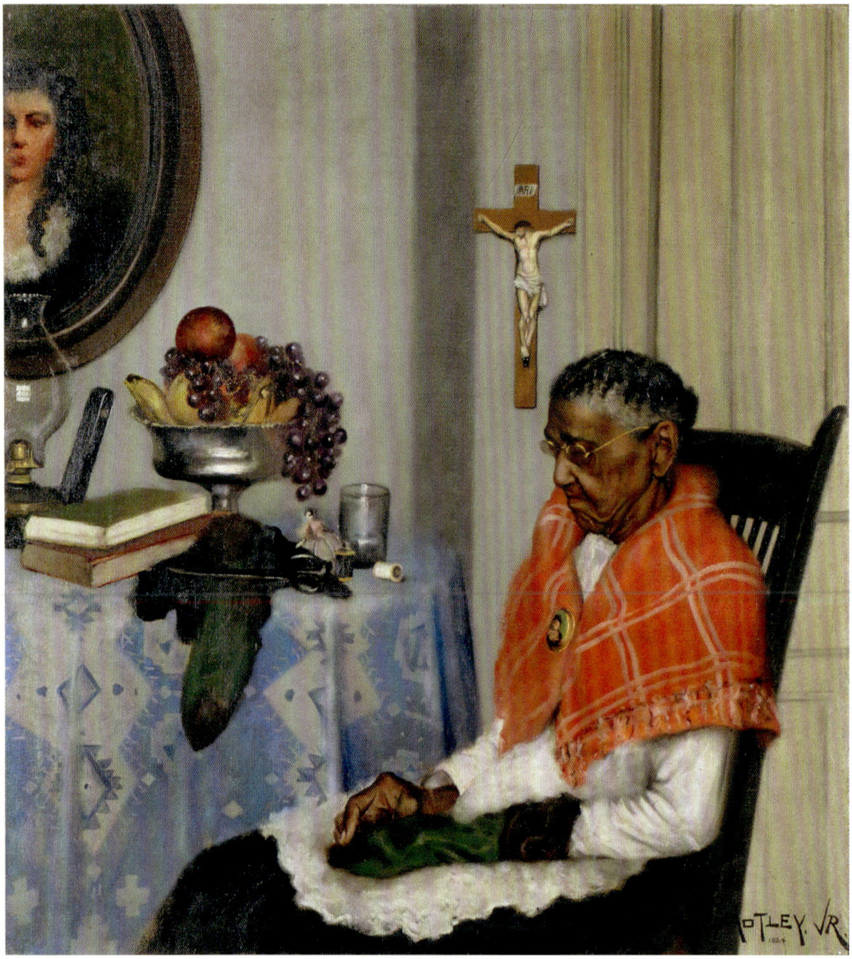

Figure 1.7. Archibald J. Motley Jr. (1891–1981), *Mending Socks*, 1924. Oil on canvas, 43⅞ × 40 in. (111.4 × 101.6 cm). Ackland Art Museum, University of North Carolina at Chapel Hill, Burton Emmett Collection. Conservation treatment for this painting, completed in 1997, was made possible by a grant from the Pforzheimer Foundation. Copyright Valerie Gerrard Brown and Mara Motley, MD.

it"[52] (fig. 1.7). Thus the individuality of any particular work "depends on" or vanishes into an assimilating vision that defines the conscientious and satisfying appraisal of blacks' creative work. Beyond symbol, there is nothing special to notice; evidences of the messenger's motives or personality merit no response. In this way *American Negro Art* enacts a form of critical attention that ennobles one specific kind of cultural activity by diminishing anything that fails its tests. In so doing, unfortunately, the book risks enfeebling the many diverse forms that share the same cultural field.

52. Ibid.

Dover's theory of attention thus "discovers" that the best practitioners of American Negro Art hail from a moral, transhistorical community of those who have divested their practices of personal interest, who understand the "creative process as a complex artist-audience interaction," not as a private affair.[53] Fundamentally outward-looking creatures with a predilection for description, "they were facing realities: they were chronicling, interpreting, and sometimes transforming. In doing so, they were meeting the needs of their own people—and the ultimate test of any work of art is its value to the society in which it is produced, not its reception by the coteries as amusing, exotic, exciting, interesting, original, or universal."[54] The proliferation of *they*s in Dover's account establishes these figures in an incontrovertible reality—the medium and objective of Dover's history. The demonstrative thrust betrays its insistently contemporary agenda: the "coteries" he mentions signify the integrated culture of modern art fomenting as he wrote. By 1960 black modernists like Clark, Norman Lewis, Romare Bearden, and Richard Hunt were already associated with that scene.

But even if, thanks to the collective, "the visual arts accordingly gained colour,"[55] a credibly black art would not alone suffice to sustain that racial-chromatic density. *American Negro Art* also had to triumph over the distractions of modernism if it was to serve as a model for neutralizing deviants.

At every point in Dover's peregrinations through the historical field, he finds opportunities to define the artist's role negatively. His preferred targets are artists who figure engagement with the "white world" by dint of methodology or mainstream appeal.[56] Along these lines, Dover suggests that Henry Ossawa Tanner's masterwork *The Banjo Lesson* (1890) is best viewed as "a token of what he could

53. Ibid., 43.

54. Ibid., 32.

55. Ibid., 33.

56. In fact, this trend accounted in Dover's negative history stretches as far back in time as he can extend it. Thus the academic bent alone of work produced by celebrated black artists of the nineteenth century—among them Edward Bannister, Robert Duncanson, Eugene Warbourg, and Tanner—earns it the label "atelier art" and a round condemnation: "They paid homage to anti-slavery and other sponsors, but failed, understandably, to contribute significantly to the progress of their own people or to the advancement of American art." See ibid., 82.

have done for his community and for American art" had Tanner been able to detach from "the standards and sentimentalities of [his] day."[57] Dover means, of course, from the standards of "the coteries" he despises.

His many disavowals of the fact aside, Dover *does* know what pictorial achievement means, but only when he wishes to set it aside in favor of dogma. And while Dover concedes that no compendium of *American Negro Art*'s scope could justifiably exclude the work of Robert Duncanson (1817–72), the widely influential naturalist, he informs the reader that Duncanson's paintings are included merely as "social relics."[58] Moreover, the continuity of "Negro Art" in Dover's appeal is shadowed by links among infidels that span vast stretches of time. Thus he scolds Hale Woodruff for invoking Duncanson's "egotistical" remark "I am not interested in color (problems), only paint." Though Duncanson's sentiment would become generic among modernists, in Dover's hands the statement becomes "the essential autobiography of a character afflicted beyond recognition of the momentous struggle around him."[59] The affliction in question? Art.

That developments in the mainstream American art culture of the late fifties directed Dover's judgment is evident in his account of Woodruff's own work, which hewed to social themes while bearing the deep imprint of Thomas Hart Benton's indolant figuration. It is the imprint, as a mark of external influence, that is the problem:

> Design is, in fact, the key word which explains all Mr. Woodruff's prints and paintings. Those who thought his stories of the Negro scene came from a genius inflamed by social awareness should look at them again with the key word in mind. Design makes sometimes grotesque stereotypes of many of his figures . . . it obscures the message of his lynching block

57. Ibid.

58. Ibid., 25. There is something showy about this in light of the artist's presentation, however, for Duncanson is the first individual to come in for ad hominem attack, again on the basis of misdirected intentions. Dover observes with circumspection that James Porter, in a 1951 reminiscence of Duncanson published in *Art in America* (October 1951), found it salutary that Duncanson's art bore "no sign of 'the least bitterness or sprit of preoccupation with other concerns than those proper to painting and industrious self-cultivation.'" Dover nods to raging arguments in the art world about these concerns' "propriety" but evidently feels that Duncanson's flagrant neglect of the black artist's mandate settles the matter: "the word for 'industrious self-cultivation' is egotism." See ibid.

59. Ibid. Parentheses in original.

> print, *Giddap* (1938), to the point where a tender spinster can miss its horror. . . . It may be, therefore, that the man who made the Atlanta School has been wise to confine himself recently to charming essays in "pure aesthetics."[60]

In Dover's treatment, the "design" that "obscures" the antilynching message also prefigures Woodruff's retreat—à la Tanner, Duncanson, and Porter. The trouble is these fellows don't know how to prevent style from compromising the didactic force, the moral integrity, of their well-chosen subject matter. "Design" in Dover's art language is equivalent to "free will" in the political vernacular. It is the taint of aesthetic independence that earned the likes of Woodruff the reputation of a delinquent. Notably, those of Dover's subjects who engage the fantasies of self-expansion that attracted many artists to modernism were his actual contemporaries, artists active in 1960 such as Woodruff, Bearden, Lewis, Barbara Chase (Riboud), and Norma Morgan. As he introduces them, Dover reminds us that the unanimity in which "most Negro artists" work is no fragile accord:

> Most Negro artists are unimpressed by the feathered phrases of escape that periodically float from Hale Woodruff's nest in Washington Square. They do not think of themselves "simply as American artists," whose primary tasks are to seek fuller "integration into American life" and "identification with mid-twentieth century internationalism." They regard themselves as Negro artists who are also American artists. They intend to rise *with* their people, not away from them. . . . In fact, no artist has ever been limited by communal loyalty, by looking with love on his brother's face.[61]

If Dover's claim were true that the confidence of "most Negro artists" amounted to "a sureness which needs no supporting parallels,"[62] then surely he could have written a book less encumbered by sketches of enemy lifeways.

In fact Dover knew that the sense of limitation answered in Woodruff's statements originated not in communal disloyalty or self-hatred but in pervasive practices of coercion that regarded any independent stance as a dereliction of duty. This is suggested

60. Ibid., 48.
61. Ibid., 44–45. Emphasis in original.
62. Ibid., 45.

in his tendency toward restatement—also in the paranoid claim that the most acute threats to black artists are the "alluring advances" from the far side of the color line: "Well-meaning white friends advise them to move, having come of age, into a larger welcoming fraternity, bound by 'the same ideals and the same characteristics which exist,' according to Walter Pach, 'among *all* groups of Americans.' The Mock-Turtle in *Alice* might have had this situation in mind."[63] Accordingly, he also portrays Norman Lewis and Beauford Delaney in terms of defection:

> Norman Lewis has moved from sympathetic, but often witty, concern with Harlem to representational or abstract designs of an immediate feminine charm and evocative quality. Often, it has been rightly noted, they are "poetic hieroglyphs." Beauford Delaney, "the amazing and invariable" bohemian of Henry Miller's doxology of blood and race, has left Greene Street for Paris, and colorful commentaries for the purities of paint and form.[64]

The same resistance informs Dover's appraisal of Norma Morgan, the painter of fantasy landscapes who apparently didn't know how to choose resources: "Her fascination for rock patterns comes, directly or indirectly, from Leonardo da Vinci. . . . By looking in this way [suggested by Leonardo] at 'a confusion of shapes the spirit is quickened to *new inventions*.' Miss Morgan's spirit is quickened into materializing ethereal shapes, but without benefit of local childhood memories and extensive reading."[65] Yet there is nothing local about the consequences of such misdirection: "Art will gain," Dover concludes, "when Miss Morgan acquires thematic control."

Dover all but acknowledges that these artists' strong aesthetics represent a conceptually insurmountable problem when, finally, he abandons Romare Bearden to the white news media, which have already picked up his story. The most ascendant black American artist of the day, Bearden was at that juncture immersed in abstraction, hard at work rethinking his practice. Dover wrote:[66]

63. Ibid., 44, 45. Emphasis in original.

64. Ibid., 50.

65. Ibid., 53. Emphasis in original.

66. This suggests a desire on Dover's part to contain any possible questions a reader might raise about the relatively warm receptions Woodruff, Delaney, and Lewis were receiving from the general art media.

> Romare Bearden is difficult to assess. He is, in the best sense, an obsessed painter, moving in widening circles around the circumstance of being a Negro persistently devoted to the causes of Negro art. His early paintings were those of a social realist with a difference, the difference being an expressionist toughness suited to the mood and conditions of the 'thirties. At much the same time, he produced several beautiful, purely decorative water colours which hinted at developments in another direction.
>
> Then came a transformed combination of the two tendencies, for out of his Negro experience, and his inclination to master colour and flat, near-abstract design, there grew *a series of plangent constructions reaching out to the common denominators that touch all men . . . .*
>
> Happily Mr. Bearden has since had an exhibition . . . which suggests that he has achieved what he has pursued for so long. Stuart Preston of the *New York Times* (23.1.60) described what he saw as the work of a "virtuoso of texture and of sumptuous and subtle color if ever there was one." Carlyle Burrows of the *Herald Tribune* (24.1.60) responded as follows: "That which materializes is not specific but remote and poetic . . . a sublimation of private experiences more than realizations of communicable subject matter."[67]

By ceding the last word on Bearden's first mature foray into abstract painting, Dover implies that the task of representing that achievement is best left to Others. The critics' language attests to the plainest available truth: what Bearden has done is not Negro Art at all but an exercise in modernist experimentation, which his earlier devotion to Negro Art had delayed. Bearden's own difficulty in defining his position during this period speaks more to the polemical efficacy of Dover's system than to any flaw in the painter's thinking. So concerted is Dover's effort to steady the craft that he follows his report on Bearden with a narratologically incongruous but duly hagiographic passage on Charles White's transcendent "interpretation of Negro Americans."[68] As if to underscore that White's commitment to his people trumps his formal gifts, Dover promises to spare us the embroidered language that Bearden had conjured in the white press. Thus no "learned-looking asides on [White's] 'sweep and strength,' massive sculpting, unmatched

67. Dover, *American Negro Art*, 49. Emphasis added.
68. Ibid., 49–50.

draughtsmanship and influences. These are evident anyway and are just as evidently subordinate to his purpose."[69]

Dover's management of sensitive subjects—such as an artist's susceptibility to suggestion from outside the race; her willful, peripatetic movement among her imaginative resources; or anything that might hinder the representational amalgamation of blackness or compromise its absolute density—indicates the extent to which the world *American Negro Art* presumes to document was being shaped not just by the mounting pursuit of integration on a public scale but by the related elaboration in black political culture of nonrepresentationalist positions. *American Negro Art* attempted to codify the aesthetic morality of a particular subject position that staunchly resists the twinned temptations of mixture and intellectual independence:

> Some Negro artists will . . . lean heavily towards being Americans; and illusions of integration, enlarged by personal acceptance within their particular circles, will encourage them to bend over till they fall down. Others will respond more to their "Negritude" than to Americanism, but a strong sense of sympathy and affinity, prompting a fresh search for values and ideas in Africa or elsewhere, can become dangerous if it develops into racialism. At the same time, the quality of affirmation in Africanism should make it more productive than Negro Americanism, in which the sterilizing element of denial is often pathetically evident.[70]

Better to embrace closure and court racism in the practice of "affirmation," concludes Dover, than enter into the difficulties inherent in one's immediate condition. Yet the infiltration of Negro culture by modes and practices of modernism meant those difficulties would continue to arise, again and again. *Design*, *pure aesthetics*, *invention*: each term encrypted a new and ramifying way of thought about acultural location, or a style of black American existence, that refused the comforts of enclosure.

If Dover's book attests his belief that art was indispensable to the work of "getting together,"[71] something "which gave fullness and

69. Ibid., 50.

70. Ibid., 36.

71. At the outset of *American Negro Art*, Dover dedicates the volume to Aaron Douglas, conveying both men's devotion to the fitness of the collective. It takes the form of a letter in which Dover thanks Douglas for introducing him to "an ex-slave, Mr. Baker, whom you were painting." Here historical continuity and cultural-spatial enclosure

the security of magic to personal and collective living,"[72] it also portrays aesthetic independence as a serious deterrent to group cohesion.[73] Dover's relentless proscriptions of "design," "pure aesthetics," and "invention" show that by 1960 the cultural dominance of black vernacular forms faced compelling new pressures from black artists throughout the culture. In September 1963, Hale Woodruff edited the feature "Leading Negro Artists" for *Ebony* magazine. *Ebony*'s editors, announcing Woodruff to readers as a "veteran artist," wrote as if they construed these developments rather differently, commending those who "have rejected the limiting confines of 'primitive' art once reserved for them by benevolent whites. Instead, America's leading Negro artists . . . have demonstrated their mastery of the full range of artistic expression, from the conventional representational to the ultra-modern abstract." This alongside another feature in the same number titled "Negro in Literature Today: Current Writers No Longer Limited to Negro Subjects."[74]

Dover wrote in full awareness of what Schapiro called "the humanity of abstract painting," which he articulated in a public address delivered, as it happens, also in 1960. Dover's project and Schapiro's shared a moment that sustained each and pushed them against one another. Both writers grasped the extent to which abstract art's humanity could inflect sociality, and both showed concern for what this said about alterations to existing social arrangements. As we have seen, what distinguishes Schapiro's writing is his sympathy with

combine in an image of arresting poignancy. It is also an *effective* image, in light of Dover's polemical ambitions and his account's total reconciliation to its subject matter: "I can still see him hurrying across his proudly cultivated farm with outstretched hands. 'Now I can see,' he said, as you introduced your friend from a faraway corner of the colored world, 'us niggers is getting together at last.' . . . What I absorbed is in the sifting of this book. In so far as it is mine, and that is very little, it is for you. . . . You will criticize it, of course, but you will recognize behind its intention the rugged figure of a grand old gentleman in Alabama [Baker] who would, I think, have seen it as another token of getting-togetherness." Ibid., 7.

72. Ibid., 12.

73. In its spiritual contribution, the best Negro American art of Dover's own time was coextensive with "the visual arts [that once] were also universals in tribal life," only now their making was confined no longer to "gifted specialists, often organized in guilds [or ateliers], who gave pictorial quality to the control of nature and the unknown . . . and perceptively adapted their skills to reducing new situations to manageable proportions." Ibid.

74. *Ebony* 18, no. 11 (September 1963): 131, 4.

those elements of abstract art that are by nature particularistic, and can only be grasped in terms of what they are and do in their circumstance, which are precisely the traits that Dover programmatically refuses. This art, Schapiro observed, "calls up more intensely than ever before the painter at work, his touch, his vitality and mood, the drama of decision in the ongoing process of art."[75] Such work, being frontloaded with contingency, psychology, and other evidences of private will, asked not to be confused with the products of a generalized culture.

> The demand for order, through which the new is condemned, is often a demand for a certain kind of order, in disregard of *the infinity of orders that painters have created and will continue to create.* I do not refer here to the desire for a new order, but rather to the requirement of an already known order, familiar and reassuring. It is like the demand for order in the brain-injured that has been described by . . . Kurt Goldstein: "The sense of order in the patient," he writes, "is an expression of his defect, an expression of his impoverishment with respect to an essentially human trait: the capacity for adequate shifting of attitude."[76]

Dover's own declaration that a prolific American Negro art would "widen our understanding of the life and thought of the American Negro people" rings hollow in light of his alarmed response to the many unambiguous proofs of expansiveness given through visual arts alone.[77] If Negro Art shored up a vision of "intensive minority living,"[78] modernism promised something linked to the unevenness and complexity of intercultural experience. In seeking participation in an open, culturally heterogeneous space, a black modernist manifested the drive toward the very zone of experience from which remediating structures such as Negro Art offered safe refuge in the guise of freedom.

The postwar period's first major political experiment to secure freedom for black Americans was under way. Popular support might not last long. There wasn't time to debate conceptualizations of freedom.

75. Schapiro, "On the Humanity of Abstract Painting" (1960), in his *Modern Art: 19th and 20th Centuries* (New York: George Braziller, 1978), 229.

76. Ibid., 232. Emphasis added.

77. The statement appears on the volume's dust jacket.

78. This was the promise of Fisk University as communicated by Aaron Douglas, who brought Dover to Fisk at the end of the Second World War. Dover, *American Negro Art*, 7.

Practical reason dictated that if art was a shortcut to action, then it made sense to demand that any black person with a creative project should unequivocally produce affirmative work.[79] Notably, there is a place in this thinking for the political-phenomenological intensity that a work of art can induce, and a thriving social fantasy life in which art compensates for lacks in the real world; there is also room for the more explicitly idealistic recognition that art offers a unique place in experience for the pursuit of ends to which it will not be prudent to expect everyone's assent. This thinking does not accommodate, but militates against in recognizing how practicing abstraction served freedom by different means—through a form of engagement with the really existing world that also suggested how it might be altered. To the extent that abstraction pointed to the dirty work of entering the intercultural fray without prejudice about the possibilities of mixture, and to a different pacing of change, abstraction was *too* political. Politics is slow, made of up of fragile legions. Affirmative culture offers speed, unity, and a clear route forward.

In the 1960s blacks became, through their own hard cultural work, the representatives and the representations they had sought in vain from a reluctant, at times unspeakably hostile white American mainstream. If the counterpositive integrity of the affirmative image proved especially compelling, it is because it is a good that at any moment can be brought about *now*. As Dover's tract makes abundantly clear, Black Art is defined by accessibility in the fullest sense; it teaches and reveals, and its content never evades. Art is allied with immediately realizable ends. Quite unlike the full integration of American institutions, or the fading of antiblack attitudes, you don't have to wait for an art that "enlarges the appreciation of the Negro minority in America" (Dover). Accordingly, the self-realized Negro artist was already the ideal emancipated individual. The rule governing his practice was not disciplined into existence; it derived from the reason given by his nature (by his origin in the craft guilds of Africa, where Dover's story begins). The magic of the Negro artist is that he already possesses the freedom not yet broadly achieved in black (or any) society as a whole. His function is to be a leader: he is

79. See Horkheimer, "Individualism," 77, 82, and notion of "independence in ideology."

an individual who specializes in the critique of egoism.[80] Even though the tribulations the Negro artist depicted were anything but relieved when Dover was writing his book (1960), Dover could celebrate these depictions as "transformations" because his spectral subject always has them in hindsight. That is to say, the air of melancholy nostalgia, that incongruous future perfect of the Negro artist, is thinkable only if we first detach that figure from the experience of the existing world, and especially the existing world of 1960.

American Negro art thrives not only in isolation from but in opposition to the integrating society, which the culture of modern art had already realized in a limited form. The modernist's distinction is that anything not derived from my own nature actually *restricts* freedom, because it binds me to something that is not myself, something alien upon which I nevertheless make myself dependent. I am conscious of cultural closure as something to be overcome rather than served. The modernist practitioner dares to take direction from the her instincts as a maker. She is one for whom everything that comes to her from outside her Negro nature counts as more than mere stimulus.[81] Thus marked by the influence of exposures deemed incongruous with her nature, her work is banished to the gallery of what Dover calls "educative ironies."

Placing black practitioners of modernism at the fringes, or beyond the limits, of politically salient activity recapitulates the common refusal to understand abstract art in terms of its practical effects, as if to deflect attention from the interracial dimension of the existence brought into view by black artists' dogged pursuit of it. To consider their situation judiciously, we must widen our view to include the intraracial politics of the movement itself, specifically the denials of representation entailed in the pursuit of formal political representation and the fervent disavowal of strong public manifestations of mixed culture. It was not the hidden politics in the art but the impatient texture of freedom-directed discourse and action that substantiated abstraction—as resistance. Abstraction pointed up the existence of contrasting points of view about the organization of black lives: it cited artists' interest to *open* closure, to redeem the human status

80. See Horkheimer, EFM, 55–56 and 57.
81. This sentence interpolates Adorno, *PMP*, 70.

upon which monolithic cultural practices preyed. In this way abstraction deterred the prime motive force of black cultural politics: speed, consolidation of consensus, achievement of symbolic density, and expedient language. Abstraction was not only a crucial defense for the individual in the midst of generalizations, a place of relief from the rushy, thrown-together, fetishistic aggregative ideal. It *represented* a decisive move across the color line, into the craggier terrain of social experiment, capturing the optimism inherent in standing down from the ideal in order to transact with what already is. (Exceptions include those few abstract artists who have volunteered themselves to Black Art as though in apology for their formalist tastes, most notably Tom Lloyd.)

Dover's response to Bearden's late 1950s equivocation between representation and abstraction is particularly interesting in this regard. Bearden expressed his difficulty in adapting to a purely nonobjective idiom as an unambiguously moral challenge: "I am trying to find out what there is in me that is common to, or touches, other men. It is hard to do and realize." If Bearden had not experienced an insight, if he had had no knowledge that another kind of moral obligation—to representation—constrained his practice, he might not have articulated in this way his attempt to embrace a more complete abstraction. Bearden knew enough to associate abstraction with resistance, and knew that his move was fraught by the implication that it pointed away from the clan and toward the fraught zone of interracial contact. In Bearden's situation, what was especially flagrant was the contradiction involved in thinking about something, steeping oneself in a form of its difficulty, when we feel (or are made to feel) we should be *doing* something about it instead.[82] The desire to modernize his practice opened Bearden up to a contradiction between the moral requirement that he disappear into the idiom of Negro Art, and the more sensuously appealing possibility of attempting through his art to access the other, to make of his art a proof of their equal humanity. Here Adorno is instructive:

> This contradiction is not one we can simply ignore. . . . In other words, where we find contradiction, where we find ourselves unable to eliminate contradictions through the stratagems of theory or conceptual devices,

82. Ibid., 9.

> what we have to do is to become conscious of them, to generate the strength to look them in the face, instead of arguing them away by more or less logical procedures.[83]

Bearden, by immersing himself in a kind of abstraction he had previously found unthinkable, fought his way through that contradiction to the most important work he would ever make (just after his return to figuration in 1963, during the Spiral group's experiments).[84] Dover, writing in 1960, could not have known this. In fact one of the last adjustments he made to his manuscript was to add the white critics' praise for Bearden's abstractions, giving him license to write Bearden into a vivid portrait of race betrayal. Bearden's is an open-shut case that shuts, sadly, with the gavel-drop of Charles White's unwavering race loyalty. But of course Dover's conception of Negro Art would be unthinkable apart from the sort of conundrum presented by Bearden.

Embedded thus in the canon of American Negro Art are case after case of how the modernist aporia opening in black culture was spatializing things. Its every manifestation raised the *question of the relation of the individual to the general* as a problem for the practice of representation. *Compensation* is the psychoanalytic term for a certitude that persists in the face of its own disproval. Facing the absence effected by traumatic loss, the mind establishes a presence to compensate. In all its varieties, black separatism was a compensatory response—the actual and rhetorical production of subjects, experiences, and forms that compensated with symbolic embodiment, and particularly epistemic certainty about blackness, for the loss of social and cultural coherency as a race—to mounting evidence that race at this juncture was "losing its composure." The compensating subject stifles racial discomposure and its attending disquiet by ratcheting up her inner violence, strengthening her bond to the categorical. "The man who is the possessor of force," wrote Simone Weil, "seems to walk through

83. Ibid.

84. See Dore Ashton, "Romare Bearden, Projections." *Quadrum* 17 (1965): 99–110; Romare Bearden, "Rectangular Structure in My Montage Paintings," *Leonardo* 2 (January 1969): 11–19; Ralph Ellison, "Romare Bearden: Paintings and Projections," *Crisis* 77 (March 1970): 80–86; Gail Gelburd and Thelma Golden, *Romare Bearden in Black and White: Photomontage Projections 1964* (New York: Whitney Museum of American Art, 1997); and, Courtney J. Martin, "From the Center: The Spiral Group 1963–1966," *Nka: Journal of Contemporary African Art* 29 (Fall 2011): 86–98.

a non-resistant element; in the human substance that surrounds him nothing has the power to interpose the impulse and the act, the tiny interval that is reflection."[85]

Compensations manage the frustrations engendered by whatever lies beyond the reach of our psychic mastery—the idea of living without a firm anchor in racial identity, for instance—by the steady production of lucid, compelling substitutions.

I am concerned here with the implications of this epistemic violence against the perception (and representation) of interracial sociality in the age of separation—the late sixties through early seventies—perhaps the primal scene of the paranoid response to widespread events of racial discomposure. Occasions to encounter mixture and its manifestations multiplied daily, placing ever greater demands on the categorical imagination. In other words, as soon as social and political expression began on a large scale to reflect the fact of mixture, specific means were devised to dis-integrate culture, to win the ongoing war with a strategy that militated against mixture on anybody's terms except the separatists' own. The prevalence of compensations to this day shows how interracial sociality unsettles instituted, idealized narratives of racial experience, frustrating the impulse to keep the races separate. Only an act of force can reduce the event of racial discomposure to an indivisible unit of substance (e.g., undiluted blackness).

Modernist activity depended on a structure of color, both literal and racial-metaphorical, that was reflective, ductile, and oriented to its changes—indeed it was conceptually wedded to the *tension* between fixity and transformation. On the ethical plane, where this activity necessarily symbolized a dynamic relationship between black and white, it manifested the races' need for each other and, still more, provided a territory apart from its violent denial through acts committed not by the state alone but by citizens of every variety.

In 1967 Raymond Saunders published a small book in response to an essay by Ishmael Reed describing the black American artist's situation.[86] As would an artist like Lawrence Weiner the next year, the

85. Simone Weil, quoted in Jacqueline Rose, *The Last Resistance* (London: Verso, 2007), 12.

86. See Ishmael Reed, "Black Artist: Calling a Spade a Spade," *Arts Magazine*, May 1967, 48–49.

had followed *Harlem on My Mind*,[90] organized by Allan Schoener for the Metropolitan Museum of Art in 1969. That exhibition had precipitated the mainstream art world's first significant collision with black cultural nationalism. The Black Emergency Cultural Coalition (BECC), formed in 1969 to protest the Met's show, was the first articulated nationalist organ in this milieu. Artist Benny Andrews, a founding cochairman of BECC (with Henri Ghent and Cliff Joseph), later recounted the group's origins:

> I thought about that strange event called the "Preview Reception for the Harlem on My Mind Exhibition," and what really stuck in my throat was the flippant and superficial attitude of the people I'd met there who were connected with the show. That episode was to enable me to sustain a sense of indignation that will be with me as long as I live. The indignation that I felt was shared by many others too; its physical expression was first manifested in a visible form in the establishment of the Black Emergency Cultural Coalition.[91]

Like Ringgold's telepathic "awareness" of black truth, Andrews's "sustained sense of indignation" tapped into a resource that was more ideological than personal. Andrews was but one of several figures on the local scene who were busy adapting nationalist rhetoric for art-world use. By the time of the Harlem show, that rhetoric had been popularized by Harold Cruse, Addison Gayle, LeRoi Jones (Amiri Baraka), Maulana Ron Karenga, Don L. Lee (Madhubuti), and Larry Neal, among others, who regarded newly created black culture as a prerequisite for revolutionary politics.[92] The black community had to free itself culturally before it could organize politically, and cultural freedom presupposed unity rooted in the color and consciousness of blackness. Karenga's widely promulgated doctrine, in which African

90. See Allon Schoener, ed., *Harlem on My Mind: Cultural Capital of Black America, 1900–1968* (New York: Random House, 1968), and the *Metropolitan Museum of Art Bulletin*, January 1969. See also Bridget R. Cooks, "Black Artists and Activism: *Harlem on My Mind* (1969)," *American Studies* 48, no. 1 (Spring 2007): 5–40.

91. Benny Andrews, "The B.E.C.C.: Black Emergency Cultural Coalition," *Arts Magazine* 44, no. 8 (Summer 1970): 18.

92. "Black artists should devote their time to expressing the needs, aspirations, philosophy, and life style of their people. They should deal with the social problems that black people are having in this racist society, *so that there will be an accurate record of our progress from an oppressed to a free people.*" Dana Chandler, quoted in *Black Art Notes*, ed. Tom Lloyd (self-published, 1971), front matter. Emphasis added.

Americans constitute a nation, assigned to blacks a preternatural need for unity, since they are "more inclined to emotion, instinct, and folk wisdom than to dispassionate intellectual rationality and a reliance on formal education for the accumulation of knowledge."[93] As its primitivizing drive indicates, this was cultural racialism, and accordingly it held division as a central tenet. "Blacks can only liberate themselves by the adoption of a unified, cohesive black culture which is completely divorced from that of the white man" (Alphonso Pinkney).[94] Potent black art would help resegregate the larger culture of the United States, putting special pressure on the black creative class. No artist would be spared. The double valence of representation in this rhetoric meant that art was uniquely susceptible to it.

The best-known tracts use a language of self-discovery and improvement through which nationalists urged upon a demoralized public their own fantasies, desires, and representational forms. Race consciousness specifically revamped the idea of the individual so that it reflected an inexorable move toward the embodiment of positive blackness. The construction was considered "positive" even though it determined the subject completely, beneficent because it was directed toward her liberation. Being a subject of racism, one's performances of self would symbolize the sloughing of a racist self-concept.

We can assess the cultural saturation of these ideas—and their dependence on a compliant visual culture—by reading a 1969 feature in the venerable monthly *School Arts*, "a national magazine committed [since 1901] to promoting excellence, advocacy, and professional support for educators in the visual arts." The feature "Art for Black Students: A Change in Objectives" begins with its author, Carolyn Lawrence of Chicago's Hirsch High School, averring that "before setting forth my objectives for the school year 1967–1968, I really had to seriously question my reasons for teaching art. I had to question my effectiveness in speaking to a classroom of black students. . . . I had

93. Joe Street, *The Culture War in the Civil Rights Movement* (Gainesville: University Press of Florida, 2007), 152.

94. As Jones/Baraka put it, "Our freedom will be in bringing Black Culture to Power. We Cannot Do This Unless We Are Cultured. That is, Consciously Black." Alphonso Pinkney, "Contemporary Black Nationalism," in *Black Life and Culture in the United States*, ed. Rhoda L. Goldstein (New York: Thomas Y. Crowell, 1971), 253. Pinkney is paraphrasing Jones/Baraka at this point in his text, which ultimately defers to the position held by Jones/Baraka.

to do something [to make them] more culturally aware."[95] "What the black student needs," she wrote, "is to produce an art that is idea-oriented. He needs to . . . look his heritage in the face and understand his racial heritage in terms of his own family history."[96] Lawrence's teaching, in her words, "emphasize[s] through cultural forms . . . a feeling for what it means to be black."[97]

The problem Lawrence diagnosed and the solution she struck upon summarize the emphatically pedagogical strategy in the Black Arts Movement. For Lawrence, as for the authors of the doctrine she recapitulates, art is indispensable as an instrument of liberation, and it is a project to be distinguished from self-discovery or -realization. Her language of needs ("I had to"; "the student needs") invokes a lack in order to satisfy it with affirmative representation: the drama of necessity conceals the force of the meanings imposed to set things right. Emergency was a style. Always, and in all things, one "had" to think, see, and act in a certain way. Art existed to establish *continuities* between black subjects and features in the larger landscape that are ours and ours alone. No amount of wandering among sources or opacity in output would be tolerated.

Simply but profoundly, Black Arts pedagogy reverses the flows of racial alienation—it's still secured through an objectification of black character, only now *black people elect this objectification.* The philosophy upon which it's based sought to do a lot of conceptual work, something along the lines of recoloration. On the one hand, a theory of vision such as the black aesthetic promises to fortify the struggle against racism by furnishing race-appropriate truths to impose any form that might present itself to "black consciousness." But total liberation from "white things" (material and immaterial) will follow only once the Black Aesthetic is reflected in and projected by black people *in their persons.*[98] Wrote Larry Neal: "If we assert that Black

95. Carolyn Lawrence, "Art for Black Students: A Change in Objectives," *School Arts* 68, no. 6 (February 1969): 19.

96. Ibid., 19. Continuing, Lawrence recognizes Black Art's promised solution to a far greater dilemma than her own or her students': "This country can't begin to solve its problems until black children begin to affirm themselves as human beings of worth."

97. Ibid. The crucial shift of referential frames, proceeding from Self to Family to Race, somehow forms a spatially and temporally elaborated, yet singular, enclosure.

98. I hasten to add that this is what it means to reproduce racism by continuing to

people are fighting for liberation, then [surely] everything that we are about, as people . . . relates to it."[99] It wouldn't be enough to depict or recover or claim black culture; one had to *become* black culture oneself. Such calls inspired numerous entrepreneurial intellectuals to devise ways to bring about the transformation of so-called Negroes into unequivocally black people. Social scientists embraced the challenge of imagining subjects for the new blackness. Time and time again, they lit upon the simplest possible conception of the individual: she would be the effective, concrete bearer of the new black institutions, bound by membership to maintain and reproduce them.

In the summer of 1971, William Cross, a PhD candidate in psychology at Princeton, offered the readers of *Black World* "a rundown of the stages and levels of awareness" involved in the "Negro-to-Black Conversion Experience"[100] (fig. 1.8). He describes the discovery of racial consciousness, which, in a majority of the subjects he observed produced an abiding need for art. "During the period in which a person immerses himself in a 'world of Blackness,'" he has "a creative burst, writing poetry, essays, plays, novels, or confessionals; a segment turns to the plastic arts or painting."[101] Cross incorporates actual testimony from artists as he describes the key "stage" of the process:

> Professional artists speak of profound and fundamental change in the quality of their work. In explaining the change, these artists state that although they were born in a Black situation, their training and pressure from society made them look for substance and content outside the black experience. For example, some wanted to be "pure" and "free," creating art for art's sake. . . . [But] with the realization of their blackness, [they] awakened to a vast and new world. . . . The artist (or scholar) simply has to look in the mirror. There occurs a turning inward and a withdrawal from everything perceived as being or representing the white world.[102]

---

produce *subjects for* racism, even if the condition to which one aspires can be very differently described.

99. Larry Neal, "Any Day Now: Black Art and Black Liberation," *Ebony* 24, no. 10 (August 1969): 55.

100. William E. Cross Jr., "The Negro-to-Black Conversion Experience," *Black World* 20, no. 9 (July 1971): 13–27. Hereafter cited as "Negro-to-Black." A cartoon in the article's heading depicts a Negro who becomes black by swapping his coat, oxford shirt, tie, and smartly parted hairdo for a dashiki and an afro. An equally real transformation, the article assures us, has occurred on the inside.

101. Ibid., 18.

102. Ibid., 19.

Toward A Psychology of Black Liberation

THE NEGRO-TO-BLACK CONVERSION EXPERIENCE

BY WILLIAM E. CROSS JR.

A rundown of the stages and levels of awareness

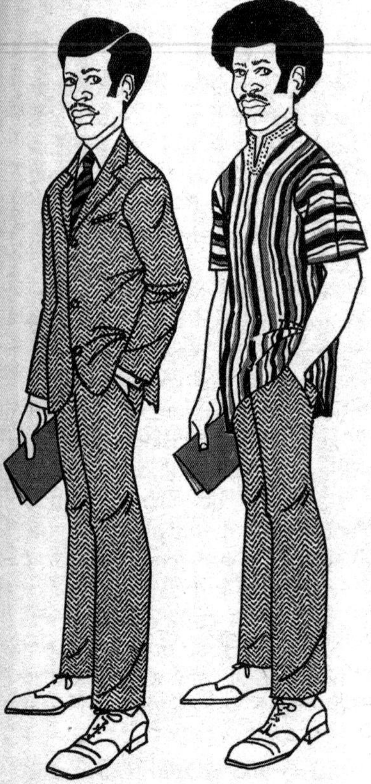

IN THE September 1970 issue of Ebony magazine, Joseph White, a Black psychologist, called for research and development of a Black psychology. Professor White stated that the so-called neutral value paradigms currently being used to evaluate and conceptualize the behavior of Black Americans are in reality weighted towards the conditions and values of white middle-class America. A Black psychology, according to White, would evolve from an understanding of the behavior of human beings within the context of Black America, *i.e.*, the psycho-social economic and cultural setting of Black communities.

A sub-heading or component of a Black psychology might be the psychology of Black liberation. In fact, one of the first concerns of Black behavioral scientists should be the creation of developmental theories, personality constructs and Black life-styles that promote psychological liberation under conditions of oppression. You will note

Figure 1.8. William E. Cross Jr., "The Negro-to-Black Conversion Experience," *Black World* 20, no. 9 (July 1971): 13.

Texts such as Brown's and Cross's may seem like slow-moving targets, but a hugely consequential and enduring structure of thought stems from them. They suggest how feverishly critics across the disciplines were devising ways to say the same thing: just as race makes the maker, so it makes her art. We see how the same idiom tacitly recognizes discomposure effects by eliding individuals, their choices and relative autonomy. We see how blackness was articulated as a structure consonant with theories of structuralism then prevalent,[103] producing a corrective discourse of blackness that sought to bind its subjects in a psychocultural vise. In countless ways the discourse substantiates such vulgar generalizations as the black mind, black temperament, and black culture. What distinguishes it from earlier models is not only the scope of its influence but its dictatorial affect. The dominant mood is policing and prohibitive. The stress continually falls on *closure* to racially "inconsistent" inputs arising in normal contact with the heterogeneous public culture of the United States. It wasn't enough to be born black. As much as anything, this discourse was about showing people how many ways there were of getting your blackness wrong. Blackness was a state of being to achieve through protracted withdrawal from "everything perceived as being or representing the white world."[104] The project of educating black desire; the aspiration to depopulate the black public of mixture signs; practices that pejoratively recoded or disappeared whatever might betray imbrication in a more complex sociality: art played a key role in all these endeavors.

If the spread of these ideas through the art world is any indication, then Pinkney was correct in crediting black nationalism with "what is probably the greatest mass base for radical social change in the

103. "A structure is not a mere collection of elements and their properties. . . . It involves laws: the structure is preserved or enriched by the interplay of its transformation laws, which never yield results external to the system or employ elements that are external to it." Jean Piaget, *Structuralism*, trans. and ed. Chaninah Maschler (London: Routledge, 1971), 7. See also Ferdinand de Saussure, *Course in General Linguistics*, ed. Charles Bally et al. (New York: McGraw-Hill, 1959); Émile Durkheim and Marcel Mauss, *Primitive Classification* (Chicago: University of Chicago Press, 1963); Claude Lévi-Strauss, *Structural Anthropology*, vol. 1 (New York: Basic, 1963), and *The Elementary Structures of Kinship* (Boston: Beacon, 1963); and Louis Millet and Madeleine Varin d'Ainvelle, *Le structuralisme* (Paris: Éditions Universitaires, 1965).

104. Cross, "Negro-to-Black," 18–19. If this account sounds fanciful, it may be to do with Cross's evident yearning to give sociopsychological grounds for his merely prejudicial foreclosure of anything that might thwart the conversion process.

society."[105] Unfortunately, its transformative effects remained almost wholly within the black population. It wasn't long before mass-media outlets adopted a stance of deference to the nationalist urge. For the April 6, 1970, issue of *Time*, the editors took "the unusual step of devoting most of [it] to a report on the condition of *black America*,"[106] and their depictions all but recommended that readers resign themselves to the "new mood" among American blacks (fig. 1.9). "Blacks are asserting a new sense of pride, self-reliance—and impatience. . . . The black sense of inequality is, if anything, growing." "Most black leaders are now committed to militancy short of violence." The editors went so far as to downplay the social perils of separatism. At least it was quieter than riots:

Figure 1.9. Cover of *Time Magazine*, April 6, 1970, featuring Jacob Lawrence's portrait of Jesse Jackson. © 1970 Time Inc. Used under license. Time Magazine and Time Inc. are not affiliated with, and do not endorse products or services of Licensee. Art © 2015 The Jacob and Gwendolyn Knight Foundation, Seattle/Artists Rights Society (ARS), New York.

> The blacks' new aggressive assertion of their separate identity helps to strengthen white segregationists, who are only too happy to keep them separate. . . . But to the extent that it celebrates black culture and nourishes black pride, it is a positive, important, and undoubtedly permanent phenomenon. To the extent that black separatism represents a retreat in hate from US society, it may only be a temporary phase.[107]

Activities on the cultural front, particularly in visual arts, gave these developments a public face. The special issue of *Time* offered black artists a generous forum and a national audience. The article "Object: Diversity" divided them into three "attitudes": "The youngest and angriest," represented by Dana Chandler, "care neither about what Whitey thinks nor about what they call the 'white man's aesthetic.' Their sole interest is to create a black art to which the black community respond"—in other words, to work from a public mandate. "Other young artists are painting or sculpting out of their sense of black [personal?] identity" and are represented by David Hammons, Malcolm Bailey, and Melvin Edwards. The third group comprises "those artists for whom the question of blackness seems to be irrelevant—they are probably the large majority—[and who] are busy establishing their own kind of individuality" (Sam Gilliam, Daniel LaRue Johnson, and Richard Hunt). "Whether their work is polemical or not, most black artists

105. Pinkney, "Contemporary Black Nationalism," 260.
106. "Black America 1970," *Time* 95, no. 14 (April 6, 1970): 15. Emphasis added.
107. Ibid., 16.

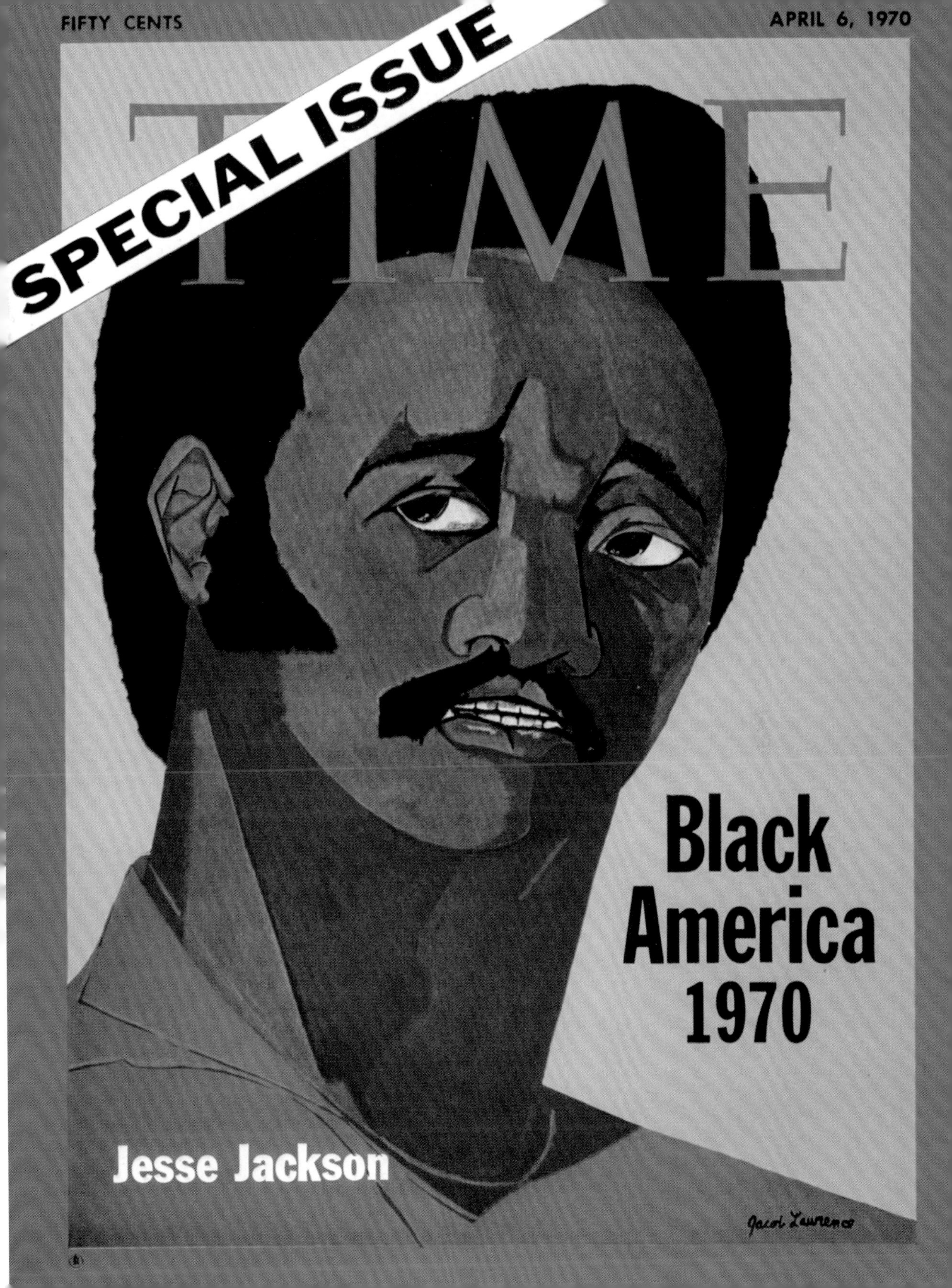
FIFTY CENTS
APRIL 6, 1970
SPECIAL ISSUE
TIME
Black America 1970
Jesse Jackson
Jacob Lawrence

feel that the art world is controlled by whites and still largely closed to them."[108]

In its haste to depict the art of "black America" with a vividness befitting the exigency to which this number of the news weekly was devoted, the coverage suppresses the great conflict among these artists. Questions of technique, ambition, or sensibility couldn't matter less. Instead the article served to confirm that, first, rapprochement between black artists and the art world was every bit as unthinkable as separatists wanted people to believe it was, and second, that the bald fact of majority dissent was somehow negligible.

In fact it had been a cause célèbre among cultural nationalists to shape the public life of color by openly castigating black artists who had demonstrated they were susceptible to nonblack influence. In winter 1971 Baraka published a searing polemic in *Ebony* magazine, "Black Art (Drama) Is the Same as Black Life." It is one of the most compact texts we have of the racialist viewpoint on aesthetics, and like its counterparts in other fields, Baraka's article considers it essential to *delineate the black artist's field of interest.* "When we have the political strength to have institutions then everything will fall into its natural order, as electrons revolving around the pulse of black life, instead of around white mineral retardation. We are all to blame . . . since we will not honestly communicate with each other and leave ego worship to sick whities [sic]."[109]

What Baraka calls "ego worship" we might otherwise describe as the practice of autonomy, of engaging the problems of art as one finds them, of declining the mandate that racialism sought to universalize. From such an outlook, the loss of cultural density threatened by the deviant "so-called artist intellectual politician"[110] would be incalculable. "All of us had better refocus on Nationalism,"[111] Baraka insists. "And don't say, 'it's my own thing.'"[112] Baraka's figure of independence is "marked" by participation in racially white culture:

108. "Object: Diversity," *Time* 95, no. 14 (April 6, 1970): 83.

109. Imamu Amiri Baraka, "Black Art (Drama) Is the Same as Black Life," *Ebony*, February 1971, 82.

110. Ibid., 78.

111. Ibid.

112. Ibid., 76.

> Niggers singing Verdi . . . niggers doing Shakespeare . . . niggers in wigs or wigs in nigger. . . . niggers talking about how they are against "Separatism," yet in the true history of the world have never been integrated with white folks to any advantage and fortunately for most of us, will not [be]. The term integration simply means that white ideas will control. And that is merely contemporary slavery.[113]

The alternative is clear: "All of black energy must be harnessed for National Liberation, as actuality. . . . Art itself is one activity. But artists must organize people and must first organize themselves around the needs of the people."[114]

Baraka may be associated with intolerant bombast, but his own art never failed to reflect his commitments. The hallmarks of his playwriting are forms that not only demonstrate the fundamental incompatibility of the races but affirm art's unique capacity to project this truth—to be the kind of "black, black art" that Ringgold forecasted in 1970. His work of this period advances several models for the violent rhetorical and representational acts through which supposedly affirmative interpretations embody the parameters of a life lived in exclusive service to black culture. According to the terms of the nationalist text, black people become a group through denials and exclusions. Only an unconscious identification of this depth and virulence can satisfy the doctrine, and Baraka's plays, like his paradigmatic black artist, strain to bring the audience to this place. As Joe Street notes in an excellent study, Baraka's white characters are uniformly mendacious and savage or guileless and foolish. "The degeneracy of these characters and the simplicity with which they are drawn are major uniting features. The black characters who consort with these whites become infected by this degeneracy. Only those who kill whites, namely the army in *Death Unit* and Black Man in *Madheart*, survive and flourish."[115]

Though much of his art depends on an indissolubly polarized relation between black and white Americans, Baraka's most effective, most dramatically crucial characterizations are black figures of racial discomposure. His plays direct huge stocks of energy to the moral

113. Ibid., 78. Emphasis in original.

114. Imamu Amiri Baraka, "Black Art (Drama) Is The Same As Black Life," *Ebony* (February 1971), 82.

115. Street, *Culture War in the Civil Rights Movement*, 130.

lessons to be drawn from those who cross the color line (fig. 1.10). *Slave Ship* (1967), still Baraka's most celebrated work, takes as its subject the misguided perversity of the integrated nonviolent movement, which is also the figurative setting for the play. In the third of four acts, a race traitor returns in the guise of a preacher in a modern business suit—an avatar of contemporary bondage. He speaks in glossolalic language of "nonviolenk," a device for Baraka to remind a black audience that had rejected integration (the audience for which he wrote) that Martin Luther King Jr. spoke neither to nor for them. Toward the play's end, the revivified bodies of dead slaves and revolutionaries form a mass, cluster around the preacher, and kill him. As *Slave Ship* nears its end, the cast engages in a jubilant dance. Black audience members are then invited to the stage to join the cast in a release of collective anger, taking the event beyond theatrics to direct experience. Nonblack audience members are meant to remain in their seats, bear witness to the collapse of life into art, and presumably speculate on what may follow. "Once the audience is comfortable with the dancing, the preacher's severed head is thrown onto the dance floor to conclude the play."[116]

Because the symbolic dilution of the race could be wrought from inside as well as from outside—by means of "color distortion" —"criticism" meant a special vigilance. To the cultural nationalist, the autonomous creator was an invaluable, seemingly unmissable opportunity to rehearse the racial deserter's intimacy with the enemy. In the vocabulary of the ardent cultural nationalist, not only was "intimacy" conceptually proximate and racially exclusive; it denoted unqualified adherence to the collective as well. In the art realm this meant granting the black art expert unchecked authority over the judgment and interpretation of works in her care even if the art itself was the least of her concerns.

In 1970 art educator Edmund Barry Gaither coined the term *new black show*, explaining its necessity by reference to the fact that "black shows" of the sixties had differed in two important respects from earlier ones: they were usually hosted by major museums and universities ("reflecting the pressure of militant arts organizations"), and they were of a much higher quality (due to "the introduction of black

116. Ibid., 133.

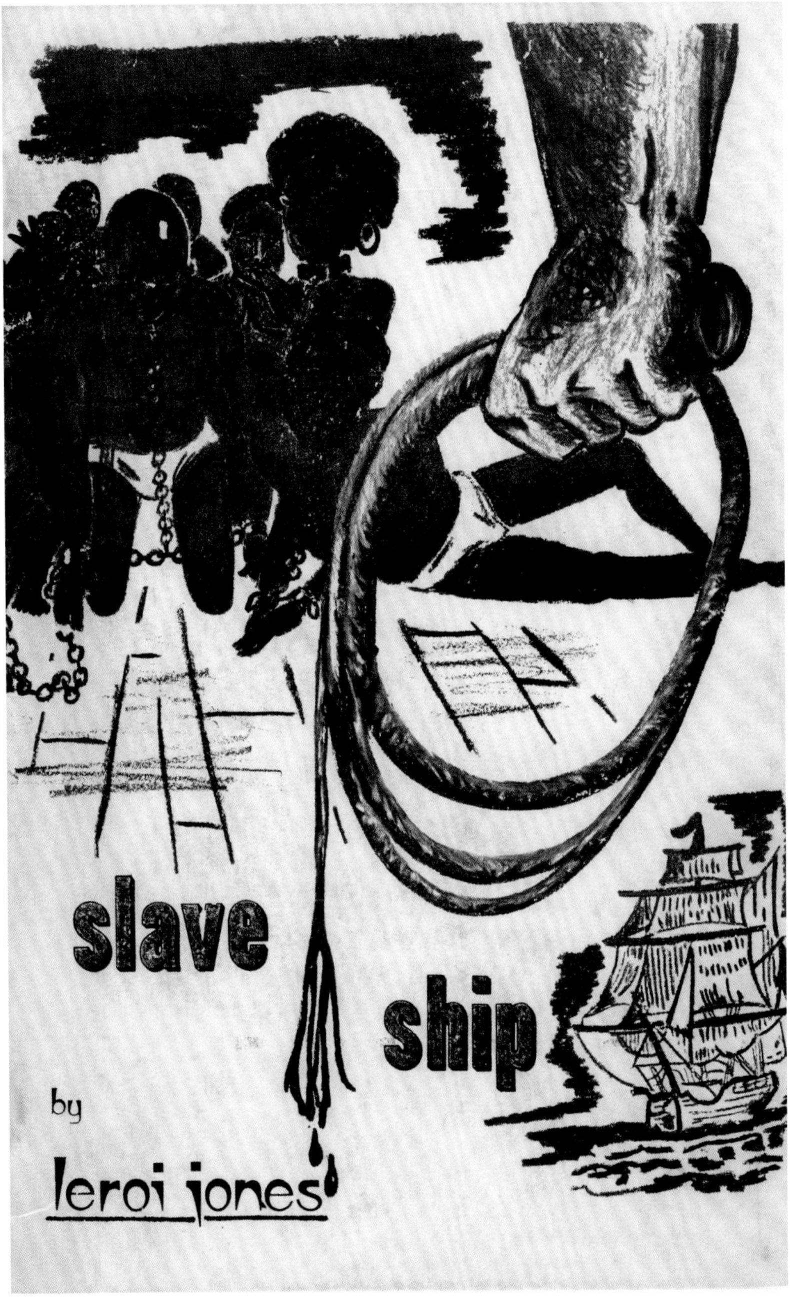

Figure 1.10. LeRoi Jones, *The Slave Ship* (Newark, NJ: Jihad Productions, ca. 1969). Yale Collection of American Literature, Beinecke Rare Book and Manuscript Library. Yale University.

organizers who have shown a greater sympathy and understanding of their fellows and have thus prevented faux pas such as *Harlem on My Mind*").[117] The interventions of cultural nationalists had finally made it possible to bring a black perspective to public presentations of black artists' works, and to those who shared Gaither's mindset, this assured a "valuable educational and cultural experience for both black and white viewers and artists."[118] A uniquely efficient cultural technology, the "new black show" fused art and essentialism and itself offered viewers a richly environmental experience. And yet art's *role* in these environments was to submit to the authority of a code or theme likely to be wholly incongruous with the work it framed. I am thinking now of the work of Malcolm Bailey, Ed Clark, Frank Bowling, Norman Lewis, Alvin Loving, Barbara Chase-Riboud, and Alma Thomas—just seven of the artists represented by abstract works in Gaither's 1970 exhibition, *Afro American Artists: New York and Boston.* Abstract art posed a particular problem for the new black show. Indeed, it is through the look and substance of this work that we become aware of the dangerous distortion of fact, the exploitation, entailed in Gaither's statement that "in his visual language, the black artist is basically a realist."[119] The claim is itself a critical weapon in the black art expert's arsenal, for it joins a racial essence to material factors that would manifestly undermine it—were they given a voice. Neither the contradiction nor the exploitation carries any consequence, and the openly conjectural character of abstract art and these artists' evident preoccupation with formal concerns have no positive value in the expert's discourse.

Those who would celebrate the emergence of the new black show as a progressive development in the history of art or museums are right to do so. Certainly it was instrumental in putting pressure on mainstream museums to become mindful of the relationship between the often extremely narrow public for which they program and the larger, very differently constituted ones they actually serve. But we also need a counternarrative that accounts for the conspicuous entitlement with which the black art expert insists, for instance, that "the

117. Edmund Barry Gaither, introduction to *Afro American Artists: New York and Boston* (Boston: Museum of Fine Arts and SMFA, 1970), n.p.

118. Ibid.

119. Ibid.

black artist may not even be aware of the extent to which blackness has influenced him, but in critical situations, the influence will inevitably surface. To the extent that any artist hides from or denies his African or African-American roots, his courage, honesty, and dignity as an artist suffer."[120] Thankfully for some, it was not up to artists to decide what counted as a "critical situation." A featured player on the nationalist stage, the black curator / art expert plays a role far more influential than that of the artist in the production of a compellingly black art.[121] It is she, after all, who performs the intervention needed to make a work of art black.

Equally important for the new black show, then, was to showcase —as it could—the sacrifice of artistic freedom that black artists were expected to make to the will of the curator. But a new black show was nothing until ratified by the black public whose authorization was supposedly discounted by *Harlem on My Mind.*[122] Benny Andrews published a response in the *New York Times* defending Gaither's exhibition against a series of critical reviews by Hilton Kramer. Kramer saw most of the art in the show as "political propaganda pure and simple, and the show itself as presenting a vivid, highly exacerbated black awareness of social problems and social aspirations, but an

120. Francis and Val Gray Ward, "The Black Artist—His Role in the Struggle," in *Black Art Notes*, ed. Tom Lloyd (self-published, 1971), 19.

121. The expert performed a crucial authorizing function as well. In 1971, Robert H. Glauber, the curator of Illinois Bell's Lobby Gallery and organizer of *Black American Artists/71*—a sprawling exhibition comprising 136 works by fifty-nine artists—assures the reader of his catalogue essay that "most of the pieces in this exhibition came to us through the organizing efforts, the publicity, the pre-screening and the patient studio and gallery guiding done by people all over the country. . . . The vast majority of them is Black and they are all experts on their own scene, personal friends, or long-term observers of the artists they have suggested. In virtually every choice in this show, I have been guided by the recommendations of local Black art experts." Robert H. Glauber, introduction to *Black American Artists/71*, exh. cat. (Chicago: Illinois Bell Telephone, 1971), unpaginated. The exhibition ran at the telephone company headquarters' Lobby Gallery from January 12 to February 5, 1971, before traveling for the next eleven months to four venues in Illinois, one in Indiana, and one in Iowa.

122. The art press immediately recognized the new black show. *New York Times* art critic Grace Glueck reported during the season of *Harlem on My Mind* that "only a few years ago, 'segregated' black exhibitions were as scarce on the white art circuit as group shows of work by Hungarians. But with the rise of black consciousness—and whites' recognition of it—such shows have become de rigueur with museums, galleries, and even corporations, all of whom are rushing to mount them." Grace Glueck, "Negroes' Art Is What's In Just Now," *New York Times*, February 27, 1969, 34.

altogether depressing lack of awareness of artistic problems."[123] In response, Andrews invokes Gaither, calling him "the black cat who can read our people even when they are keeping their cool." (Translation: he can discern what's black even in an utterly non-objective work.) Andrews had asked Gaither if black attendees were "proud of the exhibition." "Barry hesitated for a moment and said, 'Yes, they felt all those things that should be felt. But remember that you will be facing them in the gallery talks, and you'll get the answers yourself.'"[124]

Andrews dedicates most of his piece to Kramer's review of the exhibition ("it goes without saying that Kramer is unqualified to honestly evaluate this kind of exhibition"; "his inability to mentally penetrate an exhibition of this kind"; "a critic like Kramer" had "an impossible task . . . when faced with a body of work like this"). The vivisection of Kramer is a pretext for Andrews's presentation of the more comprehending vision that black people bring to such an exhibition. Here is Andrews's account of the scene in the gallery after he had explicated his own painting, *The Champion*, to a group of visitors (fig. 1.11).

> When I finished talking about my feelings and my reasons for painting, I looked into the crowd, and as I looked from one black face to another, I knew that they felt in their own way the way I felt in mine, and that it was no longer a question, "Did folks feel the exhibition"' I had those beautiful and soulful faces nodding and silently saying, "Yes, yes, indeed we understand."[125]

This is a signal example of the testimonial performativity through which this discourse establishes its authority over and against any troubling manifestation of idiosyncrasy. It engenders the desire for race consciousness by presenting scene after scene of its achievement by individuals who gladly concede their autonomous personhood to the collective.

I will underscore, again, what a toxic environment this is for art by noting how the particular qualities of the ostensibly

123. Hilton Kramer, "'Black Art' and Expedient Politics," *New York Times*, June 7, 1970, 107.

124. Benny Andrews, "On Understanding Black Art," *New York Times*, June 21, 1970, 101.

125. Ibid.

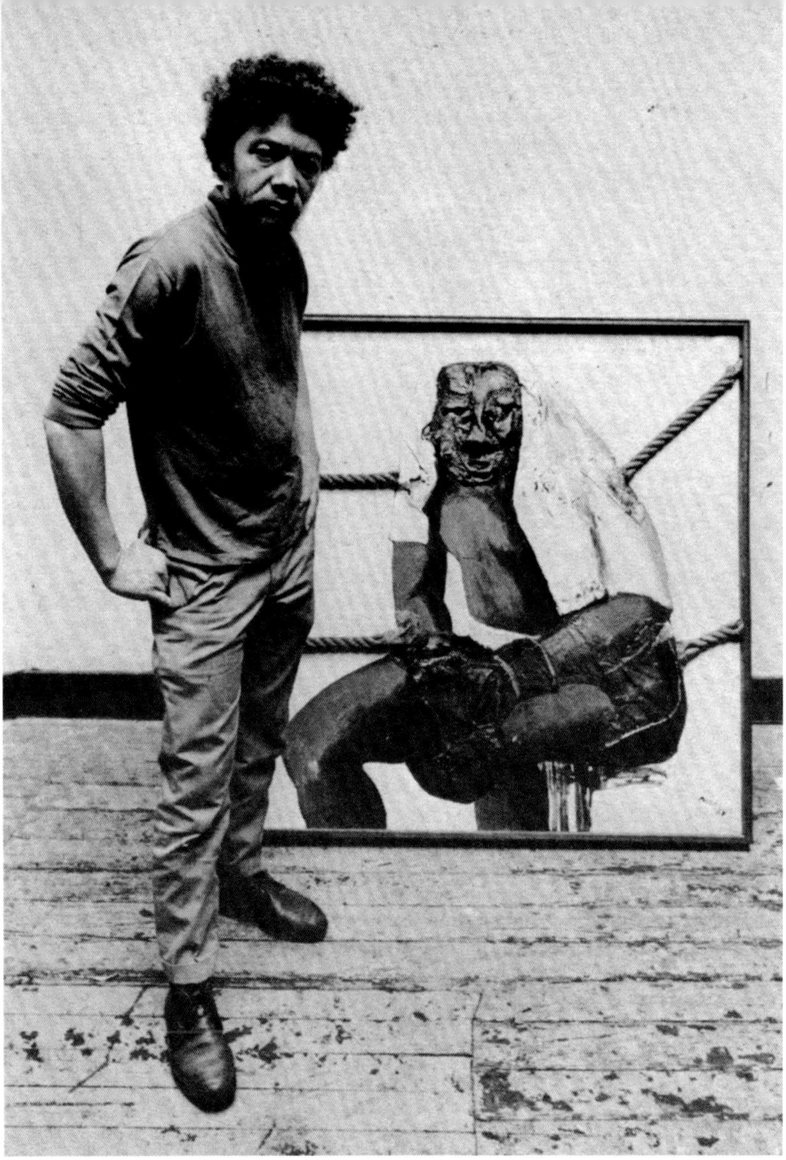

Figure 1.11. Benny Andrews with *The Champion* (1968). From the *Boston Phoenix*, May 23, 1970, 10. Amherst College Archives and Special Collections, Marshall Bloom Alternative Press Collection. Art © Estate of Benny Andrews/Licensed by VAGA, New York, NY.

consciousness-precipitating artworks leave no discernible trace on the representational condition they help bring about. Such works are props; nothing distinguishes them from the cultural work for which they provide a pretext. The discursive relay between Andrews's verbal performance of consciousness and its verification by a phantasmatic black public generates the meaning that the painter now feels it most important to communicate. As James Cunningham wrote in 1969, "The picture of artist and public that emerges is clearly a story of a vigorously mutual affair. HE AND THEY AND THE ART ARE ONE: a clear declaration of the most intimate solidarity."[126]

Certainly art-world devotees of cultural nationalism were capable of making aesthetic distinctions, but the black public was a pretext for critics to elaborate the terms of the artist's inviolable bond to the idea of race. The critics' understandable fixation on the question of representation meant a natural hegemony for figurative art. Again and again, the realist imperative imposing itself sets abstraction at a distance, conjuring "relevance" by bringing a black point of view to anything that might issue from black hands. By focusing on the black artist's activities, we come to realize that even when appreciating the scope of the struggle for public recognition at this historical juncture, recognizing this struggle's positive content is not enough; equally important is the flipside, recognizing what it rejects. The management by this discourse of abstract art in particular makes glaringly evident the element of compulsion at work in the new black show and the art history that developed in lockstep with it. More than any other phenomenon, a black artist doing abstraction undermined the explanatory power of the expert and her methods alike. To tell the full story of the historic struggle for representation taking place at this juncture, we have to track the figure of the black modernist, whose activity is precisely what the struggle rejected in order to achieve itself.

Shortly before racialist aesthetics had fully crystallized into a full-blown politics, the *New York Times* critic James R. Mellow reviewed a peculiar exhibition mounted at the Studio Museum in Harlem in 1969 that presented abstract works by four artists, three black and one white: Melvin Edwards, Sam Gilliam, Stephen Kelsey, and William T. Williams (fig. 1.12). Mellow considered abstraction's peculiar effect on black representational space. In the apparent misfit, Mellow observed a compelling tension. "The attempt to create and promote a specifically black art, as opposed to art created by black artists," he wrote, "underscores the disadvantages—and the radical integrity—of abstraction."[127] Mellow recognized the schism between the art presented and the then-new museum's explicit invitation to

126. James Cunningham, "Getting On with the Get On: Old Conflicts and New Artists," *Arts and Society* 3 (1969): 390. Emphases in original.

127. James R. Mellow, "The Black Artist, the Black Community, the White Art World," *New York Times*, June 29, 1969, D23.

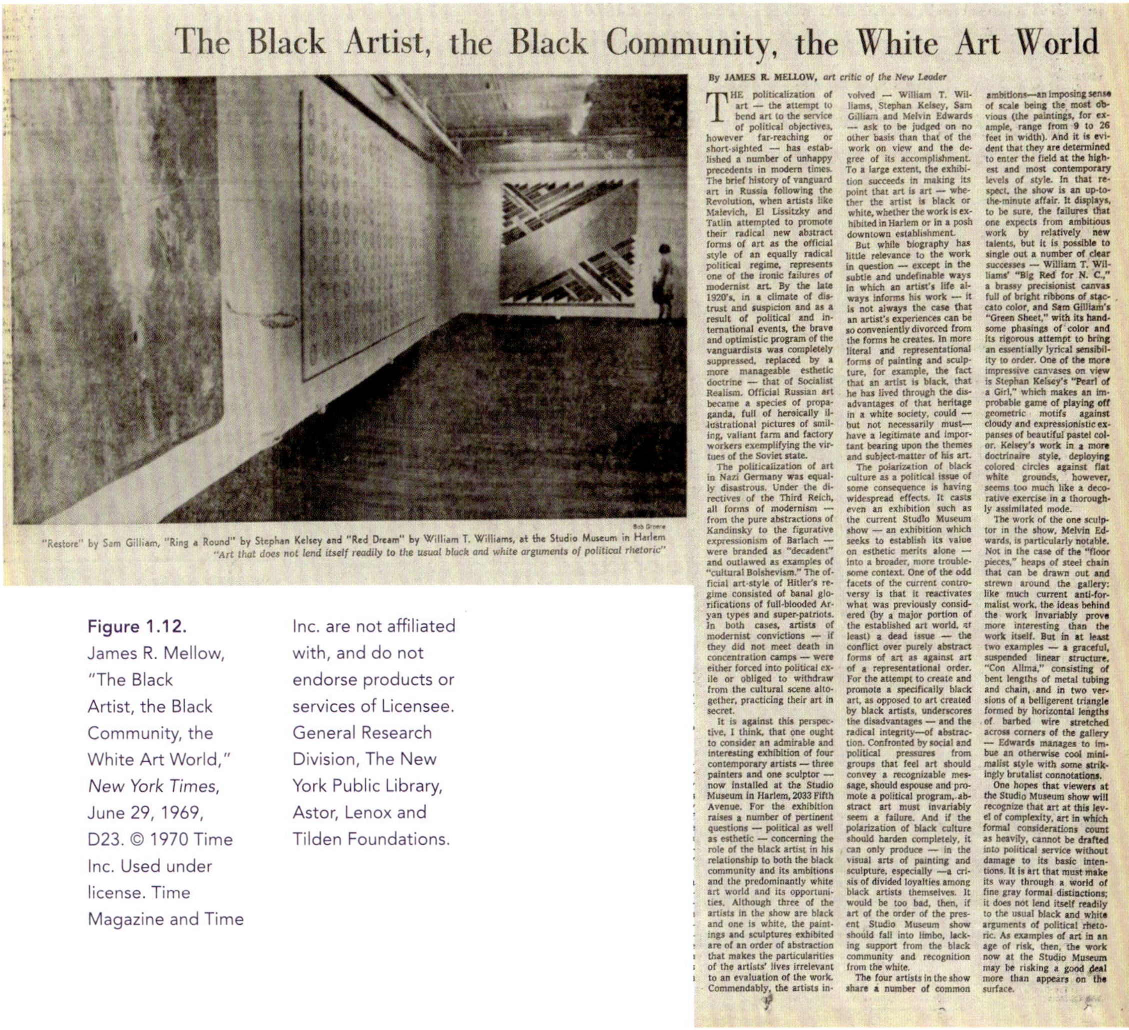

The Black Artist, the Black Community, the White Art World

By JAMES R. MELLOW, *art critic of the New Leader*

Bob Greene

"Restore" by Sam Gilliam, "Ring a Round" by Stephan Kelsey and "Red Dream" by William T. Williams, at the Studio Museum in Harlem

"Art that does not lend itself readily to the usual black and white arguments of political rhetoric"

THE politicalization of art — the attempt to bend art to the service of political objectives, however far-reaching or short-sighted — has established a number of unhappy precedents in modern times. The brief history of vanguard art in Russia following the Revolution, when artists like Malevich, El Lissitzky and Tatlin attempted to promote their radical new abstract forms of art as the official style of an equally radical political regime, represents one of the ironic failures of modernist art. By the late 1920's, in a climate of distrust and suspicion and as a result of political and international events, the brave and optimistic program of the vanguardists was completely suppressed, replaced by a more manageable esthetic doctrine — that of Socialist Realism. Official Russian art became a species of propaganda, full of heroically illustrational pictures of smiling, valiant farm and factory workers exemplifying the virtues of the Soviet state.

The politicalization of art in Nazi Germany was equally disastrous. Under the directives of the Third Reich, all forms of modernism — from the pure abstractions of Kandinsky to the figurative expressionism of Barlach — were branded as "decadent" and outlawed as examples of "cultural Bolshevism." The official art-style of Hitler's regime consisted of banal glorifications of full-blooded Aryan types and super-patriots. In both cases, artists of modernist convictions — if they did not meet death in concentration camps — were either forced into political exile or obliged to withdraw from the cultural scene altogether, practicing their art in secret.

It is against this perspective, I think, that one ought to consider an admirable and interesting exhibition of four contemporary artists — three painters and one sculptor — now installed at the Studio Museum in Harlem, 2033 Fifth Avenue. For the exhibition raises a number of pertinent questions — political as well as esthetic — concerning the role of the black artist in his relationship to both the black community and its ambitions and the predominantly white art world and its opportunities. Although three of the artists in the show are black and one is white, the paintings and sculptures exhibited are of an order of abstraction that makes the particularities of the artists' lives irrelevant to an evaluation of the work. Commendably, the artists involved — William T. Williams, Stephan Kelsey, Sam Gilliam and Melvin Edwards — ask to be judged on no other basis than that of the work on view and the degree of its accomplishment. To a large extent, the exhibition succeeds in making its point that art is art — whether the artist is black or white, whether the work is exhibited in Harlem or in a posh downtown establishment.

But while biography has little relevance to the work in question — except in the subtle and undefinable ways in which an artist's life always informs his work — it is not always the case that an artist's experiences can be so conveniently divorced from the forms he creates. In more literal and representational forms of painting and sculpture, for example, the fact that an artist is black, that he has lived through the disadvantages of that heritage in a white society, could — but not necessarily must— have a legitimate and important bearing upon the themes and subject-matter of his art.

The polarization of black culture as a political issue of some consequence is having widespread effects. It casts even an exhibition such as the current Studio Museum show — an exhibition which seeks to establish its value on esthetic merits alone — into a broader, more troublesome context. One of the odd facets of the current controversy is that it reactivates what was previously considered (by a major portion of the established art world, at least) a dead issue — the conflict over purely abstract forms of art as against art of a representational order. For the attempt to create and promote a specifically black art, as opposed to art created by black artists, underscores the disadvantages — and the radical integrity—of abstraction. Confronted by social and political pressures from groups that feel art should convey a recognizable message, should espouse and promote a political program, abstract art must invariably seem a failure. And if the polarization of black culture should harden completely, it can only produce — in the visual arts of painting and sculpture, especially —a crisis of divided loyalties among black artists themselves. It would be too bad, then, if art of the order of the present Studio Museum show should fall into limbo, lacking support from the black community and recognition from the white.

The four artists in the show share a number of common ambitions—an imposing sense of scale being the most obvious (the paintings, for example, range from 9 to 26 feet in width). And it is evident that they are determined to enter the field at the highest and most contemporary levels of style. In that respect, the show is an up-to-the-minute affair. It displays, to be sure, the failures that one expects from ambitious work by relatively new talents, but it is possible to single out a number of clear successes — William T. Williams' "Big Red for N. C.," a brassy precisionist canvas full of bright ribbons of staccato color, and Sam Gilliam's "Green Sheet," with its handsome phasings of color and its rigorous attempt to bring an essentially lyrical sensibility to order. One of the more impressive canvases on view is Stephan Kelsey's "Pearl of a Girl," which makes an improbable game of playing off geometric motifs against cloudy and expressionistic expanses of beautiful pastel color. Kelsey's work in a more doctrinaire style, deploying colored circles against flat white grounds, however, seems too much like a decorative exercise in a thoroughly assimilated mode.

The work of the one sculptor in the show, Melvin Edwards, is particularly notable. Not in the case of the "floor pieces," heaps of steel chain that can be drawn out and strewn around the gallery: like much current anti-formalist work, the ideas behind the work invariably prove more interesting than the work itself. But in at least two examples — a graceful, suspended linear structure, "Con Alima," consisting of bent lengths of metal tubing and chain, and in two versions of a belligerent triangle formed by horizontal lengths of barbed wire stretched across corners of the gallery — Edwards manages to imbue an otherwise cool minimalist style with some strikingly brutalist connotations.

One hopes that viewers at the Studio Museum show will recognize that art at this level of complexity, art in which formal considerations count as heavily, cannot be drafted into political service without damage to its basic intentions. It is art that must make its way through a world of fine gray formal distinctions; it does not lend itself readily to the usual black and white arguments of political rhetoric. As examples of art in an age of risk, then, the work now at the Studio Museum may be risking a good deal more than appears on the surface.

Figure 1.12. James R. Mellow, "The Black Artist, the Black Community, the White Art World," *New York Times*, June 29, 1969, D23. © 1970 Time Inc. Used under license. Time Magazine and Time Inc. are not affiliated with, and do not endorse products or services of Licensee. General Research Division, The New York Public Library, Astor, Lenox and Tilden Foundations.

visitors to view the work through the lens of cultural identity. He saw that abstraction compelled distinctions between cultural forms and their content, distinctions with devastating consequences for a cultural politics bent on negating the specificity of whatever came within its grasp. In addition to showing what made the medium of exhibition a particularly potent conduit for this charge, his review is one of staggeringly few contemporary efforts to think through the tension and really grapple with abstraction's challenge. Mellow determined that "abstract art must invariably seem a failure" in its confrontation with

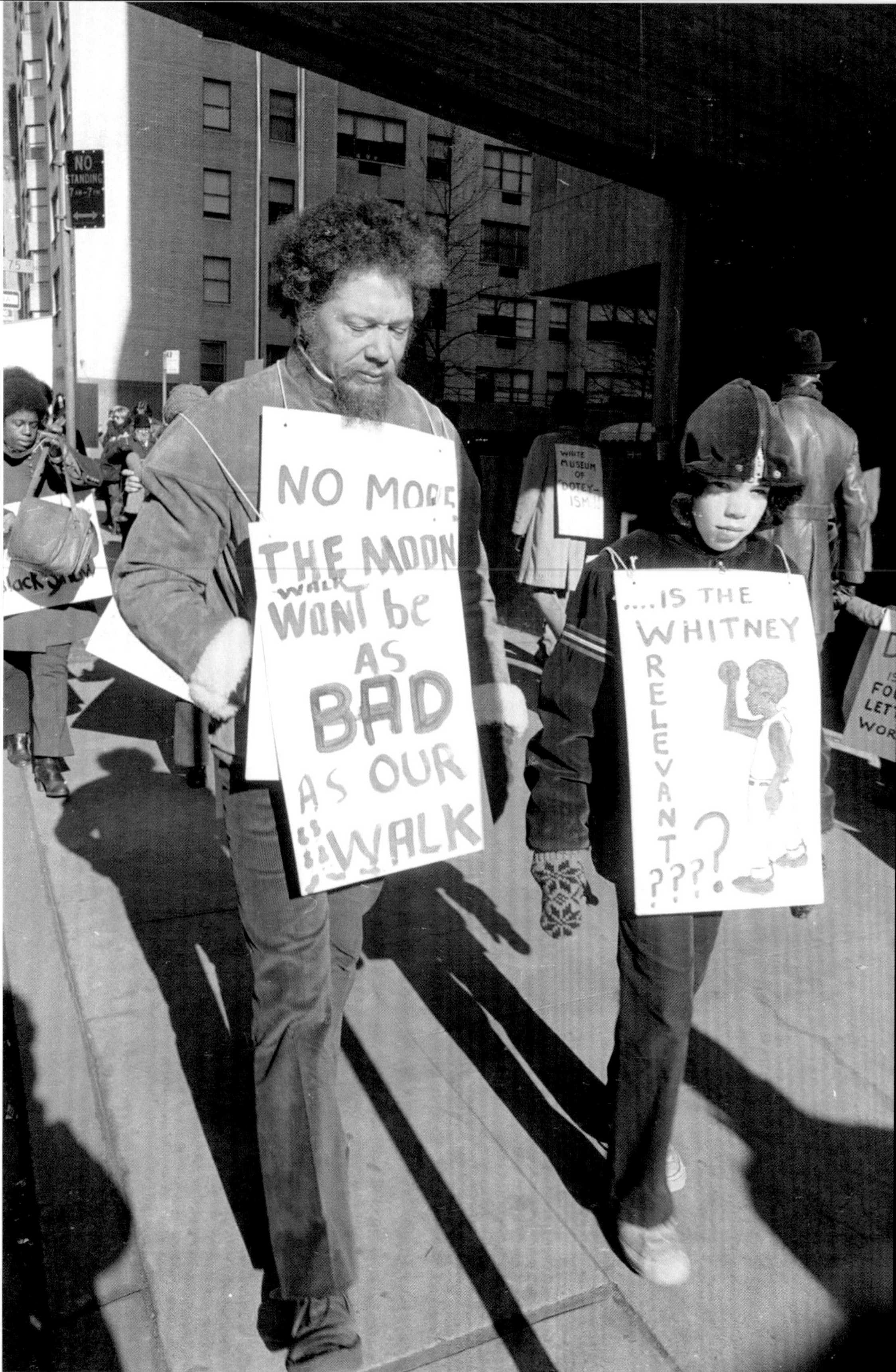
NO STANDING
NO MORE
THE MOON
WALK
WONT be
AS
BAD
AS OUR
WALK
....IS THE
WHITNEY
RELEVANT
???

Chapter 2

Making a Show of Discomposure

Contemporary Black Artists in America

As the work of a white man, *Contemporary Black Artists in America* originated in an abstraction of the black experience. How could it possibly exhibit a convincing picture of American blacks' tireless recent efforts to construct a political identity of their own? Making matters worse, the show's curator, Robert Doty, was certain that his own interest in this cause, because it was developed over several years of conversations with black artists, would yield a result important in at least two ways. It offered a cogent proof that abstract art made a critical difference in the topical but tendentious context of the new black show.[1] And it made an equally strong case for the black modernist's veritable radicality, her socially creative stance of nonfixation on racism, and her seriousness about advancing the cause by expanding the possibilities for representation. As sensitive as anyone to the dangers of letting art get swallowed up in a category, Doty further understood this art's power to evince the *difficulty* of summing up the black race in a category, let alone in a picture. And he appreciated the singular daring of black artists who elected that difficulty by choosing aesthetic independence. At least as clearly as anyone else looking

Figure 2.1. Benny Andrews (left) and child in a Black Emergency Cultural Coalition protest against the exhibition *Contemporary Black Artists in America* outside of the Whitney, January 31, 1971. Photo © Jan van Raay.

1. While I argue that abstraction was the dominant chord in the exhibition—the formal and rhetorical notes with which Doty set the tone for the show and that upon which he summarized it in the closing gallery—*Contemporary Black Artists in America* comprised a mix of stylistic approaches. Alongside the works of steadfast modernists one could also see those of James Brantley, John E. Chandler, Jacob Lawrence, Phillip Lindsay Mason, Charles Searles, Evelyn P. Terry, Heartwell Yeargens, and Charles White, among others.

around in 1971, Doty perceived in this art and its distinctive culture the traces of lived history in the present that had riven the black community very deeply.

Thus being quite a bother to routine methods of narrating the pasts of modernism and black America alike, *CBAA* has virtually no art history. What little consideration it has received invariably originates from the perspective of the Black Emergency Cultural Coalition (BECC), which occupied itself with the exhibition process for the better part of three years beginning in the spring of 1969.[2] Everything about the exhibition seemed to point *away from* the means and ends that the BECC viewed as salutary. Its openness and the social creativity of the curatorial process that brought it about actually made it infamous before it could even open, in April 1971 (fig. 2.1). As mentioned, BECC had formed in 1969 amidst protests against *Harlem on My Mind*. Discussions with Whitney officials followed shortly thereafter, focusing on what the museum could do address the needs of the black community, and especially its artists—none of whom had Allen Schoener included in *Harlem*.[3] First and foremost, they pressed for hiring a black curator or a "name" black art expert. A compelling and timely demand to make of a museum of American art with a paltry record of inclusiveness. Negotiations with Whitney officials were first publicly reported in the *New York Times* on October 2, 1969.[4] "The museum will stage a 'major' black artists' exhibition next year, and it has established a fund for the acquisition of works by the younger and lesser known among them," Grace Glueck wrote. This was said to satisfy two of the coalition's five demands. "The other three were for the establishment of at least five annual one-man shows for black artists in the small gallery off the lobby; more black representation in the Whitney Annuals, with black representation on their selection committees, and a black curatorial staff[er] at the Whitney to coordinate 'all such endeavors.'"[5]

2. For a representative account, see Susan E. Cahan, *Mounting Frustration: The Art Museum in the Age of Black Power* (Durham, NC: Duke University Press, 2016).

3. *Harlem on My Mind* closed on April 6, 1969. The first meeting between BECC and Whitney officials occurred on April 24, 1969.

4. Grace Glueck, "Whitney Museum Plans Show by Black Artists for Next Year," *New York Times*, October 2, 1969, 53.

5. Ibid.

The survey exhibition, referenced in Whitney documents as the "black show," would take two years to bring off.[6] By the time that happened, the museum had met every BECC demand except for the very one that would authenticate the exhibition in the coalition's view: the appointment of a black curator.[7] Contrary to news reports that the expert question was still in play, a September 1969 memo from Whitney director John I. H. Baur to the museum's attorney indicates that BECC had conceded this point well before Glueck's piece in the *Times* was published:

> After long discussion and two relatively minor changes in the wording of our statement—which I do not think vitiate its contents—we have parted amicably. This is an end that I believe was infinitely worth working for. . . . We have made it clear that we could not appoint a Black guest curator for the black show, the Annuals or any of our other activities. We have said only that we would consider qualified Black candidates when a regular curatorial opening occurred, but that our final choice would be based on the ability and experience of all candidates. They have accepted this position and the omission of the whole subject from the release.
>
> The only new sentence added to the R[elease] says that we will consult Black art experts in the survey phase of our large Black exhibition "wherever feasible." Steve and I left the meeting and worked out this wording very carefully.[8]

The BECC's acceptance of these terms included an acknowledgement that Whitney had selected Doty to organize the survey, with the BECC-instigated stipulation that he consult with black art experts. But the curatorial issue would prove far more volatile than either party's representatives suggested at this stage. The Whitney could meet the BECC's ultimate demand in only one way. The winter of 1969–70 saw a flurry of communications to Baur from the coalition over "the

6. The official quoted in the report to address the group show issue was the museum's director, John I. H. Baur. Baur indicated that "the show of black artists' work would be done 'in the same way that we did a California show—to document and investigate what a certain group of artists is doing.'" Ibid.

7. Cliff Joseph admitted in a 1972 interview to knowing all along that the financially strapped Whitney could never concede this point. Cliff Joseph, interviewed by Dolores Holmes, Smithsonian Archives of American Art, 1972. Oral history transcript, accessed by hyperlink on March 25, 2007.

8. Memorandum, John I. H. Baur to David M. Solinger, Esq., September 18, 1969, Frances Mulhall Achilles Library, Archives, Whitney Museum of American Art, New York (WMAA hereafter).

way the selection of art work for the proposed exhibition of works by Afro-American artists at the Whitney is being handled."[9] Already in March 1970, Henri Ghent was talking of "what could have been" about an exhibition that wouldn't open for another thirteen months:

> I wouldn't want to see such a significant gesture of recognition of the black artist jeopardized in any way. But when you insist on allowing Mac to do this thing on his own I think you are, in essence, inviting trouble. . . . Whether this persistence in ignoring capable blacks who could be of invaluable assistance to you stems from sheer resistance to the idea, or a kind of blind loyalty to Mr. Doty, I do not know. I do know that what could have been a meaningful signal of change in the unwritten policies of our Establishment museums has all the earmarks of the kind of paternalism we have come to expect.[10]

Less than a month later, Ghent wrote to Baur again: "Couldn't [WMAA] possibly allow a black to assist in the selection of the art work that will comprise the show?" And he warned, "I don't have to tell you that your present ill-advised course has all the makings of inciting even more resentment and dissension in the black community than in the past."[11]

By January 1971, Benny Andrews and Clifford Joseph had decided to take their anger public. They told Baur that BECC intended "to stage a demonstration in protest of the Whitney Museum's dishonoring of our joint agreement as it was stated in the NYT, October 2, 1969"—which, as we have seen, had misstated the outcome of the coalition's agreement with museum officials (figs. 2.2 and 2.3). Their purpose was "to bring about an effective boycott of the exhibit, one which we hope will persuade [the Whitney] . . . to re-evaluate its general policies, particularly its policy regarding the issue of black curatorial expertise."[12] Enclosed with their letter was a copy of the press release they had prepared. It read in part:

> Ignoring an earlier agreement that the work for the exhibit would be selected by a two-man committee consisting of one of the museum's curators and a qualified Black art expert acceptable to both parties, the

9. Letter, Henri Ghent to John I. H. Baur, April 21, 1970, WMAA.
10. Letter, Henri Ghent to John I. H. Baur, March 31, 1970, WMAA.
11. Letter, Ghent to Baur, April 21, 1970, WMAA.
12. Letter, BECC to John I. H. Baur, January 4, 1971, WMAA.

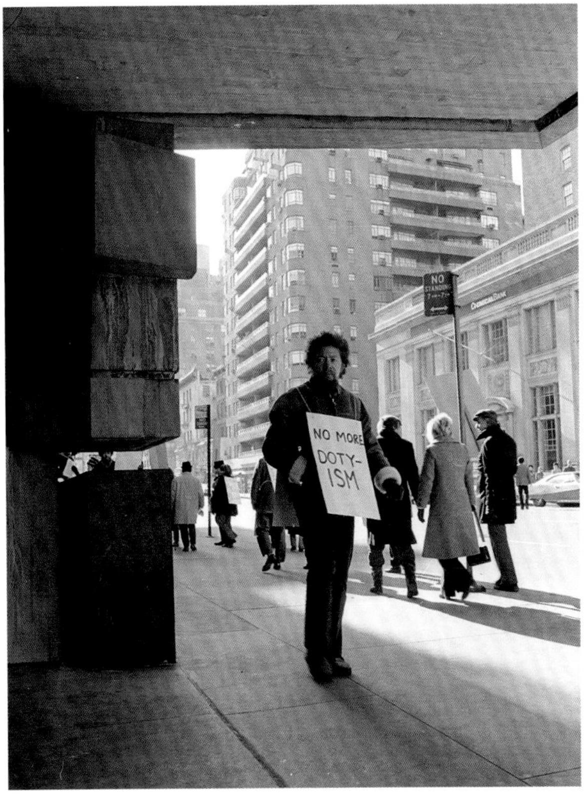

Figure 2.2. Benny Andrews holding a "No More Doty-ism" sign in a Black Emergency Cultural Coalition protest against the exhibition *Contemporary Black Artists in America* outside of the Whitney, January 31, 1971. Photo © Jan van Raay.

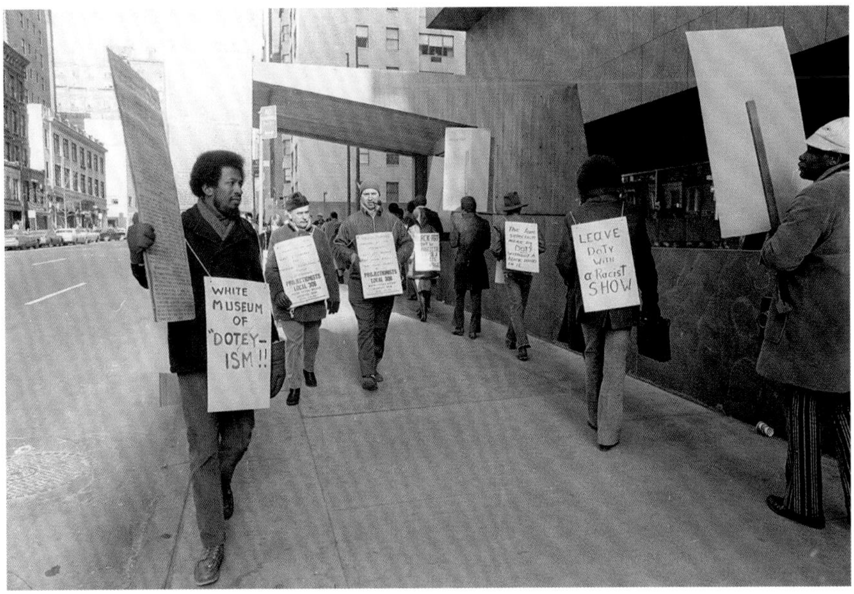

Figure 2.3. Benny Andrews (left) holding a "White Museum of Doty-ism" sign in a Black Emergency Cultural Coalition protest against the exhibition *Contemporary Black Artists in America* outside of the Whitney, January 31, 1971. Photo © Jan van Raay.

> museum declared that its own curators would choose the show, utilizing the advice of Black Art experts "Wherever feasible." We are dealing here with evidence that neither the museum's stated commitment to stage a Black Art show during the art season's prime time 1970–71, nor its grudging promise to draw upon the advice of Black Art experts have been honored. . . . We must seriously question our need to tolerate the callousness of such as the Whitney. Doty's and the Whitney's response to the community's urgent demand for complete and wholesome cultural nourishment, has from the beginning been characterized by a reluctance unbecoming an institution charged with the responsibility of providing and preserving its community's cultural health. It has thereby proven its irrelevance to the community.
>
> We of the Black Emergency Cultural Coalition, being dedicated to the principle of upholding the community's cultural integrity, see it as our responsibility to respond to these gross failures on the part of the Whitney with vigorous and relentless protest action.
>
> We are calling for a massive boycott of the Whitney Museum's Black show by all concerned Black Artists. All sympathetic members of the art community and all people concerned with cultural freedom. We call for this action in protest of policies and practices on the part of the Whitney Museum of American art, in relating to Black Artists and the Black Community, which typify it as a racist institution.[13]

The BECC spent the winter of 1970 pressing its campaign against the approaching exhibition. The protest activity culminated on January 31, 1971, in a two-hour picket along the Whitney's front sidewalk. Eventually fifteen artists would drop out of the show, some in complaint and others in solidarity (the Whitney posted the names of fourteen of the withdrawing artists on a wall near the exhibition entrance).[14] This is the sort of activity that typically counts as political in progressive histories of late art. Whatever it opposes becomes apolitical or retrograde. In such a situation, the actually progressive character of Doty's actions, and of the intellectual project he made of his assignment, becomes difficult to recover.

13. BECC press release, enclosed with ibid.

14. The posting read as follows. "The following artists were invited to participate but withdrew from the exhibition: Robert Hamilton Blackburn, Betty Blayton, Eldzier Cortor, Roy DeCarava, John Dowell, Jr., Melvin E. Edwards, Sam Gilliam, Richard Hunt, Daniel LaRue Johnson, Joseph Overstreet, John T. Scott, George Smith, David F. Stephens, William T. Williams."

In fact, the coalition's claim that Doty had failed to consult black art professionals was patently false. The museum's exhibition records reveal the scope and intensity of Doty's endeavor to learn his subject and to involve black art specialists extensively, both in this process and in the exhibition planning.[15] These efforts, which involved engagements with collectors, academics, community art center heads, and artists, seem to have occupied him fully, in fact, during the winter and spring of 1970.[16] In a memo to Baur, Doty reports,

15. Whitney and Archvies of American Art records show that Doty wrote to John Biggers, then at Texas Southern University; James Conland of the University of South Alabama; Harold Hayden of the University of Chicago and *Chicago Sun-Times*; James E. Lewis, Art Department chair at Morgan State College; and Hughie Lee-Smith, who had just succeeded James A. Porter as acting chair of Howard University's Art Department. A memo from Robert M. Doty to John I. H. Baur dated February 2, 1970 notes "anticipated travel for the exhibition of works by black artists." It details an itinerary covering Southern California ("to see the exhibition Dimensions of Black at the La Jolla Museum of Art; to work with the Black Arts Council, and area artists such as Fred Eversley"); the South ("to see the annual exhibition at Atlanta University, and to visit the Martin Luther King Jr. Institute in Atlanta; Mobile, Alabama: to visit the University of South Alabama; New Orleans, La.: to see artists of the area; and Houston, Texas, for which I have made some inquiries and which seems to have some artists of promise"); "Nashville, Tenn., for Fisk University"; "Washington, D.C. for Howard University, and area artists such as Sam Gilliam"; "Detroit, Michigan, and Chicago, Illinois: Chicago has Richard Hunt, of course. I have learned that there are several black artists working in Detroit"; "Boston, Mass.: the Director of the Institute for Contemporary Art is most willing to help. There is strong art activity in the Roxbury Ghetto. The Elma Lewis School will be important"; "meanwhile, there will be a continual checking of black studios in the New York area"; "San Francisco and the Bay Area: in the Fall, for a final selection. Work to be carried out in consultation with Mrs. Evangeline Montgomery." Memorandum, Robert M. Doty to John I. H. Baur, February 2, 1970, WMAA. That winter the Whitney made grant proposals to the Mellon Foundation and the Taconic Foundation, seeking help with exhibition-related costs. Both foundations declined the Whitney's requests.

16. None of the assembled correspondence between Whitney officials and BECC includes any address by BECC officials to Baur's challenges:

> What concerns me even more [than the BECC's allegations as such] is the spirit of your statement, which seems determined to ignore or subvert everything have been trying to do to help qualified Black artists and promising young people. You know of the work we are doing at our Art Resources Center on Cherry Street for a predominantly Black group of high school students from poor neighborhoods. Did you know that we have succeeded in finding scholarships at art schools for some who are now graduating so that they can continue their training as artists?
>
> You ignore, though I am sure you are aware of them, the one-man shows which we have given to four Black artists in our Lobby Gallery during the last year, and which we are continuing to give. You must also be aware that we have purchased the work of a number of Black artists for our permanent collection and have set up a special fund for this purpose.

Sadly the Whitney's archive no longer contains photographs of the installation.[25] But its caches are replete with evidence that reveals staggering inconsistencies between BECC's portrayals of Doty's process and the work he actually performed to realize the exhibition. By autumn 1969, Doty was mired in preparations for *CBAA*. He visited studios, went on scouting trips, and sent letters of inquiry to artists, writers, and community activists in New York, Chicago, Los Angeles, Milwaukee, Cincinnati, and several other US cities. By the end of January he was developing an organizational scheme for the exhibition. Doty wrote to Baur and Booker, who would host Doty on a scouting trip to Los Angeles: "We have not decided whether there will be many artists represented by one work each or a very few artists represented in depth. The answer to that problem will be settled by the nature of the work itself."[26]

But fears and frustrations continued to plague the project: Ghent, writing as both BECC rep and black art expert, wasted no time in dissociating himself, writing in May 1970 to insist that Baur and Doty leave out of the catalogue any mention of the help he had given them. Ghent's distance-taking made *CBAA* nearly untouchable when it came time for the Whitney to try to travel the exhibition.[27]

25. A selection of photographs of the installation, which are absent from the museum's records, eventually were made available to me, as scans in hard copy, in the final stage of this book's production. My representations of the final installation include adjustments to the manuscript made upon viewing these images, whose source remained unknown to me and which I was barred from displaying publicly until Cahan, *Mounting Frustration*, came to print. I am content with this as my concern since the start of this project in fall 2007 has been to represent to history the figure of the black modernist, those in whom she found sympathy at this juncture, and the movingly optimistic impulses from which these individuals acted and drew strength in this time of their abject maltreatment. For this reason, what takes precedence in these arguments is the exhibition that Doty imagined, planned, built, and described. I am grateful to Cahan for sharing a selection of her photographs with me and thankful for her volume's contribution to the exhibition literature.

26. Letter, Doty to Booker, January 30, 1970, WMAA.

27. Doty finalized the exhibition proposal letter on August 4, 1970, and sent it to LACMA, the Berkeley Museum, the National Collection of Fine Arts in Washington, DC, the Art Institute of Chicago, and the Detroit Institute of Arts. The letters of refusal contain a litany of polite evasions: "you do make the exhibition look as effective as possible," but "we are also planning some kind of black exhibition or festival"; "it looks as though we must decline"; "the possibility of participating in your exhibition . . . does not look very promising"; "we have decided not to participate, in favor of another direction we would prefer to take here." The most dramatic followed Peter Selz's (director of the Berkeley museum) expression of "definite interest in booking this show," when later Brenda Richardson, then associate curator of exhibitions, wrote to Doty again to decline,

More to the point, for many *CBAA* failed because, conceptually and actually, it was a matter of integration—no longer a salutary goal for radical politics. Exigency dictated perpetual deferral to representatives of mass yearnings rather than to particularly compelling, if singular, articulations. And it demanded *disregard* for the fact that Doty was creating a major stage for black artists who sought inspiration beyond the black experience, who embraced an attitude of mutual reciprocity with the general resources of art, or who dared to openly challenge racialist norms.

Nevertheless, focusing on Doty's perceived missteps was a way to disavow the more vexing truth that the spectral consensus of black artists was just that: spectral. During exchanges with Baur, Ghent called Doty's integrity into question; this was not based on Doty's qualifications but on the nature of the art presented in the solo presentations of black artists that Doty and Marcia Tucker had curated since 1969:

> It's a fact that you've given one-man shows to two black artists (and rumor has it that there'll be a third), neither of which can be said to have been a success, really.[28] When I say "success" I'm referring to general public appeal. I'm very cognizant of the fact that an artist, black or white, has to adhere to his own style—regardless of what the public thinks. However, it seems to be the policy of the Whitney to assemble shows [on] the sheer novelty of the works included with very little thought given to its [*sic*] durability and esthetic contribution as a work of art. The consensus of opinion is that the two black artists that you've given one-man shows to will not pose a threat to anyone, hence the reason for their having been chosen.[29]

For Ghent, Doty symbolized the cultural legitimation of the racial discomposure that modernists embodied. Rather than condemning the fact that some black artists were working abstractly, Ghent's "consensus" targeted the Whitney's choice to foreground these

---

saying that "under present circumstances, with which I am sure you are familiar, it seems the wisest thing at this point to follow their ['the black artists on campus and the black students union'] suggestions." Letter, Brenda Richardson to Robert Doty, December 18, 1970, WMAA.

28. These were *Alvin Loving: Paintings* (December 19 1969–January 25, 1970) and *Melvin Edwards: Works* (March 2–29, 1970). The third was *Fred Eversley: Recent Sculpture* (May 18–June 7, 1970).

29. Letter, Ghent to Baur, April 21, 1970, WMAA.

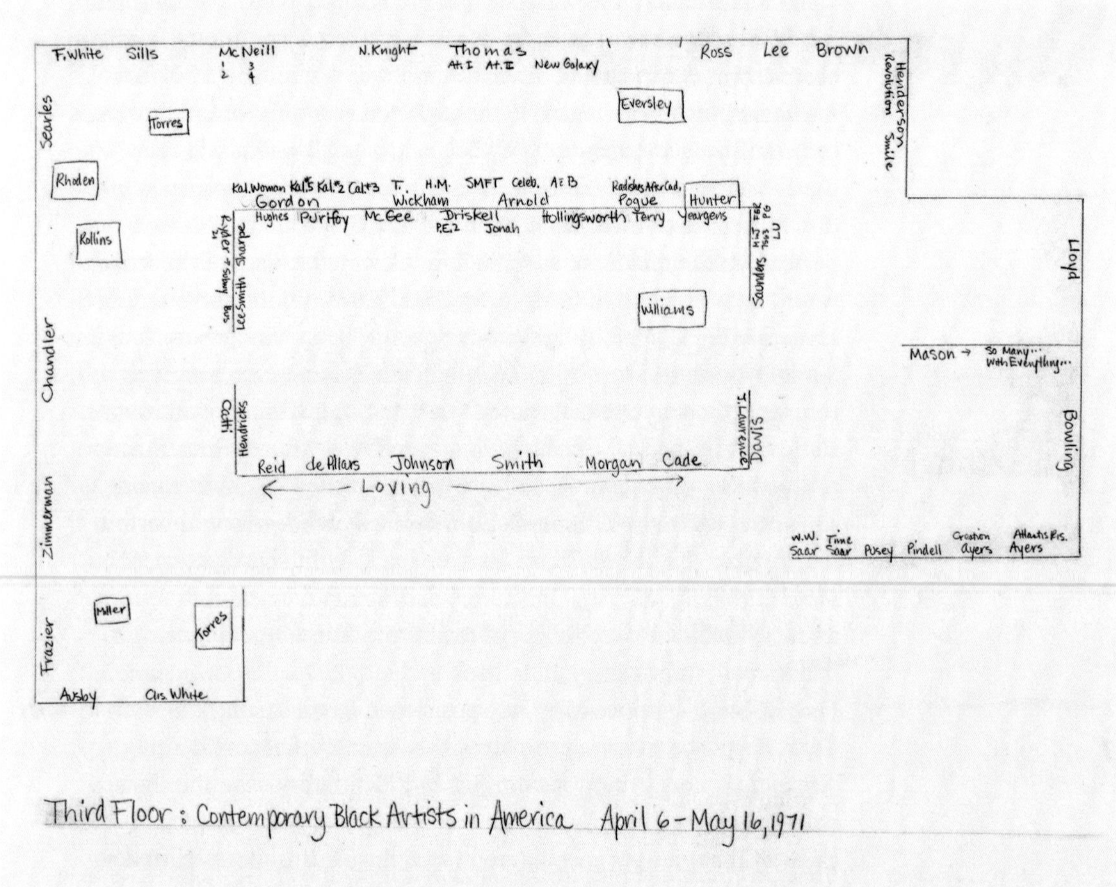

Figure 2.4. Exhibition plan for *Contemporary Black Artists in America.* Frances Mulhall Achiles Library, Archives, Whitney Museum of American Art, N.Y.

Figure 2.5. Frank Bowling (b. 1936), *Where Is Lucienne?*, 1970. Synthetic polymer on canvas, 126 × 134 in. (320 × 340.4 cm). Copyright of Frank Bowling, courtesy of Hales Gallery London. Photographed by Charles Robinson.

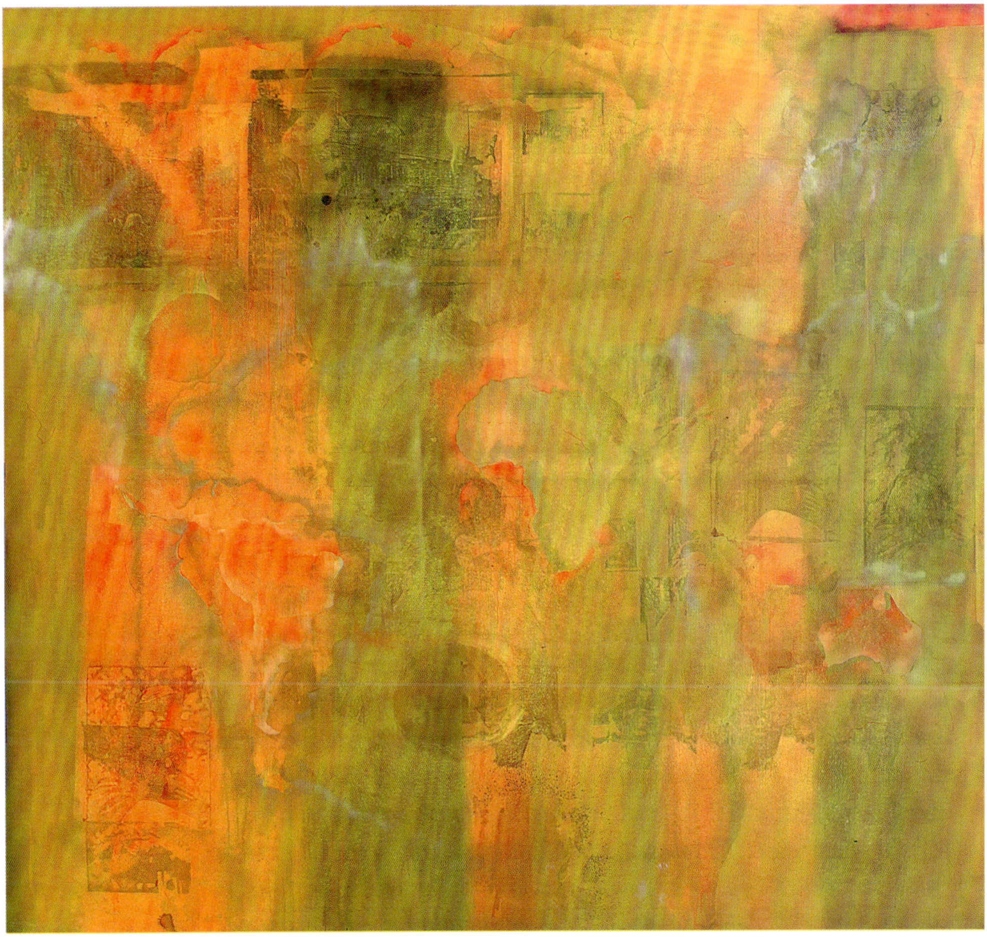

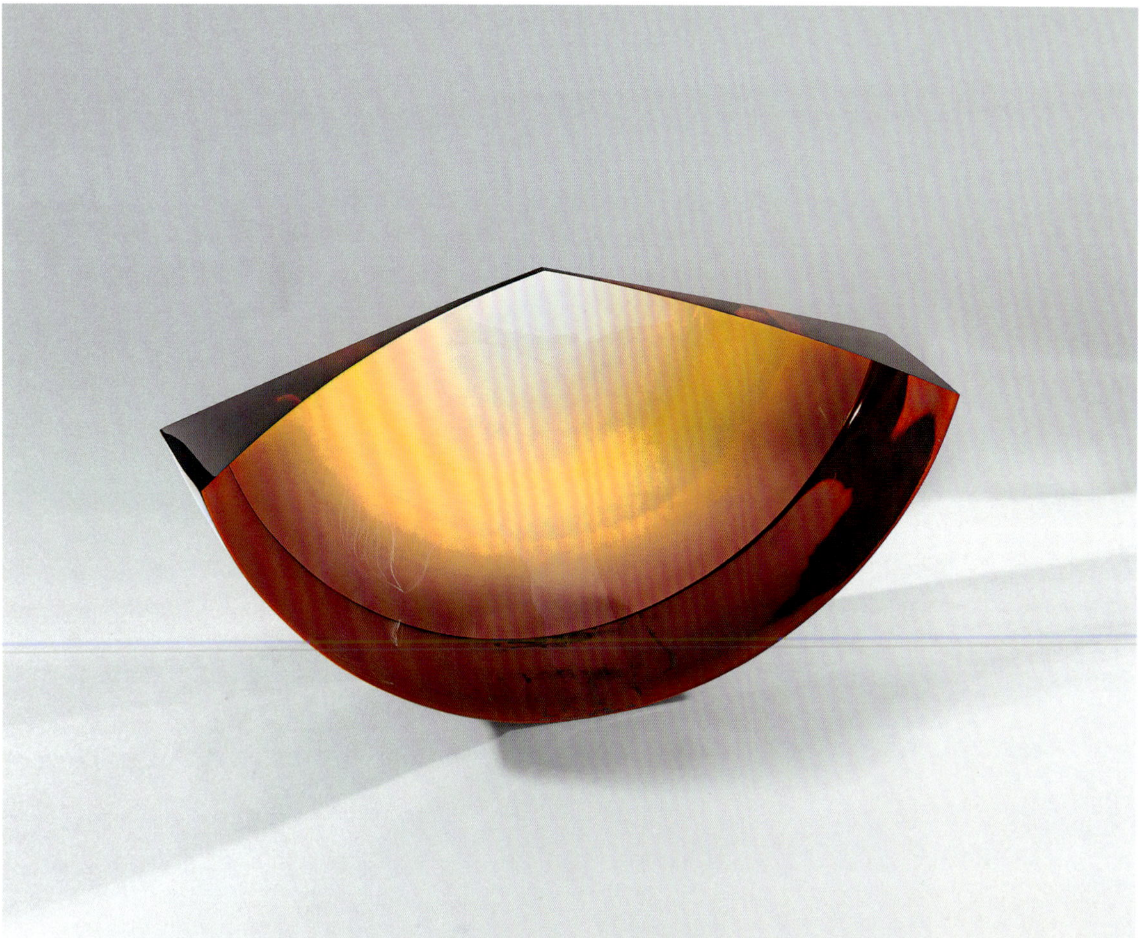

Figure 2.6. Fred Eversley, *Untitled*, 1971. Polyester resin, 20 × 38 × 8 in. (50.8 × 96.5 × 20.3). Photo: Jamie M. Stukenberg / Professional Graphics Inc., Rockford, Illinois. Collection of Nancy Church and Charles Jett. Courtesy of the artist.

Figure 2.7. Tom Lloyd, *Moussakoo (from the Electronic Refraction Series)*, ca. 1968. Light sculpture consisting of aluminum, colored light bulbs, plastic laminate, and digital controller, 54 × 64 × 15 in. (137.2 × 162.6 × 28.1 cm). The Studio Museum in Harlem; gift of the Lloyd Family and Jamilah Wilson. Photo: Marc Bernier. Courtesy of Omar Shabazz.

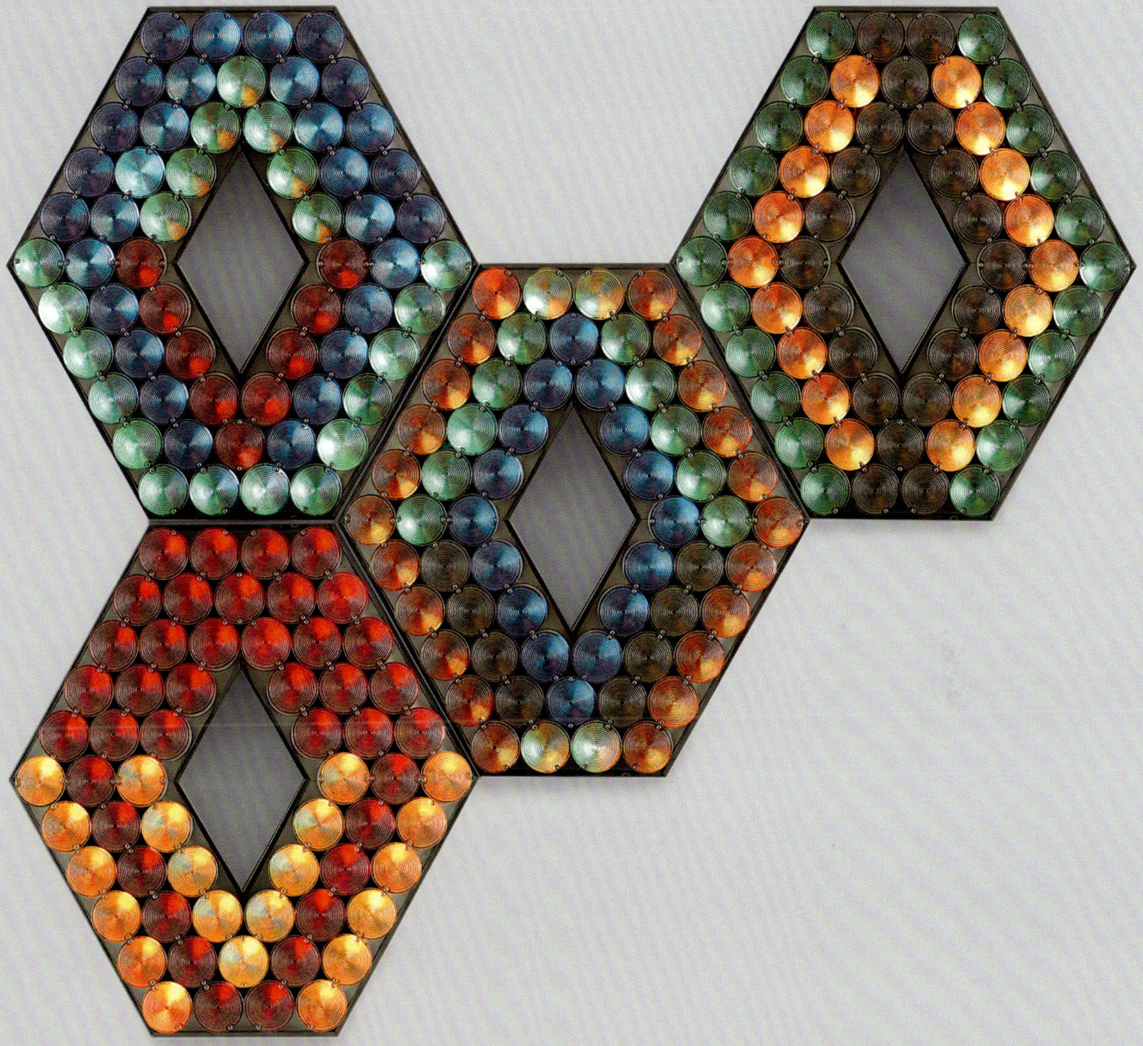

enthusiastically avowed by proponents of Black Art and reflected in the national conversation about the "race problem." And it did so without making the art *mean* its politics. So situated—whether as the aperture through which one apprehended *Contemporary Black Artists in America* or as a strong but less-than-perfectly-explicable presence within that framework—abstraction slowed the galloping consumer. It stymied sociological reading. Upon even a moment's reflection, abstraction would reveal that a dynamic of unsettlement existed not only between the races but *in and through* the "pure color situation" (Loving) that the public picture of contemporary black America served up. To stress abstraction in this setting, to underscore its emergence in the perfectly self-adequating space of black art, was implicitly to privilege its mobility over stasis. "The lines of movement in space that art represents"[35] were now spatially dispersive and anything but concentrated.

In hindsight, *CBAA* offers a lens through which to discern the contested and dynamic nature of the terrain on which stoic formations of blackness were then being established. My argument is simply part of the long reception of *CBAA*, a reminder that we still await a language in which to comprehend such phenomena historically. As we will see, Doty—by all accounts the very condensation of white-institutional insouciance—articulated the exhibition in empathy with the black modernists' autonomy and aspiration, which is itself unrepresentable using current protocols of African American art history. The exhibition invites an art history that does not understate the historically variable relationships of black artists to aesthetic formations such as modernism and even the museum institution. These artists don't need our help discovering a relationship to modernism; already in 1971, the two coconstituted the culturally queer formation whose existence *CBAA merely proves*. Doty's deployment would show that modernism provided dissident black artists—those opposed in principle or in practice to the arts of racialism—with a unification that did not totalize. *CBAA* is the optic through which we see that for them abstraction was politically crucial *as* another way of responding, through art, to pressures in the historical present, or another way of just experiencing that present—a way less oriented to suspicion and

35. Leo Bersani, "Sociality and Sexuality," *Critical Inquiry*, Summer 2000, 643.

antagonism, when such a disposition was hard to come by and still harder to pursue openly.[36]

We can reconstruct some of the experience that visitors would have had by cross-referencing the illustrated exhibition catalogue with the floor plan. These documents show an installation conspicuously short on ideology-friendly motifs and figures. The exhibition's failure to fulfill the implicit task of the new black show inhered in its critique of that cultural form. The most tangible racial presence to be experienced was simply one's knowledge that every one of the artists in the show was black. (Even this wasn't entirely true: Elyn Zimmerman, a white sculptor, was included.) Whatever unity their massing suggested was rarely confirmed by the shifting shapes, invented forms, and erratic chroma in the art. Abstraction's emergence within the space of black art undermined the very idea of the cultural representative; freedom from representation was a working principle for many of the individuals responsible for this work. They sought an audience no more specific than whoever took art seriously. They sought no control over the viewer's thoughts. And they partook fully in the modernist fantasy of self-creation extended in a viewing situation, which modernist sensibility regards as a sustained and sustaining (because repeatable) moment of recognition. Modernism was also a means of dissent. Its promotion of the dissenting artist meant that *this* black show exaggerated the individual's asymmetrical relationship to the community. The openness and vulnerability of this individual was antithetical to the nationalist disposition (to any going definition of the dissenter, really), according to which "our art [will] remind us of our distaste for the enemy."

This was in evidence from the first view to the last: from the "establishing shot" of Alvin Loving's colossal multicolored wall construction to the final gallery full of works so contemporary that the lone instance of realism, a poster-formatted oil painting by Charles White (the fourth oldest of fifty-eight artists), would have struck a loudly dissonant note.[37] The installation guaranteed that one could not rec-

36. This formulation interpolates Eve Kosofsky Sedgwick, *Touching Feeling: Affect, Pedagogy, Performativity* (Durham, NC: Duke University Press, 2003), 144.

37. The section was planned to include two works by Mahler Ryder and one each by White, John Chandler, Catti, Elyn Zimmerman (who is not black), Ernest Frazier, Ellsworth A. Ausby, Algernon Miller, and John Torres.

These arguments make much of the extent to which the discourse of Black Art discourages attention to the wild divergence between color's figurative stability and the chromatic instability of the works themselves. A few months after *CBAA* closed, Henri Ghent wrote an indignant letter to the *New York Times*, responding to a reviewer of his Rath Museum show who confessed to finding it difficult to see the black experience in all that abstraction. Ghent wrote in dismay that "traces of the 'African spirit' and the 'black experience' abound in this contemporary exhibition. If there was a single unifying factor in this diverse show, it was the artists' persistent preference for vibrant color and their consummate use of same."[47] As we have seen, it is Ghent's own *discernment* of racial content suspended in nonobjective works—to him, Sue Irons achieves this through "totally unconscious preoccupation"—that renders their artists' use of color "consummate." Absent such an "informed" observation, color is both less dense symbolically and far more arbitrary.[48] The rhetoric of racialist aesthetics recognizes an *opportunity* in color (its privileged subject) and a *threat* in abstraction (its privileged combatant). But abstraction subjects color to an antithetical type of discipline, one better described as nondescriptive and capricious. Such color resists becoming an instrument of racial enclosure with extraordinary force.

1971 was a moment of uncommon flexibility in abstract painting and sculpture. In retrospect Peter Schjeldahl saw it as a return of "relatively unexplored or recently despised byways of the American abstract tradition. Synthesis and careful eclecticism became, and remain, the keynotes of new abstract painting." Clark, Loving, Thomas, and Whitten are just four who serve to illustrate the transformation Schjeldahl described. As painters sought new expressive possibilities through peculiar visual and tactile effects, "the point is that such operations are not performed with the end in view of some pure aesthetic formulation; that sort of meaning is in desuetude."

47. Ghent, "Protesting the Instant Experts and Their 'Black Art,'" D17.

48. Here is how Jack Whitten addressed the subject of color in 1974, in his WMAA exhibition catalogue brochure: "On Lispenard Street I'd sit by the window and see a certain color on the street, a color someone was wearing on a shirt, I'd go back and grab that color and mix it and put it in. Take Smithson's *Spiral Jetty*. He uses tons of dirt; I use paint. Art comes from everywhere." Jack Whitten, interviewed by David Shapiro, in *Jack Whitten* [August 20–September 22, 1974], exh. cat. (New York: WMAA, 1974), unpaginated. Artist's file, WMAA.

The quiet that had come over the modernist milieu made an excellent environment for artists to cultivate their practices and seek audiences on the basis of feeling rather than fashion. "This is not a period of sensational innovations, but rather one of slow, individual growth and consolidation. It is a splendid time in which to look at paintings, without worrying too much about who is or isn't on the right track."[49] Such art "deals more in feelings than in analyses; the adventure of it is in its extraordinary variety of kinds of feelings." For Schjeldahl this was "a situation brought about by the artists themselves in preference to the sweepstakes hysteria of the art world in the sixties."

But the fact is that painting and sculpture of this kind were in retreat, along with the critical positions that legitimated them. 1971 was also the moment of ascendancy for engaged art practice of a type theretofore unseen in the mainstream of American art. The most exciting new art was unanchored by wall or pedestal. It might ramify over a period of time, or just happen; it might appear somewhere wholly apart from art's traditional spaces; it was thickly experiential and possibly interactive. Many influential critics of the day reserved their most strenuous endorsements for art actions resembling the BECC's activities more closely than those of the painters and sculptors who concern me here. Yet the coincidence of this play within visual formalism, the tendency Schjeldahl reviewed above, and the wider diminishment of interest in modernist dogmas (now closely affiliated with the institutions that artists were interrogating)—if this activity cast a long shadow over modernist painting and sculpture, it also made possible social experiments with this art that were unimaginable when it was de rigueur. I want to suggest that modernism's *performance* in connection to problems of political subjectivity was one crucial possibility that arose at this stage. If *CBAA* offered viewers a chance to explore an "extraordinary variety of kinds of feeling," it did so with the aesthetic dynamics of color painting and sculpture, which, in this setting, could not be dissociated from the event of racial discomposure. This art rudely disaccommodated the desire to reconcile it to some idea about the artists' capacity for a "consummate use of color." Rather, though someone black made this art, she did so toward

49. The foregoing quotations are all from Peter Schjeldahl, "New Abstract Painting: A Variety of Feelings," *New York Times*, October 13, 1974, 183.

an outcome that meaning cannot convey: the traditional pairing of the raced maker and the racial signified is now broken, suspended. No more than a strong nearness connects them.

I have referred to the practice of spectatorial multitasking, of looking at art while simultaneously looking for race. My own confidence that Doty designed *CBAA* as a rejoinder to this practice is based in part on his placement of Loving's colossal, multicolored geometric wall construction, *WYN . . . Time Trip I* on the exhibition's title wall. *Time Trip I*, the exhibition's "establishing shot," gave the viewer no way around the question "How does, how can, *this* picture *mean* Contemporary Black Artists in America?" Nor did it offer a clear way to answer it. In this arena, both race and color—two definitive products of the quantifying mind—began to lose their shape. At this point (and at many others throughout the show), one had no choice but to wonder at the wild divergence between color's symbolic stability in Black Art ideology and the extreme chromatic instability in so much of the art that discourse would explain. Acting upon color toward ambiguous outcomes, this art severed the traditional bond between the black producer and the artwork as a dependable racial signifier. And *Time Trip I* delocalized color with extraordinary force. As we will see, abstraction of the kind that preoccupied Loving at this juncture—as it did Alma Thomas, Jack Whitten, and William T. Williams—subjects color to a type of discipline completely antithetical to the ones that structure normative accounts of racial color.

Time Trip I gave the visitor no way around these dilemmas. As soon as the elevator reached the third-floor galleries and its doors parted, one's attention was seized by and fixed on the sight of this single huge and difficult object—on the work in the art on display, and the work it was doing on the color concepts with which one arrived. The perfect vehicle to engage viewers with the exhibition's questions, *Time Trip I* brought the problem of definition quickly to the fore. *What is this thing? What about the black artist in America? How will I figure it out? What does it matter?* It put color to ends that were totally incongruous with the social logic of color that we look to black artists and black shows to uphold. One reviewer harrumphed, "The first impression is of large spots of bright color, pretty enough on the white walls."[50]

50. John Canaday, "Black Artists on View in 2 Exhibitions," *New York Times*, April 7, 1971, 52.

What was clear was that *CBAA*'s account of racial color would be emphatically antifoundational.

Loving's construction, 27 feet across and 12 feet high, comprises multiple hexagonal canvases, each divided into three clearly outlined regions of color. Their combination by the artist results in a situation where chromatic harmony and discord not only combine but determine how the eye travels across the array. This movement produces questions: Is the overall picture an assembly of adjacent cubes or teeming lozenges? A multifaceted solid or an amalgam of discrete parts? The work doesn't dictate answers to these questions. Changes in hue further dynamize the relations among these units, drawing some hexagons closer together while pushing others apart. If the overall form holds, it is because the units share contours. The ambiguity of the common contour is aggravated, however, by the fact that each line has a distinct character—a different chromatic intensity, or amplitude—depending on whether we see it flatly or in deep space (that is, as the single edge of a hexagon or the outer limit of a cube), or depending on how its color is affected by the play among adjacent hues' shadows. Edges become interstices and flatness becomes depth, and the interchanges themselves also vary in interest and structural importance. Color, at most times, appears wildly disproportionate to itself: sometimes it seems poorly chosen, or not always evenly applied, and its internal tonalities shift greatly with the smallest change to one's viewing position. The spatial effect of the total composition is neither wholly convex nor concave; it comprises figures (colored shapes) that force it to work both ways.

A tremendously bold act of ambiguation, Loving's picture is a "cultural expression" completely ungoverned by a center. *Time Trip I* involves itself with the space beyond it by means of the axonometric projection Loving used to produce it. Loving turns the image's volumes obliquely, so as to suggest their (and their colors') infinite extensibility into both background and foreground space.[51] The resultant spatial ambiguity causes parts of the image to alternate between recession and projection. The picture employs axonometry

51. The same device allowed El Lissitsky, when creating the *Proun*, to employ a different axis of projection for each volume. See Yve-Alain Bois, "Metamorphoses of Axonometry," in *Het Nieuew Bouwen: Neo-Plasticism in Architecture, De Stijl*, exh. cat. (The Hague: Haags Gemeentenmuseum and Delft University Press, 1983), 152.

in a picture." He found the painting "all the stronger because, rather than idealizing or sentimentalizing members of his race, [Searles] has shown them as brutalized creatures whose explosion into violence would be vicious and unreasoning within the context of the society responsible for the brutalization."[63] If the scarcity of such works in the exhibition had created the opportunity to differently conceive the black artist's enterprise, or critique the representationalist hegemony, this was lost on most reviewers. Instead, playing up the "singularity" of Searles's picture, they brought forward the artistic caricatures of black rage that "black shows" were supposed to privilege.

The *Rebuttal* show catalogue, produced for an exhibition that ran at the same time as *CBAA*, at the Acts of Art Gallery, grasps the challenge *CBAA* posed by highlighting abstraction:

> While Black artists do sometimes concern themselves with principles of composition such as unity, contrast, repetition and so on, we are generally not believers in any so-called universal aesthetics, pure art, nor superior art. Black artists tend to see these as the same old bigoted, vague rules and laws which are created and used by Whites and are still arbitrarily applied . . . to work about which they know nothing.[64]

Nigel Jackson, who organized the *Rebuttal* show and probably wrote the catalogue text, shared with Canaday an inability to conceive of a black person who would choose to be represented by modernist art. Robert Doty's presence on the scene assured Jackson that this was a manifestation of undue white influence on the black artist, which to the nationalist mind prevented black artists from progressing "beyond the decadent sterility of that Western omnivorous monster called 'Art' and indeed [becoming] BLACK!"[65] Abstraction was anything and everything but a black artist's choice. Such an art handicaps the impulse to separate black culture from white. What self-respecting black artist would impose that predicament on her public at a time like this? As a black art expert, or enough of one, Jackson enjoyed the right to forcefully disclaim the position, very different from Ghent, who set "contemporary" works aright by pumping them with racial content.

63. Canaday, "Black Artists on View," 52.

64. "Forward" [sic], *Rebuttal to Whitney Museum Exhibition: Black Artists in Rebuttal at Acts of Art Gallery NYC*, exh. cat. (New York: Acts of Art Gallery, 1971), unpaginated.

65. Melvin Dixon, "White Critic—Black Art???" in *Black Art Notes*, ed. Tom Lloyd (self-published, 1971), 3.

Tom Lloyd took the response to another level. Just ahead of *CBAA* he self-published and distributed *Black Art Notes*, a collection of eight commissioned essays by such cultural leaders as Jeff Donaldson, Ray Elkins, and Baraka (figs. 2.9 and 2.10). Lining the volume's inside covers are quotations from voluble nationalists, each with a powerful exhortation to the black artist. Lloyd described the publication as "a concrete affirmation of Black art philosophy as interpreted by eight black artists," which meant to be a "counterstatement to the introduction in the catalog . . . of the 'Contemporary Black Artists in America' exhibition."[66] The strongest statements in the volume take direct aim at Doty personally, castigating the curator for being patronizing and racist.[67] But the essays also deal handily with artists of modernist inclination.

> If there is one lesson the post–civil rights period has taught us, it is that those most likely to shape the destiny of black Americans in the next decade are activists and artists, who may possess additional skills as organizers. When discussing the black artist and his role, we must begin by dispelling the false notion that an artist is an artist, no matter what his color, and that being black imposes no special responsibility on him.[68]

Lloyd's own essay asks, "Can the Black artist sit back and watch while white critics and white-oriented institutions dilute, polish, and whitewash Black art?" Here again, abstract art is a fluky aftereffect of unwitting black-white mixing, color distortion, and other

66. Tom Lloyd, introduction to his *Black Art Notes* (self-published, 1971), unpaginated. *Black Art Notes* included Doty's exhibition catalogue essay as an appendix. Per Lloyd's request, Doty sent the text on January 29, 1971, several months ahead of the show's opening. He included the following note: "Please find enclosed a copy of my introduction and the list of names, as you requested. Since your project serves to stimulate the spirit of free inquiry on the subject of work by black artists, it should very valuable." Letter, Robert M. Doty to Tom Lloyd, Alma W. Thomas Papers, Archives of American Art, Smithsonian Institution, Washington, DC. (AAA hereafter.) While Thomas had in her possession a copy of the above letter, her collected papers as archived do not include a copy of *Black Art Notes*.

67. "A white critic in Black art is only an outsider looking in" (2); "he is not in communion with the artist" (2–3) and displays a "constant compulsion for taking an anti-life stance" (5). Lloyd's own piece describes Doty as a "white culture-maker for the Black people" (4) and the exhibition itself as an "intrusion into the Black experience . . . justified by . . . the art for art's sake concept" (4). "Can an oppressed people afford the luxury of an 'undynamic' art? The answer is 'no'" (4).

68. Francis and Val Gray Ward, "The Black Artist—His Role in the Struggle," in *Black Art Notes*, ed. Lloyd, 19.

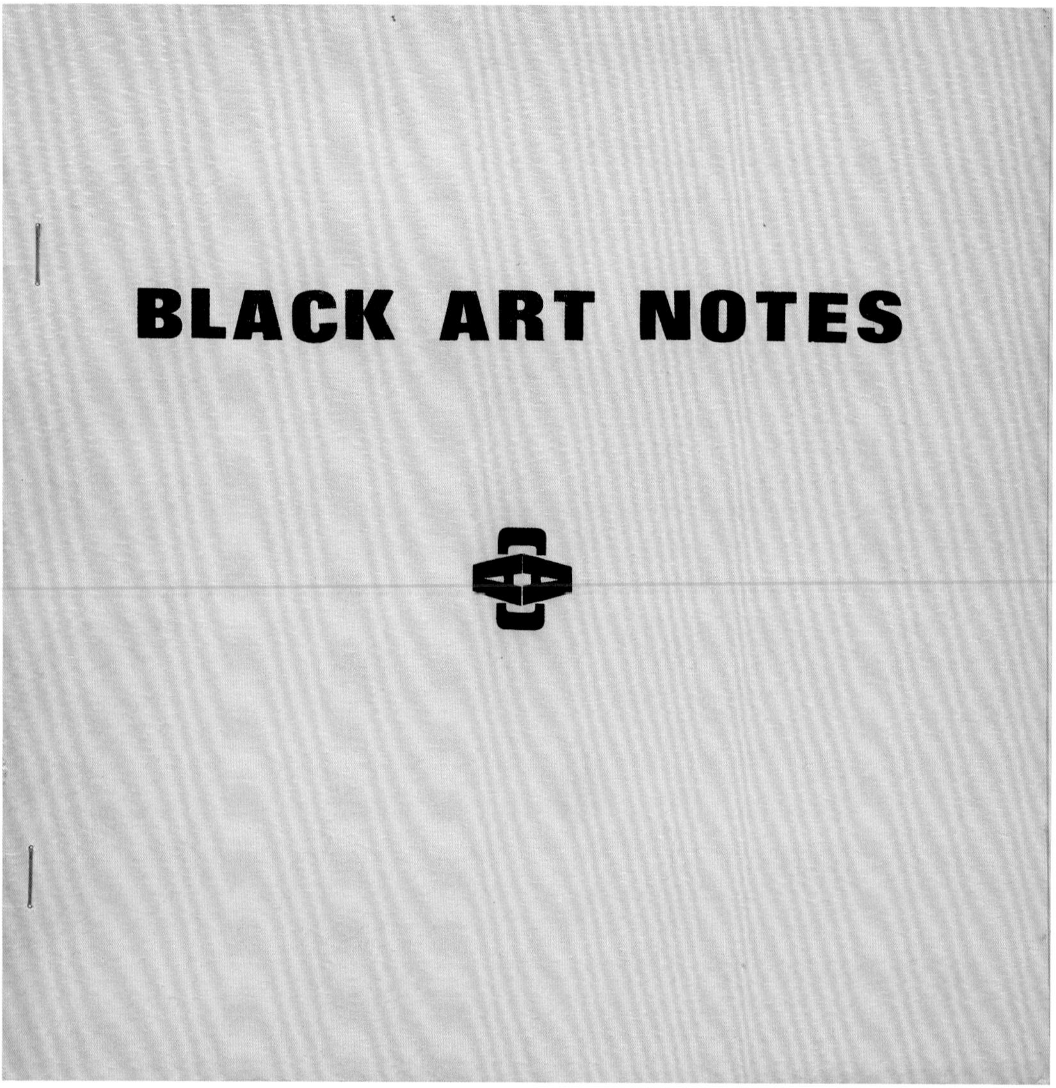

Figure 2.9. Tom Lloyd, *Black Art Notes* (1971), cover. Courtesy of the Underground Museum, Los Angeles; and Omar Shabazz.

Figure 2.10. Tom Lloyd, *Black Art Notes* (1971), table of contents. Courtesy of the Underground Museum, Los Angeles; and Omar Shabazz.

CONTENTS

forms. These were predominantly postpainterly geometric abstractions articulated as realms of interpenetrating colors that seldom involved black. The dominant activity in a given practice involved the discovery and development of the possibilities of those structures.

In a 1969 interview with the *Detroit News* on the occasion of his solo exhibition at the Whitney—in this, the first of the BECC-instigated shows, Loving showed five polyhedrons constructed from a total of 130 interchangeable canvases—Loving described the point of view from which his geometric abstraction originated (fig. 2.11). "I can't accept totally the attitude of pure color. Without some kind of rational vehicle, color becomes an indulgence."[77] At the time of Loving's show, the cube was his preferred vehicle. But the cube had a resonance for Loving that went beyond its capacity to mediate the politics of pure color. The cube stood for the place where Loving's passage through abstract expressionism had deposited him: "I became more involved with outside things," at which time "I began working with the cube as my only subject."[78] But Loving never presented the cube as an inert form. Almost always open, Loving's cube is an unnervingly mobile device.

Loving created *Septahedron 34* (1970) in the prolific season that followed his solo at the Whitney (fig. 2.12). The large-scale painting presents the eponymous form illusionistically and in optical color, perforated and fitted to a hexagonal support with which the painted figure literally fights. We view the form from an elevated oblique angle, facing the triangular surface that remains after a large section of the cube has been sheared off. The septahedron sits awkwardly in the flat space of the canvas, attached but not reconciled to its shape, whose straight directionals disagree with the figure's torqued orientation. Loving leaves the resulting tension unresolved. We experience the cube's opening of the surface's closure as quite emphatic: the septahedron appears as though held by a force, the lessening of which, by even the smallest degree, could propel the image further

exactly what it was. Modernist art was an integral component in a scene of singular plenitude, of the absolute shattering of fixed identities.

77. Alvin Loving, quoted in Joy Hakanson, "Painter Loving in Solid Solo," *Detroit News*, June 15, 1969, n.p. Clipping in artist's file, WMAA.

78. Loving, quoted in Bryna Taubman, "A World in a Cube," *New York Post*, January 15, 1970, n.p. Clipping in artist's file, WMAA.

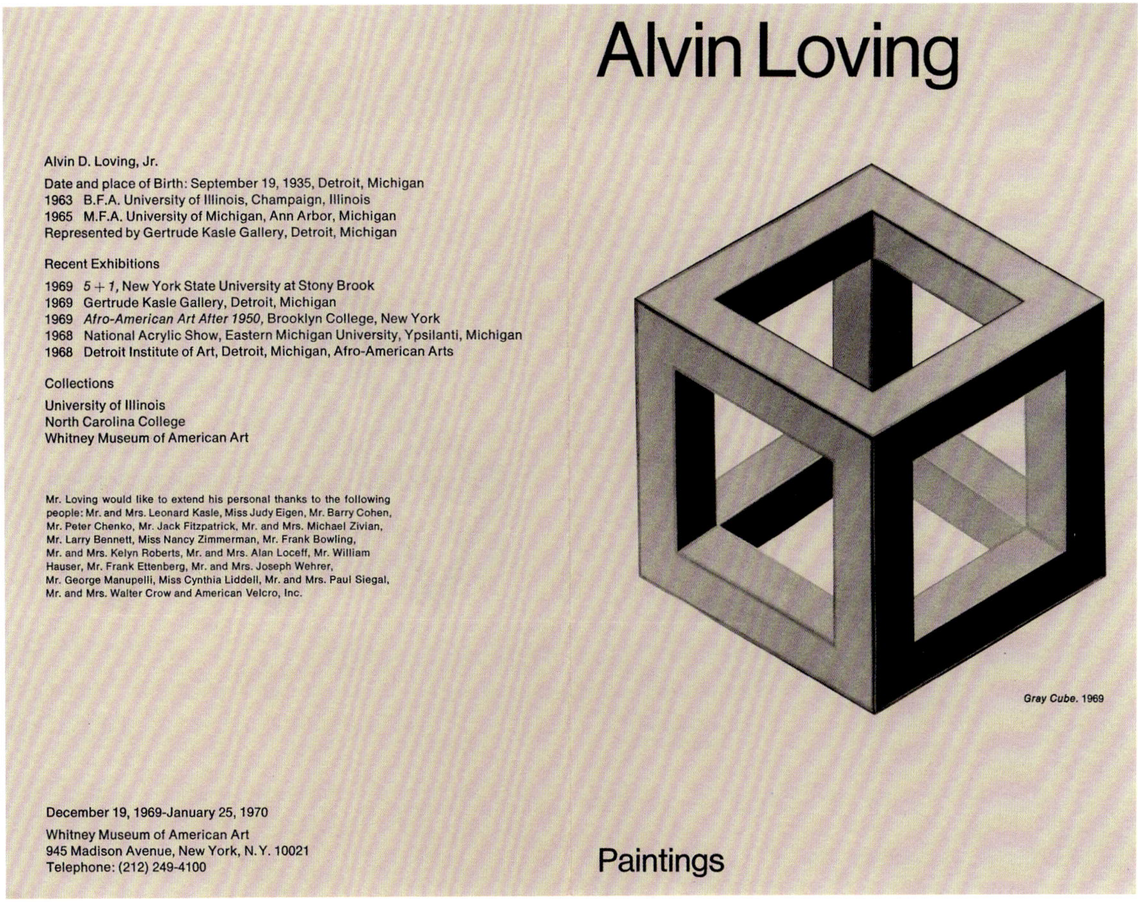

Alvin Loving

Alvin D. Loving, Jr.

Date and place of Birth: September 19, 1935, Detroit, Michigan
1963 B.F.A. University of Illinois, Champaign, Illinois
1965 M.F.A. University of Michigan, Ann Arbor, Michigan
Represented by Gertrude Kasle Gallery, Detroit, Michigan

Recent Exhibitions

1969 *5 + 1*, New York State University at Stony Brook
1969 Gertrude Kasle Gallery, Detroit, Michigan
1969 *Afro-American Art After 1950*, Brooklyn College, New York
1968 National Acrylic Show, Eastern Michigan University, Ypsilanti, Michigan
1968 Detroit Institute of Art, Detroit, Michigan, Afro-American Arts

Collections

University of Illinois
North Carolina College
Whitney Museum of American Art

Mr. Loving would like to extend his personal thanks to the following people: Mr. and Mrs. Leonard Kasle, Miss Judy Eigen, Mr. Barry Cohen, Mr. Peter Chenko, Mr. Jack Fitzpatrick, Mr. and Mrs. Michael Zivian, Mr. Larry Bennett, Miss Nancy Zimmerman, Mr. Frank Bowling, Mr. and Mrs. Kelyn Roberts, Mr. and Mrs. Alan Loceff, Mr. William Hauser, Mr. Frank Ettenberg, Mr. and Mrs. Joseph Wehrer, Mr. George Manupelli, Miss Cynthia Liddell, Mr. and Mrs. Paul Siegal, Mr. and Mrs. Walter Crow and American Velcro, Inc.

Gray Cube. 1969

December 19, 1969-January 25, 1970
Whitney Museum of American Art
945 Madison Avenue, New York, N.Y. 10021
Telephone: (212) 249-4100

Paintings

Figure 2.11. Cover of the exhibition brochure for *Alvin Loving: Paintings* (New York: Whitney Museum of American Art, 1969). Courtesy the Estate of Al Loving and Garth Greenan Gallery, NY.

off kilter, if not off the wall. A similar strain pervades the work. The septahedron's geospatial tension has a certain echo in the optical colors (cadmium red light, pink, orange, yellow, and blue) applied by Loving in varying densities to the "exterior" and "interior" surfaces of the painted form, which comprises a medley of geometric shapes, due to the sheared corner and the obstructed view of the open cube's inner surfaces.

In 1970 Loving called the cube "a self-portrait that offers a means of expressing horizontal feelings toward things."[79] "I can't stand pictures that just sit there," he said.[80] Indeed, an encounter with

79. Ibid.

80. Loving, quoted in Joy Hakanson, "His Paintings Have a Beat," *Detroit News*, September 20, 1970, n.p. Clipping in artist's file, WMAA.

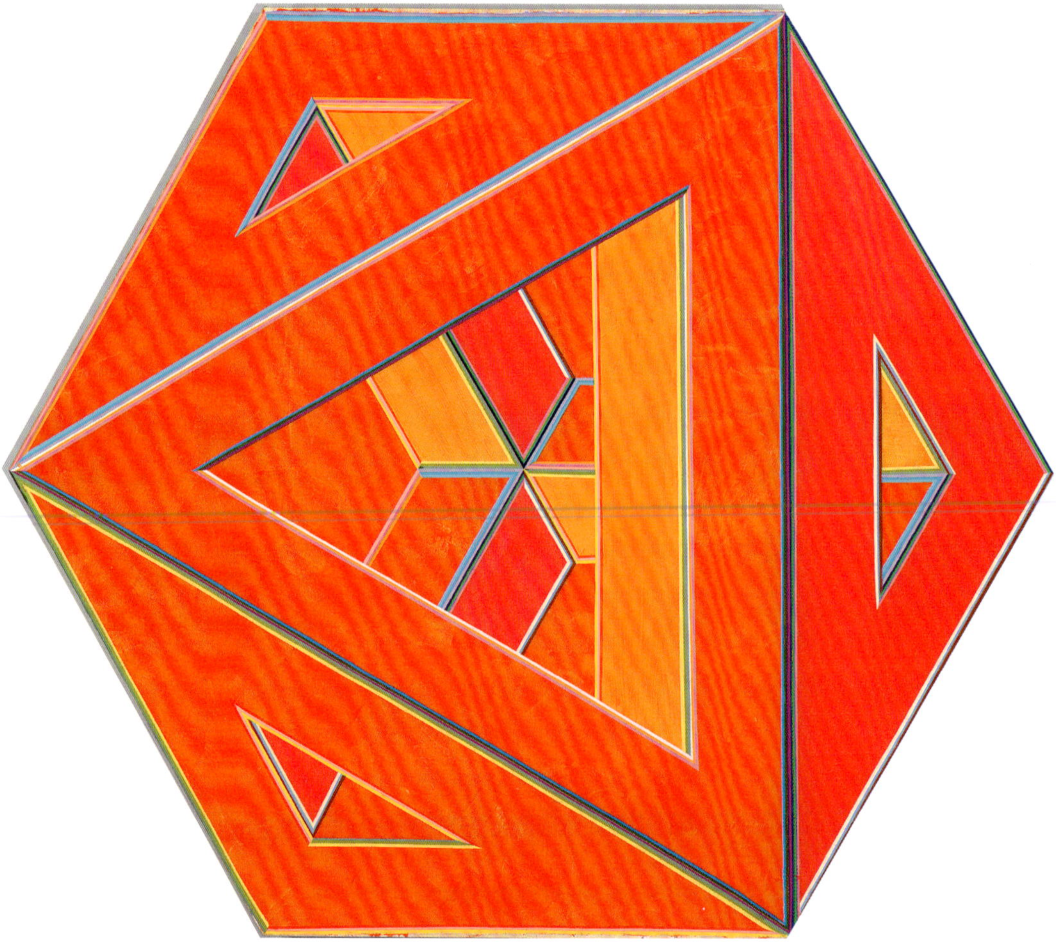

Figure 2.12. Alvin Loving (1935–2005), *Septahedron 34*, 1970. Acrylic on shaped canvas, overall (irregular): 88⅝ × 102½ in. (225.1 × 260.4 cm). Whitney Museum of American Art, New York. Gift of William Zierler, Inc. in honor of John I. H. Baur (74.65). Digital image © Whitney Museum, NY. Courtesy the Estate of Al Loving and Garth Greenan Gallery, NY.

Septahedron 34 promotes horizontal feeling of a strong, strange kind —in the body's registration not of a self-affirming equality with the hexagonal support, but of the septahedron's inclination to wrest free of it. One reaches this understanding through two distinct perceptual actions, both demanded by the illusion. Though seemingly lost to the painting's dysmorphosis, ultimately the cube qua cube is recoverable by the mind. The cube's Gestalt dictates that we can recover the known cube from the presented septahedron. However one recovers it, one comes to understand what Loving has done, one comes to the significance of this form, by reference to the convention it alters. The second action is comparatively incidental. It carries us "past" the painting's surface and through the large triangular aperture facing us at the cube's severed corner. Such a gesture might be utterly without consequence, were it not for its explicitly horizontal directionality. This rhyme with Loving's language for *feelings toward things* is almost harshly literal. But it is from within this unexpectedly plausible interior that one best apprehends how Loving constructed *Septahedron 34* so as to accentuate its reality as a painted, not a built, thing. Its tectonic inconsistency says the structure would never hold, with its rough edges, nonaligned rays, tonal shifts that don't track to logic, and paint surface alternating from flat to stippled (loosening and tightening surface). It remains solid only for as long as one feels in sync with the broken, *a*symmetrical form Loving excavates from the symmetrical schema. And that isn't long.

Time Travel I and *Septahedron 34* both recall a few of the innumerable ways in which structures—generally—fail to capture phenomena experienced in their mobility and proliferation. There's no describing the bright, bizarre constructions on the wall that doesn't pass through some structural crisis in which a specific formal convention and Loving's adjustments to it form the two halves of a terminally fraught whole. More, the paintings become objects of our experience by demanding from us a practical relationship to vision—not just dumb sight of the sort that overwhelms the particulars by, say, recovering a cube from Loving's adulterations. The high degree of viewer involvement that Loving's geometry requires merely extends the artist's own effort to *explore* structure rather than just assert it, to depict the modulations, blind spots, decompressions, and delocalizations upon which all structures tremble. Throughout this period Loving continually staged disclosures of structures' interiors, not to reveal them but to destabilize something fixed—for instance, "I'm enclosing internal spaces in the cube so that I can do more with color."[81]

Loving's art and statements suggest that he imagined not his eccentric geometry alone, but the whole experiential apparatus of which it was a part, as a refutation of the "pure color attitude." We cannot say whether he was aware or ignorant that these remarks gain a special resonance from their historical coincidence with nationalist languages for art. But surely the instituted order among black artists—from which Loving was but one of many deviators—could also be called a "pure color attitude." The two have a strong conceptual nearness that we would do well to acknowledge and take seriously but not overdetermine.[82] As we have seen, racial blackness was meant to be experienced as a structure it was neither desirable nor possible to exceed, with artists, objects, and entire exhibitions expected to embody and ennoble that ideal. Artists like Loving upended that structure in two ways, one literal (by working beyond the strict thematic boundaries of black art) and the other metaphorical (by working with color but not toward meaning). But the coincidence invites us to think color, in both its senses, as relational rather than substantial in nature. Its structures, rather than being determined by essential characteristics, are determined by differences, to whose presence we are constantly alerted by the vividness of the materials, hues, shapes, textures, and effects that give these artworks their character.

Most of Loving's other work in this mode shows that he had but one way to explicate the cube's interest for him: by *opening* it. *The effort was to explore structure rather than assert it*, to depict the modulations and blind spots upon which it stood. Manifestations of this interest in Loving's work strike me, too, as more imaginative than analytic or even para-analytic (à la Sol LeWitt). I say this because of the formal inconsistency thematized in his geometric work and because of

81. Ibid.

82. Later I will consider the more directly artistic resonances of this term as given by modernist activities in connection to postpainterly abstraction. In very general terms, Loving makes his statement too long after the fact to be plausibly understood as directing himself to that development, which Clement Greenberg named in 1964 to describe a style that had already become historical by the time of his writing.

the high degree of viewer involvement that his structures summon, even in the everyday form of puzzling them out (as one does, say, the diagrammatic illustrations of M. C. Escher). The historically concrete task I suggest Loving's art performed again and again, and thus asks the viewer to engage, is the practical use of imagination to reckon critically with structure and to model a sociality that exceeded structure. For Loving, abstraction was a social practice.

We know that Loving intensified his relation to the cube ("a self-portrait") with social language at the same time his thinking shifted toward "outside things." The work in *Time Travel I* and *Septahedron 34* suggests that we understand this shift less in terms of the outside things themselves than in terms of the turn toward them. In other words, the significance of this operation is given by the *displacement* of which Loving's color work is most expressive. Self, structure, color: these are its terms, but the pivotal event is the opening of a self onto existence as complex contingency, presumably in defiance of instituted forms of being.[83] Recall that "pure color" was Loving's term for the structure in question. Loving's art and statements suggest how he imagined not his eccentric geometry alone, but the whole experiential apparatus of which it was a part, as a destruction of pure color. We cannot say whether he was aware that his blackness would give these remarks a special resonance, but we can observe his obvious aesthetic deviance from the "pure color situation" to which the instituted order aspired. To be sure, political projections of blackness contained and entailed an "attitude of pure color."

The work requires that we think color, in both of the senses in play here, as relational rather than substantial or completely for-itself in nature. Its structures, rather than being determined by characteristics essential to them, are determined in a field structured by differences to whose presence we are alerted by the interplay of materials, colors, shapes, choices, and other forces constituting the identity of the work of art.

We ought to think about their art, then—the stuff they made and the fantasies of self-expansion that drove that making—in terms

83. "I am still an expressionist," Loving told Joy Hakanson, critic for the *Detroit News*, on the occasion of his first-ever solo show, at Gertrude Kasle Gallery in Detroit. Hakanson, "Painter Loving in Solid Solo." The Whitney had purchased "Rational Irrationalism" for its collection shortly before the opening.

of its consequences for the ostensive structural consistency of black aesthetics. The important historical point concerns the impacts such art (and its attendant fantasies) would have had upon the felt experience of the cultural and symbolic space reserved for Black Art. Was this nearness strong enough to provoke an awareness of the threat black modernists posed to the coherency of the new cultural ideal? Was it evident, or even thinkable within this realm, that abstraction was a token for deviance, the residue of a specific practice of freedom?

If other black modernists' statements available in the historical record are any indication, it was barely thinkable. Again and again, they explained their choice of an abstract idiom (a step their non-black counterparts didn't have to bother with) by electing a discourse in which the creative act was simultaneously aesthetic and social, identified with relationality and spatialization. Their languages for abstraction show that for them, while black art and its discourses were both palpable and limiting, modernism meant they didn't have to experience them as insurmountable constraints. There were other ways of being and working; abstraction made *that* more expansive actuality palpable too. Among the terms they chose, then, there is a rigorously race-critical dimension, but not a crabby one. It matters that these terms are married to visual art practices centered on dispersed and ambiguated color structures.

It is in this connection that we can begin to think of modernism —again—as a social practice. Through it, practitioners achieved a particular imaginative and intersubjective possibility specially foreclosed to the black artist who could be persuaded to withdraw her affections from "everything perceived as being or representing the white world." One finds among black modernists a wholly different attitude toward representation, one distinguishable from the norm by its ameliorative mood.

For example, Alma Thomas talked in 1970 to an interviewer from *Art Gallery* magazine for a special feature on black artists' "approaches to inhumanity." She said, "Painting released me from the limitations of the past and opened *the door to progressive creativity*. Creative art is for all time and is therefore independent of time. It is of all ages, of every land, and if by this we mean that the creative spirit in man which produces a picture or a statue is a common to the whole civilized world, independent of age, race and nationality, the statement may stand unchallenged."[84]

Jack Whitten, who withdrew from *CBAA* but had a solo exhibition at the Whitney in 1974, would later speak of his art in these terms:

> My paintings teach me how to live. That's what they're about. How to go out there and carve out a space for myself in society. My paintings teach me that.
>
> You know what attracted me to painting in the first place, and to art? Being in the South, when you're black and the white people own everything and you're always in the back, and you can't do anything until they say. . . . When I first started getting a scope on what this thing "Art" was, my thinking was that you go out and paint a picture. You do a little landscape or you try to make it look like somebody so that everybody says, "Well, that looks just like your Mama, boy." That was the extent of my thinking as far as what "Art" was. But then I started reading more about the meaning of art and its relation to history and cultures and how it shapes people's lives and started reading the lives of other artists. And then coming to New York for the first time. And then meeting artists. And then coming to New York and reading more and going to a museum for the first time. And then meeting artists—meeting Bill de Kooning and Franz Kline and all the abstract expressionist painters. And I'm starting to get a picture that, "Man, this is about much more than painting this tree and trying to make this thing look like your mama." That's when I started saying, "This is fantastic! This is an amazing kind of freedom. You can actually build this thing the way you want to build it." And *that's* what really just zeroed me in on it.[85]

This describes Whitten's turns, first to art and then to abstraction, with a succession of barriers leveled. But the story's distinguishing feature is not crashing a boundary so much as the mobility and affinities that follow it. Whitten is describing openings of mind and other effects of the shift from racially delineated space to the contact zone. Running in parallel is Whitten's distinction between two "kinds of freedom," which he establishes when comparing the prior discovery of art qua art to the (for him) more intensive freedom that abstraction offered. Whitten identifies abstraction with autonomy but,

84. Alma Thomas in "Interviews: Four Afro-American Artists," *Art Gallery* 13, no. 7 (April 1970): 36. Emphasis added.

85. Jack Whitten interviewed by Beryl J. Wright, in *Jack Whitten* (Newark, NJ: Newark Museum, 1990), 12–13. Artist's file, WMAA.

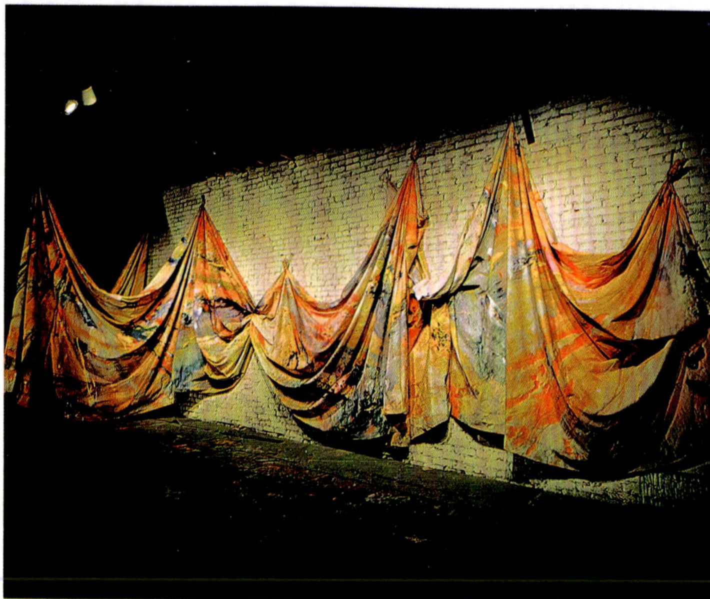

SAM GILLIAM: CERTAIN ATTITUDES

Sam Gilliam, *Carousel Change*, acrylics w/powdered aluminum on canvas, 10 x 75′, 1970.

LeGRACE G. BENSON

The presumptive categories "painting," and "sculpture" do not apply to the recent works of Sam Gilliam; nor do such otherwise useful hybrid terms as "shaped canvas," or "combines." The word "situation" seems appropriate, carrying as it does connotations of place or locality and also of conditions and circumstances that are only metaphorically spatial.

Draping painted canvas out into the space of a room came out of necessity and after a long period of experimentation. The form did not arise from the desire to devise a new type of art object, but out of the pressures of deeply felt visual, kinetic, tactile emotional experience. For a time, Gilliam actually seems to have resisted the urge to let the paintings move:

". . . . but the point was that there is a tradition involved that you could not [ignore]. *You know it's hard for a painter to think in terms of sculpture. And after pushing it back and forth, I got very romantic about Baroque, you know, you think about Rubens' S-curves . . . and the structural problems. But then this whole thing just does not matter—I don't really think about it that way. I didn't really want to be a sculptor.* [He didn't wish to look at sculpture or painting in terms of translating one into the other.]. . . *but if I could just stay with it, and just be very thoughtful and let it happen, let it come kind of new, then I wouldn't have to worry. A sculptor was in here one day and he said, 'Well, all bad painters eventually become sculptors,' and that really made me mad. But it was good kidding. It was good in the sense that then I began to discuss it more."*

He had experimented with the color and space effects of folding and rolling small watercolors for several years, then *". . . the idea just occurred to me as I was finding with the watercolors, . . . why not just remove the support, why don't I use the form, let the form. This in the sense of trying to believe in the materials or the kind of tools that I actually use and let them excite the kinds of possibilities, and not to get too mental, you know, about what's really going on. Just to sort of sit back and observe what you're doing as much as you can, you know—just work and let things go. So that I got this whole kind of idea of really sitting back and looking at curtains . . . and with the one here* [one of the large Carousels] *of actually going to the top* [of the painting] *and kind of breaking the frame and* [thus] *getting into the shape. Suddenly I felt myself constructing kinds of traverse rods and actually hanging the paintings, so that all these problems of trying to structure and of letting* them *move and create the kind of forms I really wanted* [could be worked out that way]."

The process became too cumbersome with its pieces of wood, hardware, etc., and in order to get past those limitations he began to hang the fabric from nails driven into the studio wall and from beams and posts, eventually utilizing all the space of the studio. Once with canvas not yet stretched he went into Rock Creek Park and experimented with situating fifteen foot lengths of painted canvas in meadows or unfurling them down rock faces.

The painting process established several years ago continues to be employed, that is, pouring, 56

Figure 2.13. LeGrace Benson, "Sam Gilliam: Certain Attitudes," *Artforum*, September 1970, 56.

inheres in the pivot of its meaning away from the recognizable, resonant, or relevant toward—what? Listen to Edwards describing the sculptural work in barbed wire featured in his Whitney exhibition (fig. 2.16a–b): "I have always understood the brutalist connotations inherent in materials like barbed wire and links of chain," he said. "My creative thoughts have always anticipated the beauty of utilizing that necessary complexity which arises from [their] use . . . in what

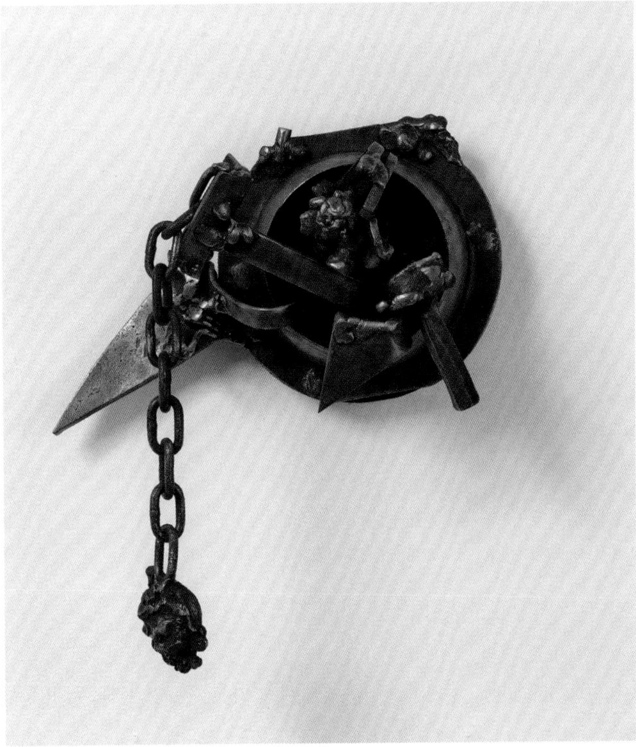

Figure 2.14. Melvin Edwards (b. 1937), *Some Bright Morning*, 1963. Welded steel, 14½ × 9¼ × 5 in. (36.8 × 23.5 × 12.7 cm). Image courtesy Alexander Gray Associates, New York. © 2014 Melvin Edwards / Artist Rights Society (ARS), New York.

Figure 2.15. Melvin Edwards, *Cotton Hangup*, 1966. Welded steel, 32 × 30 × 20 in. (81.3 × 76.2 × 76.2 cm). The Studio Museum in Harlem; gift of Mr. and Mrs. Hans Burkhardt. Image courtesy Alexander Gray Associates, New York. © 2014 Melvin Edwards / Artist Rights Society (ARS), New York.

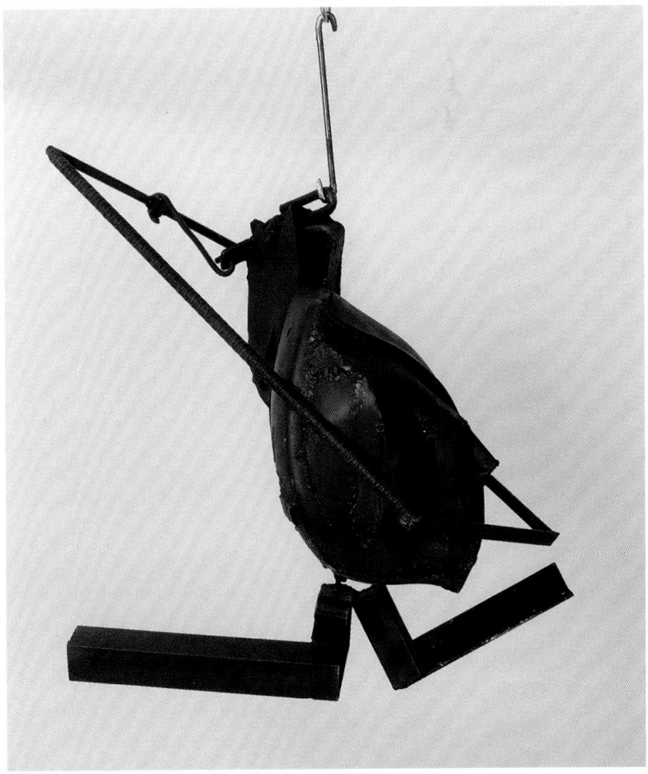

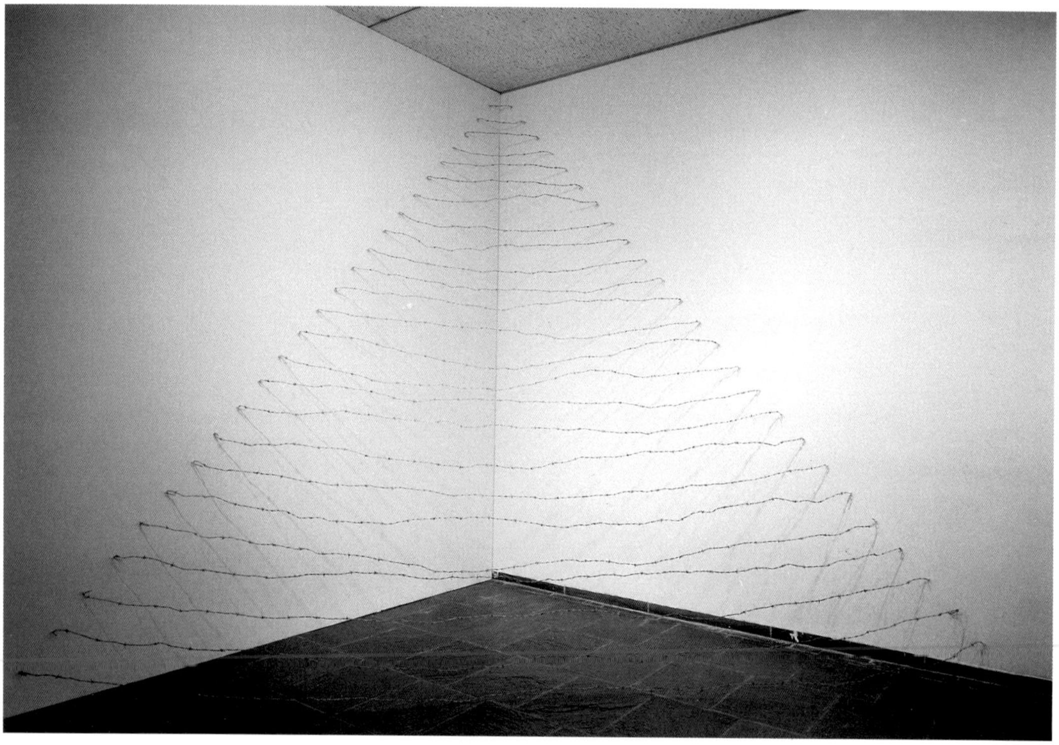

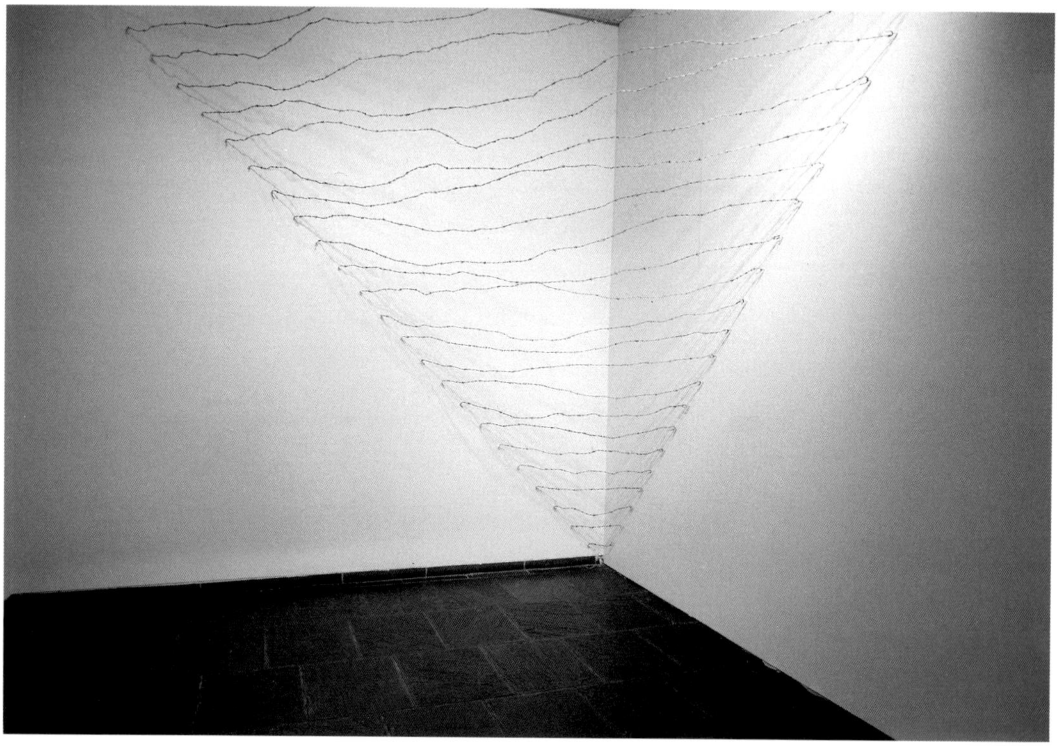

2.16a–b.
Melvin Edwards, *Pyramid Up and Down*, 1969. Barbed wire, dimensions variable. Images courtesy Alexander Gray Associates, New York. © 2014 Melvin Edwards/ Artist Rights Society (ARS), New York.

could be called straight[-]ahead formal works."[90] For Edwards, who devised this language in correspondence with Doty (who curated his Whitney solo), making meant a way beyond connotation, a path to a more complex signification in which only traces of literal meaning remain. The emphasis falls on "anticipated beauty," a locution pointing us to the realms of signification in which these tragically charged materials might otherwise dwell.

Edwards's statement avows the necessity of thinking alternatives. So did his most characteristic sculptures of this period. Largely made up of scrapped cast metal, they evoke instruments of violence as these have been turned by the various, possibly arbitrary manual inflections recorded in the compressed, fragmented, and stacked, knotted, melted materials—not merely against functionality but toward an as-yet-formless order that follows, but does not forget, social tragedy. His materials' association with racial degradation is thus one kind of truth,[91] but the evidence of Edwards's involvement with these materials requires us to notice that abstraction as process allows the artist to access other figures of truth. They make tangible Edwards's confidence about the changeability of things.

Eversley adopted similarly expansive terms to describe his activity at the time. His measured words accentuate his objects' portability and internal dynamics to explain their capacity to overcome the static self-sufficiency that their monolithic character suggests. As we've seen, Eversley's work of the period takes the form of richly colored blocks of color-layered polyester acrylic, alternately transparent and opaque, solid and pearlescent. But Eversley *meant them* to engender a certain intimacy. "I am attempting to [focus] the spectator into perceiving the complex nature of reality, both physical and social, and through these perceptions, forming new kinds of subjective meanings."[92] Eversley's statement for the Whitney, where he showed in May 1970 in an exhibition Tucker organized, all but instructed the viewer to disregard his sculptures' redoubtable independence:

90. Ibid.

91. For example, in August 1955 Emmett Till's killers reportedly attempted to sink his lynched corpse in the Tallahatchie River by attaching it with barbed wire to a cotton-gin fan.

92. Frederick Eversley, "Statement of the Artist," in *Frederick Eversley* (Palm Springs, CA: Palm Springs Desert Museum, 1978), n.p.. Artist's file, WMAA.

on aesthetic freedom, then, to also demonstrate what creative work in the relative absence of those constraints could look like. Art *meant* the relative absence of constraints: art was a place away from them and a means of doing something about them. A vital component of this demonstration, of course, was its enactment before witnesses. The artists' statements themselves, the event of exhibition, the culturally queer act of laying claim to autonomous progress through one's own destiny: all these constituted practices of freedom that gained meaning through performance. Hence the cruciality of the stage that *CBAA* provided.

Practice of freedom is a term used to contrast abstraction in this milieu and the well-known practices of liberation associated with figures such as Baraka, Neal, Nikki Giovanni, and others. In this distinction between practices of liberation and practices of freedom I follow Michel Foucault, who in an interview from the period observed that "liberation is not in itself sufficient to define the practices of freedom that will *still* be needed if . . . individuals are to succeed in creating admissible . . . forms of existence or political society." This, Foucault says, "is why I emphasize practices of freedom over processes of liberation."[97] Foucault recognized that because not everyone will perceive or capitalize liberation identically, even in a "liberated" condition one remains subject to discipline or domination in the range of power relationships organizing one's experience with others and institutions. With this model, liberation harbors a potential that waits to be actualized as freedom through specific acts and procedures.
Of course, such an absence may be found only in improvised or provisional social arrangements. Which is what makes the forging of such arrangements both so crucial and so difficult to historicize: frequently they are social experiments that never aggregate as movements or even as events. So while Black Art has come to signify liberation historically, its functional operation in the culture, as the only choice a nonpathological black artist can make, and as the most likely referent for everything she does—obligates us to consider whether its greatest effectiveness may be as a formal impediment to the very achievement it is seen to represent.

97. Michel Foucault, *Ethics: Subjectivity and Truth*, ed. Paul Rabinow, trans. Robert Hurley et al. (New York: New Press, 1997), 282–83. Emphasis added.

Unlike liberation schemes that instruct "authentic" blacks to reflect and express the racial-objective, a practice of freedom puts the subjective into play against the objective.[98] It is often founded on, and coextensive with, a subject's movement toward what Foucault called the "care of the self."[99] Importantly, a practice of freedom also presupposes dynamic relationships with others; it entails the cultivation of modes of relating. Invoking the care of the self in this context allows me to suggest that abstraction at this time belonged to the range of activities undertaken across racial lines in pursuit of positive affects. In this respect it was a social process initiated and undertaken in a spirit of mobility by individuals besieged by the divisive affects that racialist regimes promoted. In addition to allowing a very different conceptualization of freedom, modernism sounded a dissonant tone in the space of black culture because it originated in the pursuit of positive affects—namely, the commitment to productive interraciality as well as to sustainable pleasures not rooted in a transient escape from suffering. Probably what has contributed much to the historical invisibility of this dimension of black modernists' activity is that its unhurried mood and tone were so out of sync with pessimistic rhetorics of polarization. In such a situation, abstraction provided "little" more than an affirmation that *other options existed* for combating racism, and that they might include cooperation with white people, and vigorous engagement with cultural practices (wrongly) seen to be exclusively theirs.

When Robert Doty gave the lion's share of exhibition space to black artists making abstraction, *CBAA* became a *fragmented and therefore*

98. A practice of freedom is concerned with individuation only to the extent that it refuses forced identifications, compulsory collectivity, and other. It reflects individual freedom neither as an entitlement nor as an accession but rather as ethics. On Foucault's account, a practice of freedom is "the mode in which individual freedom . . . [is] reflected as an ethics." See ibid., 284.

99. Foucault notes that at certain points in history, "the care of the self becomes suspect. . . . Being concerned with oneself [is] readily denounced as a form of . . . selfishness or self-interest in contradiction with the interest to be shown in . . . self-sacrifice" (ibid.). As we have seen, the very same movement shaped the reception of black modernists' art: abstraction became an acute problem for politics at the very moment it was possible to think of blackness as a condition to be claimed and cultivated, expressed and reflected, imposed and extended, an instrument of power believed to be impotent unless explicitly figured.

representative picture of the black artist's situation circa 1971. The exhibition was an eloquent argument defending artistic freedom against the increasing narrowness of liberationist thought structures. An exhibition designed to introduce black artists to a public asks that public to see art *as* race. It was that forced simultaneity, the risks it poses to art and human experience alike, into which Doty's deployment of abstraction intervened.

Abstraction compelled reflection and the making of distinctions. Thus it did not merely document the constraints besetting the subject of liberation. It afforded a close look at a particular experiment in lifting and superseding them. Loving's language for his geometric wall constructions literalized the effect of Doty's installation: "My interest in composition: composing a wall finds more options with the use of a shape. Repetition of that shape breaks the horizontality, rectangularity, verticality, and depth of normal confines."[100] Doubtless there is projection in my insinuation that by "normal confines" Loving means those binding the black artist to representation or to otherwise explicitly political work. But it is Doty himself who, through the exhibition layout and the astonishing catalogue essay, first patiently *articulated* this claim. There Doty posited abstraction as a critical program. His decision to grant abstraction a defining position in the exhibition also publicly recognized it in the face of black cultural politics. As a kind of amplification and countersignature of the black modernist's claim, *CBAA* became an example in microcosm of the integrated culture that was the object of racialism's most passionate foreclosures.

Many worried then about divided loyalties among black artists, and that division shapes the scant literature on the exhibition as well.[101] But *CBAA* represents a courageous if imperfect attempt to *understand* this. Doty understood that in the highly policed thought-space of the black American artist, the fantasies of self-extension that modernism opened up had the status of a felt necessity for many.

100. This counts among the "random thoughts" printed in the WMAA brochure for Loving's exhibition. Artist's file, WMAA.

101. See Kellie Jones, "'It's Not Enough to Say 'Black is Beautiful'': Abstraction at the Whitney, 1969–1974," in *Discrepant Abstraction*, ed. Kobena Mercer (Cambridge, MA: MIT Press with INiVA, 2005); and Bridget R. Cooks, *Exhibiting Blackness: African Americans and the American Art Museum* (Amherst: University of Massachusetts Press, 2011).

The exhibition he made shows that Doty did not take fright at this discord. Rather he felt, or acted and wrote as though he felt, that this was a consequential historical development with which audiences needed to reckon—and one that found its most concrete expression in the figure of the black modernist. Doty understood that figure to be a new kind of historical subject, an improbable manner of being within black culture as then conceived, and yet a literal effect of the expanding contact zone. The curator welcomed this development in an Arendtian awareness that "to watch the agents of history play their roles in the drama of necessity was to miss the central political capacity of [human beings]: action, the capacity to begin something new whose outcome is unpredictable."[102] Doty was certainly aware of the mandates that black artists should filter their perceptions of such activity. His frank formulations of abstraction as a counterdevelopment—"inevitably an artist reacts to the ideas and techniques which constitute the current mode, sensing and assimilating new directions of thought and vision"[103]—have a modesty that belies their consequences for the idea of black culture.

It is the catalogue essay that proves Doty did not underestimate the difficulties facing the internal dissenter. Doty understood that abstraction was a particularly subtle way to respond through art to real pressures in the historical present. Nearly every vector in the essay supports reading it and the show it accompanies as pointed efforts, grounded in Doty's empathy for these cultural dissidents, to complicate the public picture of black America by placing them squarely inside it without diminishing their particularity. The essay begins:

> This exhibition is devoted to commitment—to pictures and objects which affirm hard work, faith, patience, imagination, and aesthetic integrity; to creation, bringing forth life or causing life to be realized anew; to human values, both intellectual and emotional.
>
> It is devoted to American artists who are black. Creative individuals, with widely disparate intentions, ideas and goals; artists whose works are categorized . . . despite the fact that diversity is their universal trait.

102. Quoted in Elisabeth Young-Bruehl, *Hannah Arendt: For Love of the World* (New Haven, CT: Yale University Press, 1982), 323.

103. Doty, *Contemporary Black Artists in America*, exh. cat. (New York: Whitney Museum of American Art, 1970), 12.

> It is devoted to concepts of self: self-awareness, self-understanding, and self-pride—emerging attitudes which . . . have profound implications for the redress of social grievances.[104]

Doty wields a political vocabulary at the end of this chain of devotions, behind aesthetic diversity, which itself follows the factor of creation and its generative moment in individualized labor. At only one point does Doty inveigh openly against the forces arrayed against individuality, citing both Barry Gaither's and the Black Panther culture minister's "extremist exhortations" drafting black artists into service. The essay's formulations of aesthetic difference as social dissent, of abstraction as a counterdevelopment, have a modesty that belies their penetrating insight into the condition of US culture in 1971. For instance, in an oblique but devastating blow to Black Art ideology, Doty observes that

> a rational approach to complex [artistic] problems is neither convenient nor expedient for the Black artist. [But] some . . . are facing the dilemma. Their command of means is significant, but it is their ambition and integrity which demand respect. . . . Ultimately the Black artist and his audience must respond to "the authority of the created thing," that unique quality . . . which flourishes under a spirit of free inquiry. The need for that freedom was never greater.[105]

What made the "need for that freedom" seem greater than ever, of course, was the proliferation of coercions directed at artistic freedom.

It is not enough to call Doty's language inoffensive. It comprises numerous proofs of his patient attempt to *bring out the desire* of many black artists who "refused" either "to be subjugated to collective aims" or "to believe that art should be subjected to the necessity of conveying a political message."[106] The essay is a conscious attempt to clear conceptual space for these individuals' own representational purposes and ambitions within the clotted construction "black America," or at least to show how their presence dimensionalized that construction. Naming Malcolm Bailey, Chase-Riboud, and Raymond Saunders (all abstract artists), Doty observes that for them "freedom

104. Ibid., 7.
105. Ibid., 13. Emphasis added.
106. Ibid., 11.

of expression signifies freedom for the individual."[107] It seems that the effort was to encourage on an audience disinclined to presuppose it a conception of art that *presupposes* freedom for the individual.

From Doty's perspective, the largest measure of group benefit will come from the kind of rigorous care of the self that the pursuit of art makes uniquely available and that was exemplified by modernism. In this rhetorical representation, "black America" is not a homogenous urge; it is a cluster of motives. One comes to know it by considering the singularity of each person and her circumstances, which teaches us that maybe there is no such thing as a single motive as both racialist aesthetics and racial commonsense would have us believe.[108] Simply to process the notion of a black artist doing modernism pierced the intellectual bubble of racialist ideology. If race isn't applicable to everything the black artist makes, then how to think about the remainder? Doty elected a noncatastrophic approach to this question. He was inspired at one point to remind his audience that "so long as Black artists are inspired to create, they will continue to testify to the 'Black experience,' the special conditions, heritage and emotions which delineate the life of Black people. But creative devices cannot be channeled."[109] Black Art will go on, he suggested, but there's violence in mightily exacting it from everyone and everything. Thus the need to distinguish "a new generation of Black artists, who inherited their own culture *and* sought the . . . canons of the visual arts." He spoke of those artists in terms of the epochal shift that the elaboration of an intercultural element in black America properly signaled. "Their task," Doty continued, "will be the assimilation, or rejection, of venerable emotions and new stimuli."[110]

But what made these practices distinctive were not simply their origins in private agency. The copresence of long-alienated, habitually separated cultural forms lent them a powerful distinction as well. It was not as though cultural difference vanished with the formation of a critical mass of abstract art. Rather, this conferred and preserved its *complexity* in an especially vivid way. It is in this sense that

107. Ibid., 11.

108. This formulation interpolates Jacqueline Rose, "Deadly Embrace," in *The Last Resistance* (London: Verso, 2007), 134.

109. Doty, *Contemporary Black Artists in America*, 12.

110. Ibid., 12. Emphasis added.

Doty shows what it means to make "concepts of self" a matter of "devotion." In 1976 he would adopt similar terms to describe Alma Thomas's achievement: "Resolution, knowledge and ardor, all have sustained Alma Thomas during a lifetime as a painter," he wrote. "Her work is distinguished by a rational and coherent development. . . . But most important of all, she holds steadfast to the personal conviction, courage, and sense of purpose which have made her a major American artist."[111]

Doty's shrewd, historically precise conception of the black artist could not stand out more starkly from its contemporary surround. He understands the black artist not as a given but as a discursive form given by history, long unquestioned, and yet by 1971 facing a profound transformation as an ever greater number of individuals formulated their projects at a certain distance from the clan. Without being a collective action, their output pointed up the exaggerated coherence of race representations while also embodying modernism's function as a medium of productive interaction between the races. Such a recognition did not attack black culture, but it did imply a radically different way of conceiving it. Coming to terms with this meant acknowledging the alternatives being posed to business as usual for black artists: given the concepts on which they were drawing, their points of reference, and the shapes of meaning engendered by this "new" mode of cultural work, interpretation would be a profoundly open-ended and intercultural affair. The artists' immersion in a comparably unrestricted set of resources meant that their work manifested the psychoanalytic truth that you *are* the others among whom you dwell:

> We only exist through the others who make up the storehouse of the mind: models in our first tentative steps towards identity, objects of our desires, helpers and foes. The mind [here the work of art] is a palimpsest in which the traces of these figures will jostle and rearrange themselves for evermore.[112]

Doty's advocacy of the modernist spirit thriving among black artists circa 1971, therefore, is anything but a formalist imposition seeking to detach their art from the events that led to its production, or

111. Robert M. Doty, untitled essay in *Alma W. Thomas: Recent Paintings 1975–76*, exh. cat. (New York: Martha Jackson West, 1976), n.p.

112. Rose, "Mass Psychology," in *The Last Resistance*, 62.

to recast it in an unconsciousness of those events. It doesn't "push" modernism so much as insist on the black artist's right to it, to the progressive model of self-determination it typified. But there is far more to Doty's exposition. The text evinces his impression that he shared a conviction with the artists about whom he wrote: The proper authority on this scene is "the created thing." Anyone who took art seriously, black or not, could see that. Doty's essay is unequivocal, even florid, in portraying thriving affinities among individuals connected by a belief in the possibilities for invention and self-creation, *at least in the very circumscribed domain of art*; in the meaning-giving capacity of the objects they considered worthy of devotion; and in the apartness of this meaning from those ostensibly underwriting difference. The essay is historically crucial, then, as an event of integration, a scene of mutual recognitions where *a whole manner of being which then seemed improbable surfaced in direct connection with the work that art does.*

What's more, Doty constructed an exhibition that made the best insights of his dauntless essay available to viewer experience. For the first time in what Grace Glueck characterized as a "rash of black shows" mounted since 1967, *CBAA* foregrounded the dissensus among black American artists. Modernists established a salient and substantive, rather than aberrant, presence. Because *CBAA* brought out the divisions separating individual practitioners, it showed that art functioned for some to confirm and extend being *without* the immediate burdens of meaning, logical clarity, or consistency with a "group experience" vastly out of scale with the individual. It proved that this aspiration was representable. The critical mass of abstraction said that large numbers of individuals were choosing to create themselves through art rather than be enacted by politics: they were seizing sources of their own choosing, confidently indulging private notions about the ends of representation, and devising personal formal languages, often out of radically independent ideas about color. In this way Doty's experiment stressed the subjective over the social. Its picture of the social made it harder to wish away *the question of its relationship to subjective experience.*[113] Importantly, the construction

113. Doty deepened the resonance of this strategy by writing his essay in a stridently personal voice.

when "blackness" became a key axis in American political culture. None of these artists expressed the slightest intention to offer up their work as a foil to race essentialism. But their works, deeds, and words—as well as those of their nonblack advocates—produce a number of logics that cultural history should be compelled to follow through.

A last word about modernism and the political. What made *CBAA* activist, and what continues to make it inspiring, was not its orchestration of a grievance but the care with which it exploited the flexibility and dimensionality that color, and color structures, had begun to acquire in the late civil rights era. It showed with an uncommon clarity how the culture was metabolizing color. By also pointing to a bevy of other forms that radical imagination could take, it substantially enlarged the public's view of the moment of subjective creativity. Too, it exploded the prevailing image of black culture by bringing its representation to that decisive point at which it is, in fact, indistinguishable from American culture per se. By these means, *Contemporary Black Artists in America* also exhibited the instituting agency of art itself, its ability to create new significations, and its inclination continually to put its own laws of existence into question. There was more than art on show. Together, black modernist painters and sculptors and the people who supported and showed them inadvertently had made a politics out of optimism.

INSTITUTE FOR THE ARTS, RICE UNIVERSITY P. O. BOX 1892, HOUSTON, TEXAS 77001 TELEPHONE (713) 528-4141

Dear Vincent:

We're planning an exhibition in a poor section of Houston. The object is to bring first-rate art to people who don't usually attend shows. Hence our intention to rent a large space, a church, a ballroom, an empty warehouse. It will be of easy access to housewives, children, laborers; the people. Those who usually attend exhibitions will find the location through publicity and advertisements; their visits will bring life to an otherwise neglected part of town.

I'm inviting:

Darby Bannard	Bob Gordon	Jules Olitski
Anthony Caro	Richard Hunt	Larry Poons
Dan Christensen	Daniel Johnson	Barbara Riboud
Edward Clark	Virginia Jaramillo	Michael Steiner
David Diao	Al Loving	William Williams
Sam Gilliam	Kenneth Noland	

I hope you can submit two works until September, when all will be returned. If you have photos available, of yourself and of your work (black and white 8 x 10 glossies, or transparencies), we'll be that much ahead; otherwise they'll be shot in Houston. Transportation and insurance are paid by Rice University's Institute for the Arts. We'll do a catalogue if there's time, otherwise a printed checklist.

Publicity on the show will be sent to all major publications and museums of the world. I'd like the show to travel. This depends on obtaining a grant. We'll keep you posted.

Peter Bradley
Guest Curator
652 Broadway, New York 677-3732

P.S. H. D. Olendorf will pick up. Label your package, Warehouse Show, Institute for the Arts, Rice University, % Dreyer, Stockton St. and University Blvd., Houston, Texas 77001

July 22, 1971

Chapter 3

Local Color and Its Discontents

The DeLuxe Show

On July 22, 1971, Peter Bradley sent a letter to eighteen fellow artists in New York, Los Angeles, and Paris (fig. 3.1):

> We're planning an exhibition in a poor section of Houston. The object is to bring first-rate art to people who don't usually attend shows. Hence our intention to rent a large space, a church, a ballroom, an empty warehouse. It will be of easy access to housewives, children, laborers; the people. Those who usually attend exhibitions will find the location through publicity and advertisements; their visits will bring life to an otherwise neglected part of town.
>
> I'm inviting: Darby Bannard, Anthony Caro, Dan Christensen, Edward Clark, David Diao, Sam Gilliam, Bob Gordon, Richard Hunt, Daniel Johnson, Virginia Jaramillo, Al Loving, Kenneth Noland, Jules Olitski, Larry Poons, Barbara Riboud, Michael Steiner, William Williams.[1]

1. Letter, Peter Bradley to Vincent Dacosta Smith, July 22, 1971, DeLuxe archive, Menil Collection, Houston, Texas. With the exception of David Diao, each of the artists listed in Bradley's letter was represented in the exhibition. Frank Davis, Craig Kaufmann, and James Wolfe were invited subsequently. I hasten to add that from the time they arrived in Houston (in 1941, having already left Paris for New York after the outbreak of World War II), Dominique de Menil emphasized through her and her family foundation's philanthropy and projects what she took her stated "policy of independence of mind" to mean (memorandum, Dominique de Menil to Menil Foundation board membership, October 16, 1976, Menil Foundation archive, Menil Collection, Houston, Texas). She saw as a critical necessity that excellent art be totally and immediately accessible by the public. Comparing what she saw in Texas with the European situation, she observed that "in Europe the poorest person can enjoy the most beautiful works of art without having to spend a cent—art is everywhere—there is not a village that doesn't have a lovely old church, an impressive castle. In Paris there is Notre Dame and the Louvre available for everybody. Art is . . . just like the air one breathes. We

Figure 3.1. Peter Bradley's letter inviting artists to participate in *The DeLuxe Show*, July 22, 1971. Menil Archives, The Menil Collection, Houston. Photo: Hickey-Robertson, Houston.

Bradley then requested a loan of two works "until September" and asked his invitee to forward to Houston the appropriate photography, while assuring her or him not only that pictures would be taken in Houston but transportation and insurance costs would be covered. There were also plans for a catalogue. Only the possibility of a tour depended on a grant that was still up in the air.

Bradley posted this missive just three weeks after the progressive Houston-based art patrons John and Dominique de Menil received a letter from Ronald Hobbs, a black literary agent, describing the project that Bradley would, by late July, make his own.[2] "Might it

---

become conscious of it when we lack it. I became conscious of art and particularly of beautiful architecture when we made our home in Houston." Dominique de Menil, quoted in Pamela G. Smart, "Aesthetics as a Vocation," in *Art and Activism: Projects of John and Dominique de Menil* (Houston: Menil Foundation; New Haven, CT: Yale University Press, 2010), 23–24.

2. Alvia J. Wardlaw, "John and Dominique de Menil and the Houston Civil Rights Movement" (in *Art and Activism*, 103–13) is a thorough and sensitive account of the de Menils' larger engagement with civil rights in the segregated city of Houston. The art historian William Camfield, who worked closely with the de Menils from 1963, details the evolution of *The DeLuxe Show* from the exhibition program Dominique initiated in 1970 at the Rice University Institute for the Arts (initially an experiment in "progressive education in avant-garde art" for which the de Menils had provided seed money): "The de Menils' concern for civil and human rights was a prominent theme in their second year at Rice. Dominique's first exhibition . . . , 'Conversations with the Dead,' September 1970, featured Danny Lyon's wrenching photographs of inmates in the Texas prison system. She followed that in February 1971 with 'Some American History,' a provocative [and controversial] presentation of slavery in the United States featuring the work of artist Larry Rivers but bolstered by the work of several African American artists. That exhibition attracted numerous visitors from Houston's black community, who would continue to come to the Institute for the Arts exhibitions. Their turnout two months later for the enchanting exhibition 'For Children' prompted literary agent and John de Menil confidant Ronald Hobbs to suggest mounting exhibitions in one of the black areas of Houston." William A. Camfield, "Two Museums and Two Universities: Towards the Menil Collection," in *Art and Activism*, 68–69. Hobbs's letter reads as follows:

> Dear Dominique and Jean,
> Might it not be effective to contemplate some sort of minor, yet effective exhibition, right in the heart of the black Houston community. All I mean is that if the Forward Times has finally come forward, hold onto their good will. Maybe there is a good local artist who can produce a sculpture in memory of the black youth recently gunned down or a memorable character in black history. It would be a gas if in a prominent black community intersection, one could come upon a symbol of pride, dignity, and high artistic achievement, realized through the skill of local black talent. I hope you find a kernel here.
> Yours,
> Ronald Hobbs

Letter, Ronald Hobbs to Mr. & Mrs. John de Menil, July 7, 1971, DeLuxe archive, Menil Collection, Houston, Texas.

not be effective," Hobbs wrote from New York, "to contemplate some sort of minor, yet effective exhibition, right in the heart of the black Houston community[?]" The prospect excited Hobbs: "It would be a gas if in a prominent black community intersection, one could come upon a symbol of pride, dignity, and high artistic achievement."[3] It was with Hobbs's vision in tow that, shortly thereafter, John de Menil flew to New York to pitch Bradley on the idea of organizing the exhibition.[4] Bradley, a color painter by night and associate director of the *haut* Perls Gallery by day, had an idea of "effectiveness" that differed dramatically from Hobbs's, and the conversation de Menil had with Bradley was a game changer.[5] As the de Menils' publicist later

3. Letter, Hobbs to Mr. & Mrs. de Menil.

4. It is not clear what Hobbs thought of the exhibition that eventually took shape, but an August 17 letter from John de Menil to Hobbs gives some sense of Hobbs's disappointment:

> Dear, Dear Ron:
> You told Simone that the DeLuxe Show is throwing a bone to black people.
> For once you're completely wrong. A show by local black artists would have been a pacifier because they are from mediocre to bad, and it would have been endorsing something in which we don't believe. Instead we are showing good artists of the younger generation, black, white and brown together. Artists of the younger generation, promising artists. The choice was made by Peter Bradley in complete freedom. *Thus it is a show with a point of view*, just like the show of Henry Geldzahler's was at the Metropolitan, but it is honest art. The artists invited by Peter responded with enthusiasm. And so do the black people who are working on the project here, including the black contractor who remodeled the DeLuxe Theater in a record 18 days, working two shifts. The project is entirely directed by blacks. We provided the original idea and the money without strings attached. I believe the community will respond: we'll soon know about that.
> I had some static from [Melvin] Huckaby and Earl Allen who resented not having been the chosen instrument. I explained to them that the artists would not have wanted to come under the local black art establishment. They wanted direct access to the street. . . .
> I'd like to see you.
> Yours,
> John de Menil

Letter, John de Menil to Ronald Hobbs, August 17, 1971, DeLuxe archive, Menil Collection, Houston, Texas. Emphasis added.

5. The de Menils knew of Bradley from his involvement with Larry Rivers's 1970 exhibition at Rice University's Institute for the Arts, *Some American History*, which had originated as a Dominique de Menil–commissioned solo exhibition of Rivers's work, but at Rivers's initiative became a group show in which Bradley, Joe Overstreet, and others participated. They knew Bradley, too, through Klaus Perls, owner of Perls Galleries and Bradley's employer since Bradley left the Guggenheim following a major exhibition of Alexander Calder, then represented by Perls.

recalled, "First, there was a question of putting together, hastily and informally, an exhibition of black art in a poor part of Houston; then the idea was discussed with [Bradley]."[6] Certain that "no serious black artist today would accept to be included in an exclusively black show" and that any exhibition he organized would have to include nonblack artists as well, Bradley proposed a competing vision.[7] "This selection," said Bradley, "breaks down the barriers that create this whole theory of black shows and white shows. The *DeLuxe Show* marks the first time that good black artists share the attention and the tribute with good [nonblack] artists."[8]

But the shape Bradley imparted to the exhibition, which took its name from the disused movie theater that he selected to house it, owed as much to timing as to principle (fig. 3.2a–d). From the first, the project was caught up in his own frustrated response to *Contemporary Black Artists in America.* Bradley had declined to participate on the grounds that it merely extended the separatist trend. The reception of Doty's exhibition, he felt, confirmed his hunch:

> We've put too much of our life into our work, and we don't want to be lumped politically. We were proven to be right, at least as far as art criticism is concerned; for you'll remember that press coverage of the all-Black Whitney show concentrated on Black political stances. Hardly a word was said of the art! It embittered many artists who, happy to accept recognition from a museum devoted entirely to American art,

6. Simone Swan, "Conversation with Peter Bradley, Curator of the Deluxe Show," August 1971, typescript in DeLuxe archive, Menil Collection, Houston, Texas, 5.

7. A July 1971 memorandum detailing the first practical steps leading to the exhibition notes that Bradley "accept[ed] this job because of its importance, and [said] that he didn't want any honorarium." "Memorandum: DeLuxe Art Show and the Black Art Center, July 1971," DeLuxe archive, Menil Collection, Houston, Texas.

8. Peter Bradley, quoted in a press release issued in winter 1972 to announce the publication of the *DeLuxe Show* catalogue. DeLuxe Show archive, Menil Collection, Houston. This was not exactly true. The spring 1969 exhibition at the Studio Museum of Harlem featuring the works of Sam Gilliam, Stephen Kelsey, and William T. Williams was one signal precedent. So was the benefit-exhibition hosted by the Museum of Modern Art as a memorial to Martin Luther King Jr. Eighty-one "leading American artists contributed works to the show, which took place over four days from 31 October to 3 November 1968, and pledged proceeds from works for sale to the Southern Christian Leadership Conference." Press releases 98 and 98a, archives of the Museum of Modern Art, New York. *The DeLuxe Show* represents the first time an exhibition was organized with the express intention of showing together recognized, celebrated artists from both sides of the color line. James R. Mellow, "The Black Artist, the Black Community, the White Art World" (*New York Times*, June 29, 1969, D23) is an extraordinarily generous review of this event.

> ended up being used as a socio-political football. . . . Many artists felt trapped and cursed themselves for not having been wiser. They felt used. Anyway, while talking to John de Menil, I explained that danger. So he asked, "Well, what would you do?" and I told him. Two days later he called me and asked if I would be willing to put a show together.[9]

Though Bradley conceived of *DeLuxe* interracially, his "we" also involved a corps of artists who agreed that another variation on the new black show would do more harm than good. Bradley's "we" were among those for whom art was a continuously varying part of the work of a singular life, a conviction trivialized when the racialist insistence on representation goes unquestioned. *DeLuxe* suggested a way through the conundrum into which contemporary black politics had thrust art by relentlessly placing the artist's prerogative on the defensive. It means much that Bradley supported the idea of siting *The DeLuxe Show* "in a poor section of town" while demanding that it be organized "without any involvement with the local black art establishment."[10] Situated where Bradley believed it would be particularly welcome, or "effective," *DeLuxe* eluded such enclosures by providing "good art"—all of it modernist abstraction—as a resource for individuals-in-formation, which is how he viewed the children of the Fifth Ward.

Mickey Leland, a Houston community organizer and a close associate of John de Menil,[11] agreed to coordinate local transactions and scout possible locations. These were submitted to Bradley, who selected the DeLuxe Theater, a vacant movie house at 3303 Lyons

9. Peter Bradley, interview by Simone Swan, in *The DeLuxe Show*, exh. cat. (Houston, TX: Menil Foundation, 1971), 68–69.

10. [Author unnamed], "Memorandum: DeLuxe Art Show and the Black Art Center, July 1971," DeLuxe archive, Menil Collection, Houston, Texas.

11. In a 1991 *Town and Country* magazine feature on Dominique de Menil, Anne Holmes wrote, "Knowing that one person can spark a reform, [John] gave Mickey the encouragement and financial help necessary to get his education. Racial tensions were running high at the time, remembers Richard Murray, a political scientist at the University of Houston: "Mickey Leland was considered the most dangerous political leader. But John taught Mickey, and Mickey was like his son. That frightened some people who thought the de Menils limousine liberals." Ann Holmes, quoted in Smart, "Aesthetics as a Vocation," in *Art and Activism*, 31. Of John de Menil, Leland later recalled, "He took me, a militant who hated all white people, and made me into a humanitarian." Leland, quoted in Marguerite Johnson, "The de Menils: They Made Houston a More Beautiful Place in Which to Live," pt. 3, *Houston Post*, January 11, 1977), n.p.

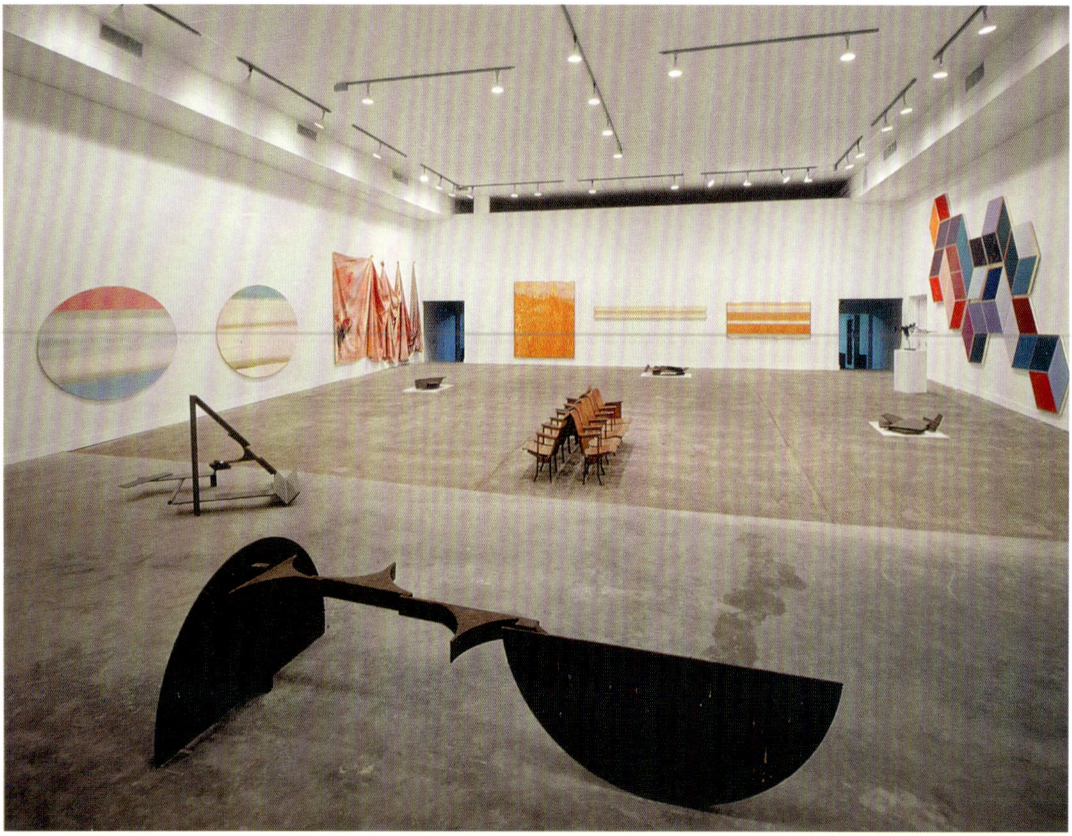

Figure 3.2a–d. Installation photography from *The DeLuxe Show*. Menil Archives, The Menil Collection, Houston. Photo: Hickey-Robertson, Houston. See also gatefold following page 212.

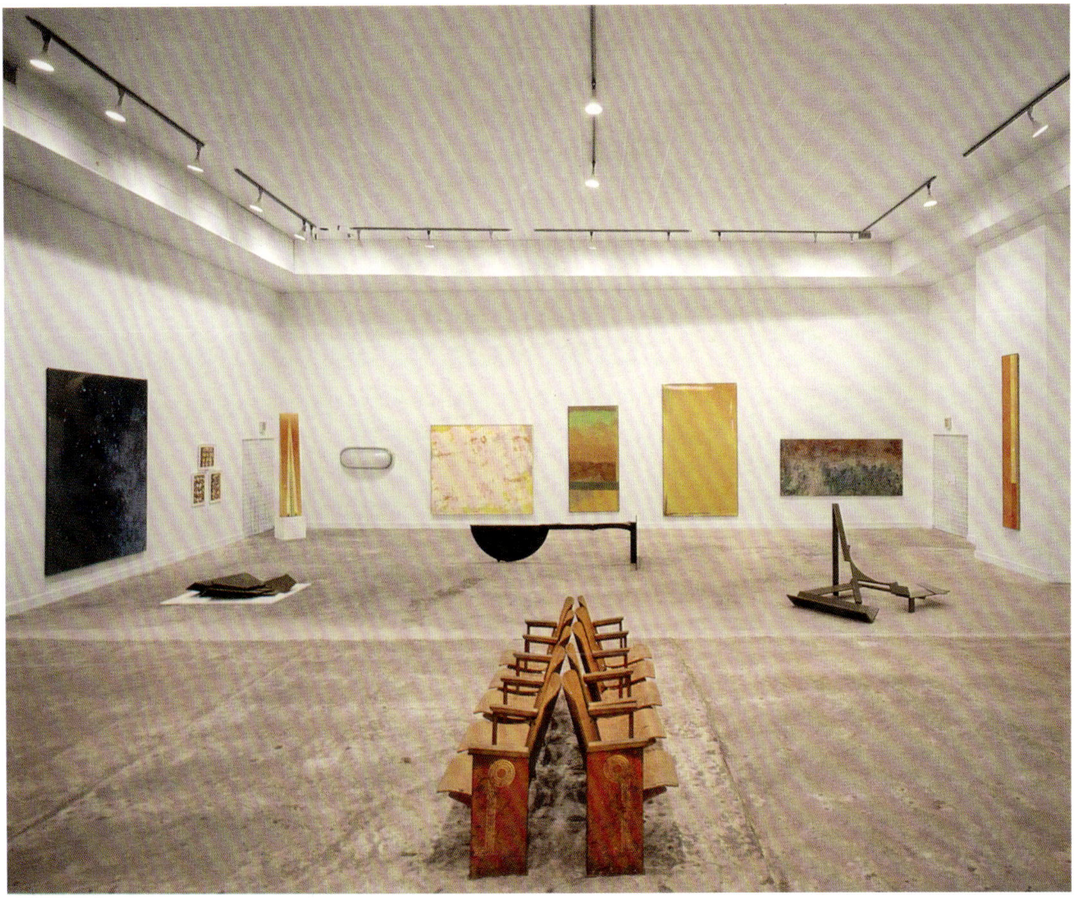

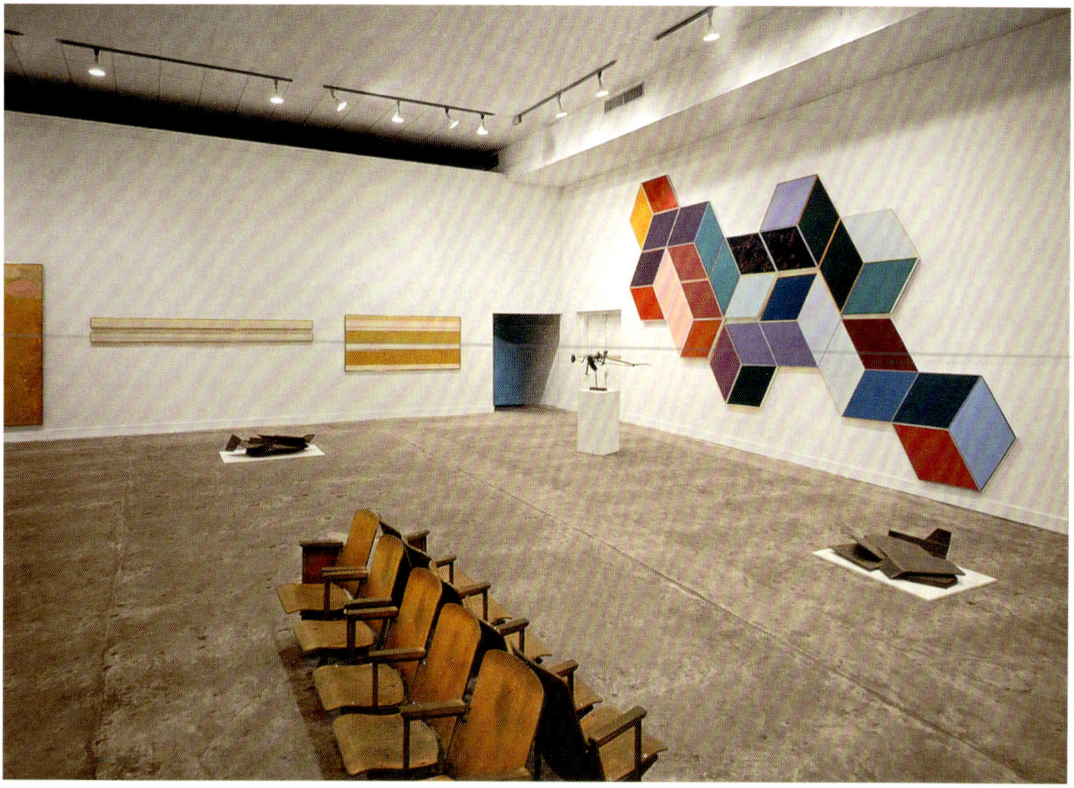

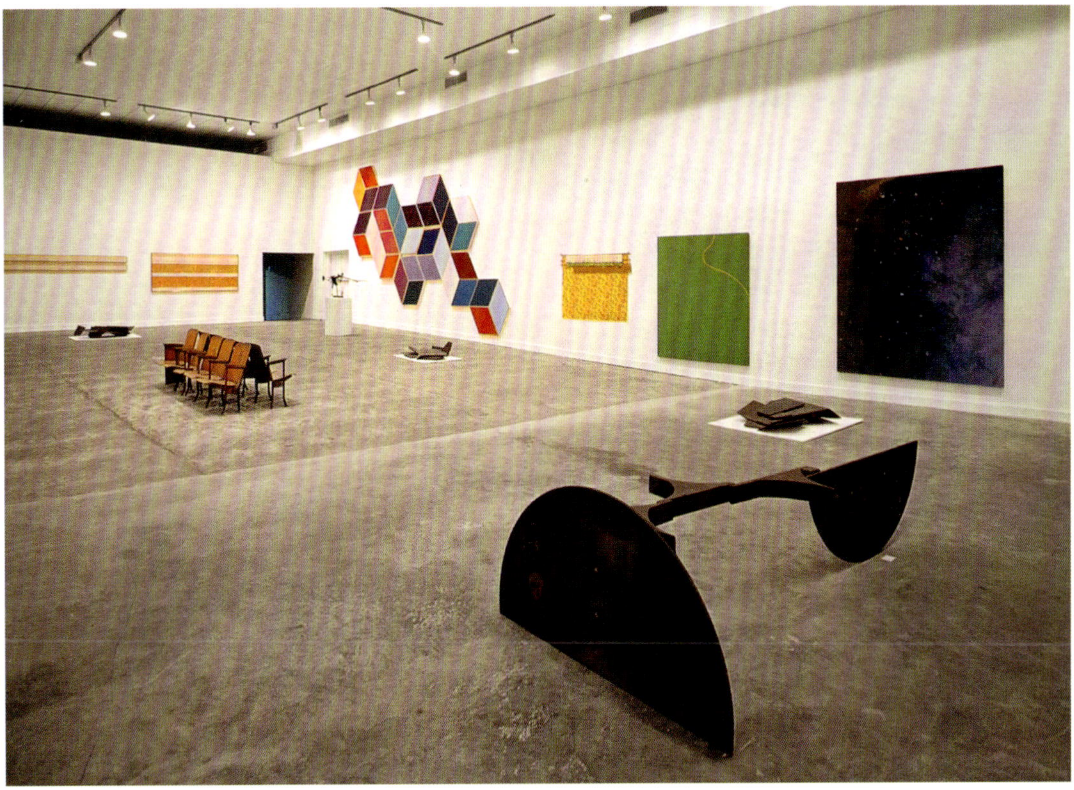

discourse and the show's somewhat eclectic mix of formats and stylistic categories did not matter for much. Rather, "the object is to bring first-rate art to people who don't usually attend shows." Wrote one sympathetic reviewer of the exhibition, "From one viewpoint it's just one more good art show; from another it could have an effect not so quickly determined. It could reveal all Heaven to a responsive person who may never have been to a museum or a gallery."[14]

In fact the sentiment echoes Bradley's, whose other statements give further insight into his equation of vulnerability and freedom with the experience of high modernist art, and color painting in particular. Bradley regarded local children, who didn't know that this art was deemed asymmetric with their experience, as the ideal viewers of his exhibition. Like the art, their minds were "honest and wide open," and so still susceptible to inspiration:

> The young kids are *really* the ones that get something out of it. The kids between 7 and 10, maybe 12, because they haven't yet been indoctrinated by bad art, or ethnic art which I think is bad. There's a chance that they can read the art better than most people who frequent museums. . . . They have a much better chance to appreciate the art and the space. This is all light and airy and free.

In a recorded conversation, a Menil employee asks Bradley, "Are you talking about black people?" to which he replies, "Who else?"[15]

14. Ann Holmes, "Behind a Battered Marquee Waits Dazzling American Art," *Houston Chronicle*, August 24, 1971, n.p.

15. "Conversation with Peter Bradley, Curator of the Deluxe Show," interview by Simone Swan, August 1971, typescript in DeLuxe archive, Menil Collection, Houston, Texas, 7–8. Emphasis in original. In fact sometimes the child in these representations is Bradley himself. *Houston Chronicle* Fine Arts editor Ann Holmes reported that "Bradley wishes his own early life might have been blessed with such a show to prod his imagination" (see Holmes, "Behind a Battered Marquee Waits Dazzling American Art"). The pitch to *Black Enterprise* for coverage of the exhibition included this mention of Bradley: "Peter knew he was putting together a milestone exhibit—the first time art of this calibre has been brought into a depressed area—and he felt a personal interest as well realizing the potential effect of art works upon neighborhood children, exposure he was denied as a child." Letter, Lys McLaughlin to Pat Patterson / *Black Enterprise*, September 24, 1971, DeLuxe archive, Menil Collection, Houston, Texas. Steve Cannon, a New York–based essayist contracted by Bradley to write the introduction to the exhibition catalogue, produced instead a meandering 150-page memoir of his discussions with Bradley and visits to Houston (an introduction was later excavated from this text). In it he relates that "the good thing about it is that they are trying to stir up some sort of serious interest in the community, the area that Peter Bradley had chosen for the show. Slowly I was beginning

DeLuxe's message, as Bradley imagined it, was utterly consistent with its form as a sited social experiment: it advanced a new cultural model, doing so provisionally by inviting visitors to recognize alternative forms of relations, types of necessity, and ways of perceiving reality—all within a notable absence of determinant images and messages. *DeLuxe* placed its faith in the possibility *alone* that an encounter with modern art in a congenial surround might spur the youngest among Houston's black poor to recognize a larger imaginative and experiential horizon than people in their circumstances were regularly associated with. This optimism registered the intense hope and expectation of *DeLuxe*'s organizer that the exhibition would engender a whole other idea about the terrain and texture of social life: a scene of representation notably lacking in avatars, scripts for living, or even images. Visitors would find themselves embedded in a scene where an event of the new and different opened limitless potentials for individual and social growth. Here too, color painting could recover its former identification with the new and different while also escaping the constraints of aesthetic formalism.

DeLuxe was an attempt to implement the specifically modernist aspiration to give the beholder something irreducibly original to the experience of *this* work of art, here and now. *DeLuxe* thus represents an insistence on the sociality of a mode of ambition that once wanted nothing more than to set the aesthetic apart: "In this condition there may be discoverable under new forms certain spiritual illuminations," wrote Hart Crane in 1925. "It is as though a poem gave the reader as he left it a single, new *word*, never before spoken and impossible to actually enunciate, but self-evident as an active principle in the reader's consciousness henceforward."[16]

In Houston, this aspiration became a politics by reference to the political medium in which Bradley deployed it. On this scene, modernist sensibility was anything but abstract or impersonal. An open

---

to get the feel for his reasoning. He was later to say to me, 'If I were a little boy, growing up in a neighborhood like this, I would like to see beautiful things, pictures, from the outside world too. Aside from all the ones that are constantly going on inside my head.' Slowly, it was making sense." Steve Cannon, "American Notes / A Matter of Taste: An Art Exhibition in Houston," unpublished typescript, DeLuxe archive, Menil Collection, Houston, Texas.

16. Hart Crane, "General Aims and Theories," quoted in Michael Fried, *Morris Louis* (New York: Abrams, 1970), 41. Emphasis in original.

refusal to engage the false empowerments of cultural generalization—to which assent was perpetually encouraged and regularly granted—culturally speaking, it was more like an act of war.

I take this aspiration to be elemental in Bradley's vision for *DeLuxe*—its lucidity, for him, enhanced all the more by his own incredulity in the face of his interlocutor's vision. For Bradley, this art's particular ways of signifying *the open* made it a practicable way to counteract cultural operations that risked immobilizing the interest of younger inhabitants of the Fifth Ward. Modernist art was a way *very locally* to alter the scene of relations in which they formed a worldview. In directing *DeLuxe* toward the youngest population within that ecology, Bradley betrayed his sincere belief in such art's capacity to impede the closure of mind that submits the self to some "higher" representational purpose.

Bradley reminds us that modernism harbors a particular, and specifically political, style of imagining, one whose political valence gets quickly lost in the narrowly formalistic genealogies and syntaxes developed for this art. The Fifth Ward, we might say, gave *this* modernism something precise and extended to do:[17] promote the kind of experience that accumulates through perceptual and reflective acts when they are "free of obstruction." The stuff it comprised didn't dictate its significance; it stood or fell on the quality of interest it stimulated in viewers, for the event demanded as many explanations as there were encounters. *DeLuxe* meant a *chance*, and nothing more, to cultivate sovereign consciousness, through the recognition of creative work that gets done when individuality forms, or finds itself, out of place.

We have seen that modernist practitioners signify mobile interest by their difference and that mobile interest is anarchical. It frustrates cultural coherency by stimulating heterogeneity and inhibiting formations of consensus. When black art history recognizes this element, it does so not through acknowledgment but rather through *a variant treatment*; modernists populate a history of exceptions. But we may look upon that treatment otherwise, for instance as a history of *the few individuals* established within that orbit—mere fads in comparison to those who served their people through fealty to representation.

17. As noted above, this formulation is T. J. Clark's.

Though a foreign presence in the established cultural firmament, their presence, once detected, is magmatic. It introduces shifts into a troublingly static medium. More, it insists that we remember we are speaking of a human ecology, where interests and commitments vary, and self-realization regularly fails to sync up with symbolic conventions. In a real social ecology, individuals particularize particularity, dissemble culture, compel a perhaps maddeningly idiosyncratic language of differences, desires, deferrals, and delays. And through them the weight and scope of the black normative comes into view.

When we assessed the assimilative pedagogy that forged new cultural forms after the "failure" of integration, we saw it systematically seek to limit individuals' distorting impacts on cultural expression. We saw its defining compensations elide individuals in order, paradoxically, to figure culture. Thus "the Negro has come to recognize that he can achieve equal opportunities only through the concerted action of the Negro community. We can't do it one by one anymore."[18] We saw the notion of survival placed at the center of the formally and conceptually distinct issue of the community form, so that sociologists could speak of the "ethic of cooperation" that does not merely bind members of the black community who "share with one another because of the urgency of their needs" as "kin and friends who exchange and give and obligate one another,"[19] but also provides a seemingly unshakable moral basis for the discouragement of idiosyncratic subjective development.

Let's not think for a second that any of these resonant period voices ever described objective reality. When, as writers on culture, we ignore the *genealogy* of this "only," of this singular "recognition," and of the collective sight that they enfold—whenever we pass up the opportunity to pose the question of their necessity—we again purchase our subjects at the cost of the individual. The loss of art soon follows. Like that of the modernist practitioner throughout this study, Bradley's "art" represents an unusually strenuous and unselfconscious effort to conserve individuality in a cultural space and moment that militated against it. *DeLuxe* placed in the heart of Houston's

18. Ossie Davis, "The English Language Is My Enemy," *American Teacher* 51, no. 8 (April 1967): 18.

19. Carol B. Stack, *All Our Kin: Strategies for Survival in a Black Community* (New York: Harper and Row, 1974), 32.

black ghetto an art event that could scarcely be thought of as cultural in the accepted sense.

Pressing the factor of audience receptivity, Bradley's attestations understand that popular public representations *imputed to that audience* a horizon of possibility limited to the supposedly inexhaustible symbolic riches of blackness—for which "ethnic art" served him as a proxy. Bradley also understood that there was nothing particularly rich about the blackness that contemporary *rhetorical* figurations of the ghetto constructed. To another way of thinking, not Bradley's alone, modernist art offered to makers and viewers alike a concrete framework for reformation and recognition of the individual's relation to place and culture. But if within black communities there existed any conventional wisdom concerning modernist art, it was anything but sympathetic. When abstract art had gained notoriety in like settings, it was for being at variance with the generalized cultural landscape—precisely because it evoked the person who steps outside of the circle.

Circa 1971, the black ghetto was a particularly color-stable entity, reinforced from inside and outside, that provided the national conversation on race with one of its most crucial rhetorical supports, an emblem of race's resolutely Manichaean structure. The recruitment of persons to this model—period representations of the black child, for instance, regularly locate her crisis condition within a ghetto mise-en-scène—is but one mechanism through which fundamental realities of race linked to corporeality, chiefly color, are comprehensively structured into conventional wisdom about who we are and how society is shaped.[20]

The works presented in *The DeLuxe Show* imposed a sweepingly different sense of space, one characterized by color indetermination and material variation, and scaled to the individual viewer. Among the most salient images *DeLuxe* throws up is that of a spatially expansive nucleus of turbulent color opened in the midst of a politically monochromatic territory. In *DeLuxe*, then, two radically divergent conceptions of color came briefly into intimate contact. This chapter tries to

20. See Howard Winant, review of *Race and the Politics of Solidarity* by Juliet Hooker, *Contemporary Sociology* 39, no. 5 (September 2010): 580.

understand the conceptual dynamics of that momentous encounter. To a bird's-eye view, *DeLuxe* instantiated racial discomposure in a metaphorical dimension of the sense introduced at this book's outset: a cultural expression that manifested those involutions of color that are constantly under way in the social but are legislated away by "theories" of racial culture and expedient sketches of the racial situation.[21] Compared with conventional politics, *DeLuxe* sought a more dramatically localized revision of the human environment, achieved as the individual negotiated an irregular succession of color paintings. If only for a moment, the dimensional color suffusing this art invited an experience massively at odds with the vocabularies of color that ghetto life naturalized.

Bradley's statement that "the artists in this exhibition depict in their works the urge for complete exploration"[22] expressed his hope that viewers would find in the work a space of belonging, of community apart from the laws or necessities of home and meaning. Because it claimed no contiguous relationship to home, this art affirmed a total freedom irrespective of place.[23] The child represented to Bradley the kind of open-ended mindfulness that is supremely capable of *the instance*:

> I think it is sometimes felt, by those angered or suspicious of such paintings, that no object the actual making of which is so unimportant could conceivably bear the major importance we have attached to works of art. It is true that their existence as instances is carried on their face: labor is not in them; they look as if they might as well have been made instantaneously, and that their use should take no longer. But the fact

21. E.g.: "For the most part our cities are circular in shape, developed in rough concentric circles running outward from a core of offices and governmental centers. The most abject portions of these circles are blacktowns—areas that expand irresistibly with family growth and migrants from rural America. They expand, that is, until they bump into that green and leafy ring closing the circle on all sides, the suburbs. This is a barrier that is virtually unpassable except to a few blacks, a they-shall-not-pass miles thick and getting thicker. So blacktown, no matter how it grows, will have to stop at the signs reading City Limits. Thus, the growing blackness of our central cities is a result ordained by whites, like all major matters affecting blacks." W. H. Ferry, "Farewell to Integration," *Center Magazine* 1, no. 3 (March 1968): 35.

22. Bradley, quoted in "Art Goes to the People," 14.

23. If coming to consciousness in the ghetto meant *being at one with the world* (existence according to type), the fleeting worldliness of art (*a* world) acquainted one with contingency and separateness, as well as the need for connection with what one finds absolutely different from oneself and unavailable to understanding.

> about an instance, when it happens, is that it poses a permanent beauty, if we are capable of it.[24]

Taken as a whole, *The DeLuxe Show* looks like nothing so much as Bradley's attempt to elaborate his artistic sensibility, not only as a progressive individualist but also as a modernist color painter, into something that could pose a challenge to the monochromy dominating black cultural politics. Indeed, the actual work color was doing in much of the art in *The DeLuxe Show* bears a heavy burden in these arguments, which suggests that color—in all its physical and metaphorical capacities—provided a site and vehicle for Bradley's intervention.

Bradley included in *DeLuxe* two large paintings of his own, *Hemming* (1971, acrylic on canvas, 108 × 84 in; fig. 3.4) and *Marble Face* (1971, acrylic on canvas, 50 × 112 in). Though the two paintings seem to have little in common, the latter hung to the right of Olitski's *Loosha One* of 1970 (acrylic on canvas, 114 × 66½ in; fig. 3.5). *Marble Face* is oriented horizontally and has a coarse surface texture and fervid contrasts. *Hemming*, on the other hand, openly demonstrates Bradley's debt to Olitski. The painting presents a dark-bluish field flecked with touches of white, pink, peach, and teal at every point except the lower right corner. At this point gathers one of two cloudlike forms that reach toward the canvas's center, their hues seeming to recede into the ground as they go. Each is in crescendo, a not-yet-completed color statement—one buoyant, lavenderish, and rising; the other marginally heavier, with shades of amber and bright yellow, and thus falling—that one takes to be either disclosing more fully or gradually concealing the center. Occupying the canvas like curtains parted before a stage, the cloudlike forms finally seem arranged to spare the geometric center of incident—and give us someplace to go. *Hemming* gives to our perception the plurivocality of color expressly in terms of its spatializing effects.

The ideas that shaped Bradley's practice from the mid-1960s had their origins in the color effects that Jules Olitski began to achieve when, in 1965, he found in the compressor-powered commercial spray gun an end to his search for a way to spray color in the air so

24. Stanley Cavell, *The World Viewed: Reflections on the Ontology of Film* (New York: Vintage, 1971), 117.

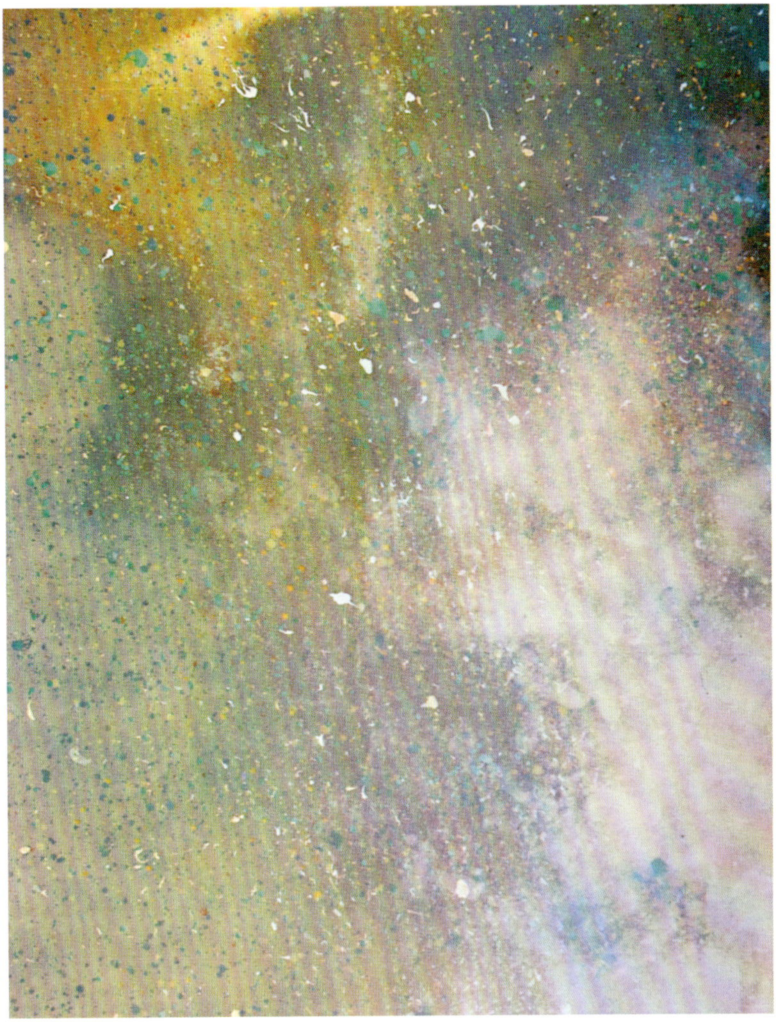

Figure 3.4.
Peter Bradley (b. 1940), *Hemming*, 1971. Acrylic on canvas, 108 × 84 in. (274.3 × 213.4 cm). Courtesy of the artist.

that it stayed there.[25] The idea was to leave the openness the two painters saw in color undelimited: *open*. In the finest examples of both painters' work in this highly circumscribed vein, airborne clouds of sprayed color became films of color when they reached the canvas

25. This is how Olitski related his ambition to Kenworth Moffett, who reports it anecdotally in *Jules Olitski* (Boston: Museum of Fine Arts, 1973), 34. Karen Wilkin records the same anecdote in her *Color as Field: American Painting, 1950–1975* (New Haven, CT: American Federation of the Arts in association with Yale University Press, 2007), 49. Olitski showed his first spray paintings at Poindexter Gallery in New York (October 26–November 13, 1965) and David Mirvish Gallery in Toronto (November 11–December 5, 1965).

surface.[26] Works from this period by both painters take what has been described as a vehemently antistructural attitude toward color, wresting it from its historical association with design and other factors of image construction. They track to a subtle but important transformation that occurred *within* the field of practice we know as postpainterly abstraction. In the narrative to which Bradley adheres, Olitski's sprayed color factors centrally. This color is to be distinguished from the "open" and often stained color—first seen in influential solo exhibitions of Louis, Noland, and Olitski in the spring of 1962, events which Greenberg's "After Abstract Expressionism" had registered like a seismograph.[27] The approach defines works that Helen Frankenthaler, Morris Louis, Noland, and Olitski produced until 1965, which had displaced the multihued skeins of abstract expressionism.

In 1960 Greenberg had praised Louis's turn to open color for diminishing tactility to a degree that made his paintings ever more "purely visual fields": "The closer color could be identified with its ground, the freer it would be of . . . tactile associations; the way to achieve this closer identification was by adopting watercolor technique to oil and using thin paint on an absorbent surface."[28] By using acrylic paints stained into unprimed canvas, painters would intensify these effects, as well as this critical vocabulary's purchase on their output. But while open color helped bind painting more closely to transparent acrylic paint itself, it became the opinion of those who had enthusiastically welcomed it that this development actually heightened, rather than shook, painting's historical dependency on image.[29] For all its

26. Cf. Adrian Stokes on "film color" versus "surface" color. Film colors, according to Stokes, are "indefinite in location . . . since the eye goes into them looking for the resistant surface more usually associated with color." Stokes, "Colour and Form" [1937], in *The Critical Writings of Adrian Stokes*, vol. 2, *1937–1958* (London: Thames and Hudson, 1978), 14.

27. Clement Greenberg, "After Abstract Expressionism" (*Art International*, October 25, 1962), in *CEC*, 4:121–33. See also Clement Greenberg, *Post-painterly Abstraction*, exh. cat. (Los Angeles: LACMA, 1964).

28. Clement Greenberg, "Louis and Noland," in *CEC*, 4:97.

29. On one occasion in 1965, even Greenberg lumped his beloved postpainterly abstractionists, only three years later the brazen pioneers of open color, into a "nominal stylistic consensus," which they cohabited with practitioners of Pop and assemblage. To Greenberg, the lot of them accentuated "clarity, flatness, openness, linearity, renunciation of thick paint and turbid color." Greenberg, "America Takes the Lead," in *CEC*, 4:215.

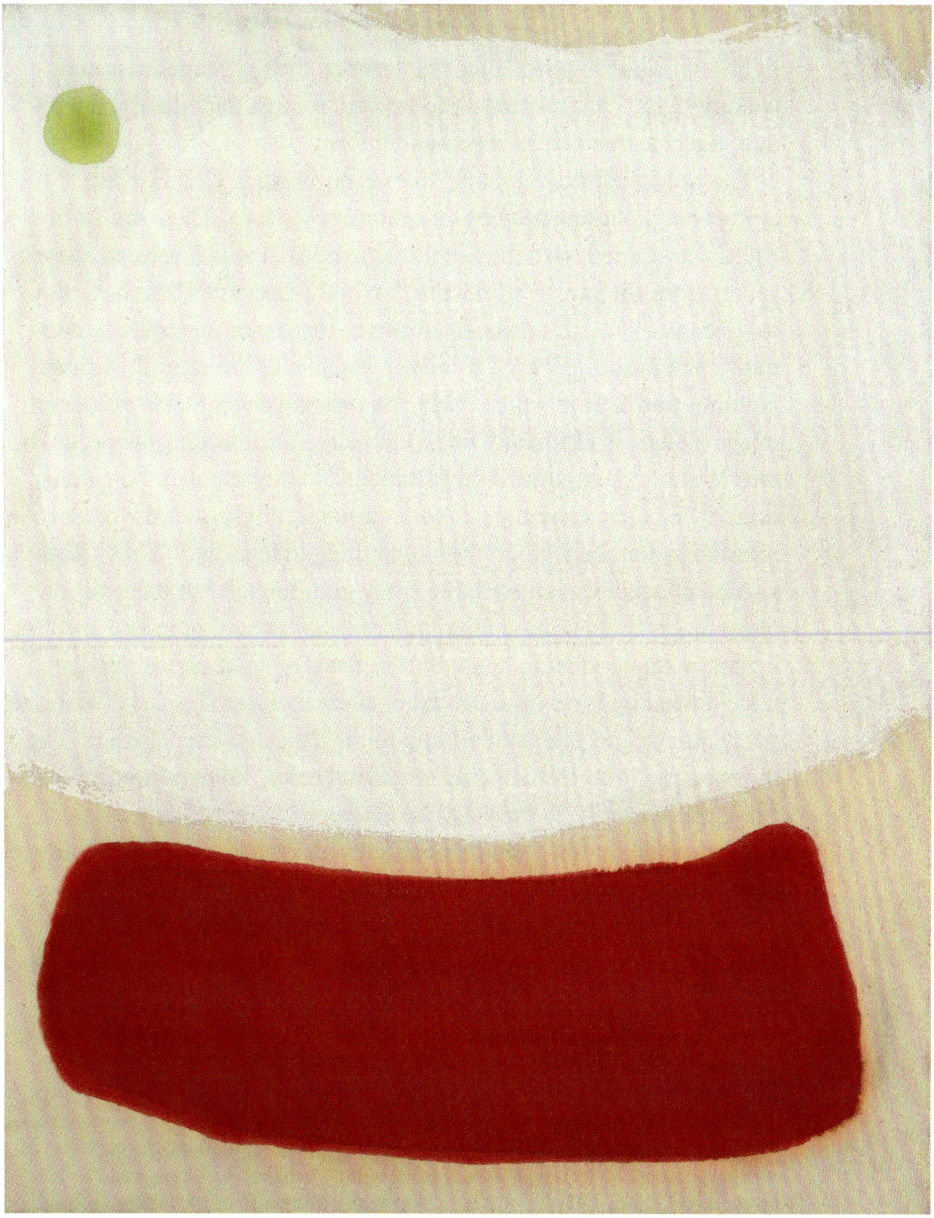

Figure 3.5. Jules Olitski, *Jackpot*, 1963. Magna acrylic on canvas, 34½ × 25¾ in. (87.6 × 65.4 cm). Art © Estate of Jules Olitski / Licensed by VAGA, New York, NY. Photo: Arthur Evans.

Figure 3.6. Jules Olitski (1922–2007), *Loosha One*, 1970. Water-based acrylic, 116 × 66½ in. (294.6 × 168.9 cm). Collection of the Kenneth Noland Foundation. Art © Estate of Jules Olitski / Licensed by VAGA, New York, NY. Photograph courtesy The Museum of Fine Arts, Houston.

DeLuxe, owed an obvious debt to Olitski's innovation. But only Bradley wielded the spray gun with anything like Olitski's concentrated intentness. Others, especially Bowling, Clark, and Gilliam, sought spatializing color effects by different means and usually featured other devices just as prominently (symbolic motifs, shaped canvas, etc.). Yet Olitski's post–spray gun paintings inform accounts of color's fate in modernist art *after* postpainterly abstraction more than any other single practice or mode. Color painting in this mode—this strategy which directed Bradley's studio practice during the period immediately preceding *DeLuxe*, and which Noland characterized in 1968 as painting in which "structure is nowhere evident, or nowhere self-declaring"[32]—presents the canvas as a monumental field, an expressly integrated space totally defined by the mobility and depth of an apparently boundless terrain of color. The terms *mobility* and *depth* allow one to emphasize the viewing effects of peculiar material and visual properties of many paintings of this kind. The sequence of observations in a 1967 review of Olitski's spray paintings gives some indication not so much of their color as such as of the kind of surprise it entails. After first characterizing Olitski's pictures as "large color-generated reliefs," Kermit Champa records an altogether different perception. In pointed contrast to the suspended, solid whole he first described, a subsequent account tells of "open, ambiguous, intractable images." We practically see the critic shift to a position near enough to the pictures to see how they disclose the inadequacy of the term *relief* to something into which one feels oneself projected.[33] Champa's evocative amendment recalls Bradley's own statement regarding the spray gun: "With the gun I can see more color," in which *to see* simultaneously means to actualize *and* to perceive. The benefits of this color, as Bradley sees it, are available to maker and viewer alike. So disposed, color literally gives more to see than its superficial identity allows—as placed, flat, unitary—where *more* acknowledges the unforeseen but irreducible difference between color identity and the experience of sprayed colors.

The novelty of Olitski's technique inhered in the tactility with

32. Kenneth Noland, quoted in Philip Leider, "'The Thing in Painting Is Color,'" *New York Times*, August 25, 1968, D21.

33. Kermit Champa, "Nothing But Color," *Art News* 66, no. 3 (May 1966): 76.

which it invested color.[34] Fried would be Olitski's most enduring champion, in part because of the way the *intension* of Olitski's sprayed color ("the concentration or density of a given color at any point"[35]) amplified his pictures' presentness-effects.[36] But the concept of presentness, in fact, annihilates the most remarkable thing about Olitski's color, which is precisely *the resistance its matter serves up* to that kind of at-onceness. Olitski's color aggrandizes the complexity of color perception by its incontrovertible materiality.[37]

What would secure Olitski's reputation among other modernists, including Rosalind Krauss and Bradley, were the viewer effects wrought by the *extensiveness* of the paintings' tactile color. These compelled Greenberg to describe "a world of color and light

34. Michael Fried described Olitski's spray technique in 1967: "He lays a length of unprimed and unsized canvas on the floor and sprays into it acrylic paint of different colors from as many as three spray-guns powered by an electric air-compressor. By the time he stops working, often with two spray-guns simultaneously, the raw canvas is no longer visible except, in rare cases, toward the edges. In some paintings the surface of the canvas consists of small flecks of different colors which, depending on the wetness of the surfaces at the moment they were sprayed on, are distinct or slightly blurred or almost dissolved into adjacent flecks, and depending on the size of the droplets in a given burst of spray, fluctuate in size from extremely fine points to larger though still minute splashes or beads of pigment. In other paintings the droplets seem to have flowed into one another completely and there are no flecks at all." Michael Fried, quoted in Rosalind Krauss, *Jules Olitski: Recent Paintings* (Philadelphia: Institute of Contemporary Art, 1968), unpaginated, n2. See also Michael Fried, *Jules Olitski: Paintings 1963–67* (Washington, DC: Corcoran Gallery, 1967), 5.

35. Fried, *Jules Olitski*, 6.

36. Fried would later account for this quality in terms of its, for him, explicit function within the dialectic of modernist painting:

> That is how I understand what has seemed to me the compulsion of certain recent painting of major ambition to affirm that the entire surface, which is to say *every bit* of it, is spread out before the beholder—that every grain or particle or atom of surface *competes for presentness* with every other. The emphasis on surface in these paintings is not so much on its expansion as on its concentration; not so much on its extension as on its *in*tension. Perhaps more accurately it is an emphasis on the second of each pair of terms as a vehicle for the first: as if the convincingness of the 'outward' spread of surface across the picture depended ultimately on the convincingness of its 'inward' spread across the same expanse. (Fried, "Larry Poons' New Paintings," *Artforum* 10, no. 7 [1971] 50, emphases in original)

Poons's *Firstwild* (1971) illustrates Fried's review, and Poons also sent it, sans title, to *The DeLuxe Show*.

37. It's like Philip Guston said: "Without this resistance, you would just vanish into either meaning or clarity." Philip Guston, interviewed by David Sylvester in his *Interviews with American Artists* (New Haven, CT: Yale University Press, 2001), 87.

differentiations,"[38] a world to which other influential viewers felt themselves accommodated still more literally. Krauss wrote a remarkable essay in 1968 for an exhibition of seventeen works produced by Olitski over the two preceding years. The essay's claims find their ground in a phenomenology Krauss developed on the basis of the *dimensionality* of the color Olitski achieved in those paintings.[39] For Krauss's Olitski,

> armature-like structures and local color would, in the end, package and delimit the openness of color. [They] would make color function as part of the grammar used to locate discrete objects. By reconceiving the role of color, he could change the syntax of the question "where?" That question would then point toward an answer outside the limits of positive location. . . . By turning to the logic of color, Olitski found himself outside the circle of the logic of place.[40]

Krauss explicates Olitski's syntactical transformation of the question "Where?" with reference to the "radical relationship" in which Olitski's color instantiates the viewer. For her, the radicality of this relation is given by history:

> In front of Raphael's fresco the viewer is a detached observer. Before Titian's altarpiece [the Assunta (1516–18)], as before a work of Rembrandt's, he is a witness, or rather he is obliged to bear witness. Inasmuch as painting is inherently and exclusively a visual art, the question "where?" is one it always asks. Olitski's question . . . is the same as it was for colorists of the past. But the syntax of his question is new. Olitski's phrasing, and the order of experience it projects, places the viewer in a radical relationship to painting.[41]

The linchpin of Krauss's account is an experience that is anything but "exclusively visual." In the disorientation she describes, the very

38. Greenberg, "Introduction to Jules Olitski at the Venice Biennale [1966]," in *CEC*, 4:230.

39. Ultimately Krauss opted for dialectical terms to articulate Olitski's achievement, which, she suggested, reduced to "the conflict between the struggle for pictorial shape taking place at the perimeters of the painting and the effortless presence of the film of color in the rest of the surface." Krauss, *Jules Olitski.* Of the countless differences between Krauss and Fried's approaches to Olitski, none counts more than the status the former accords to the viewer, by her systematic emphasis on the peculiar effects of film color. For more on film color, see Stokes, "Colour and Form."

40. Krauss, *Jules Olitski.*

41. Ibid.

form that one conceives *in advance of looking* as "the painting" becomes spatialized by its color into a territory one feels oneself to inhabit. Color plays the key role in questioning our assurance that a painting is a coherent aggregation of matter occupying a space distinct from our own. It is as though one feels indistinct from *this* color: the painting, after all, "in all its literalness poses a question about where the surface is." And it does so in the same way any specific "phrasing" that grabs our attention immediately "locates" language. What alters the syntax of the question "Where?" is the felt, or perceived, location of the questioner.

Viewers are generally accustomed to differentiated areas of color, but spray painting presents color seemingly in medias res—that is, color not as a stationary but as a variegating visual field. Color discomposed: colors, plural, coming in and out of being as they exchange places in the field of vision, troubling that field of vision, breaking it up, rupturing it before our eyes. Krauss describes the sight of various colors

> not as they spread or flood across a two-dimensional plane, but as they seem to lie behind each other along a single line or point of vision. Like sighting down the surface of a painting from a point at the edge, the colors seem stacked up or telescoped.
>
> Because the seeing of the surface is tied to the perception of a kind of color which so opens and expands that surface toward the viewer that it might be characterized as foreshortened, the very seeing of the painting in all its literalness poses a question about where the surface is. To see Olitski's color means to see the surface itself as elusive and unaligned. And this means seeing it this way over the whole surface and for every moment of one's looking; for the color which permeates that surface has the capacity to destroy its identity as inert, discrete, locatable, and objective.[42]

In other words, Olitski carries the challenge to local color off the canvas and into the realm of the body. The color Krauss describes in its movement beyond the surface plane undermines the viewer's emplacement of the painting on the wall, or at least resists her efforts to maintain it. But it further undermines her tendency to affix color to its customary localizing, denotative function. Such color was unforeseeable by no less a figure than Adrian Stokes, who wrote in 1937 that

42. Ibid. Emphasis added.

"we can never succeed in catching even a faint trace of the feeling that [local surface color] is something belonging to our own bodies."[43]

Descriptions of these pictures routinely invoke films of color and mists of spray, and not only to speak of their obviously atmospheric character.[44] The spatialization of color about which Krauss is particularly insistent depends upon the plurality of values as well as hues present within a given canvas though not strongly contrasted or bounded, so one experiences a succession of color perceptions like shifts within a volume or indistinct phases in a cycle. Fried, in his Corcoran catalogue essay, relates the "dramatic" fluctuations in value within a single hue that Olitski managed with the spray gun. But Fried writes these events as he witnessed them from a position that lay squarely outside, and to a degree opposed to, the picture. Krauss's analysis introduces a difference into the late modernist color vocabulary—the difference a body makes. Krauss positions the body of the beholder, or rather permits it to keep its place, squarely within the "work." In this way it assimilates bodily impacts to the peculiar "order of experience" that this modernism made available. The unprecedented dimensionality of Olitski's color—"indefinite in location . . . one goes into [it] looking for the resistant surface more usually associated with color"[45]—authorized modernism to convey its desire to express in positive terms the whole-bodily dimension of beholding. The unknown in color; its capacity for surprise; the reconciliation of reality with its experienced variability—if this painting made such timeless latencies of color evident, it was the body that told one this was so. The question "Where?" now belongs to painter and viewer alike. Where once "'matter painting'[46] obstructed the exploration of color," the beholder of Olitski's sprayed color literally sees herself *in* color,[47] which is to say, immersed in its changes.

43. Stokes, "Colour and Form," 15.

44. See for example Andrew Hudson, "A Painter Breaks New Ground," *Washington Post*, April 9, 1967, H8; Barbara Rose, "Abstract Illusionism," *Artforum* 6, no. 2 (October 1967): 33–37; and Sidney Tillim, "Scale and the Future of Modernism," *Artforum* 6, no. 2 (October 1967): 14–18.

45. Stokes, "Colour and Form," 14.

46. According to an uncredited quotation appearing in Krauss's essay, "matter painting" was Olitski's coinage for figuration. See Krauss, *Jules Olitski*.

47. On a related theme, see Frantz Fanon, "The Fact of Blackness," in his *Black Skin, White Masks*, trans. Charles Lam Markmann (New York: Grove, 1967), 109–40.

Scale helped secure these effects of color: the seventeen paintings in the exhibition for which Krauss wrote had average dimensions of 6½ by 13 feet. All of the wall-bound works in *DeLuxe* more or less held this scale, the largest being a construction by Alvin Loving made up of eleven hexagonal canvases each measuring 50¼ inches across. This consistent ambition of scale, then, points out another advantage of the child viewer: that she occupied a scale readily swallowed by such pictures all but guaranteed her access. Does not this detail make plausible Bradley's claim about viewers to whom the art would actually "*look like*" what he called "the new world we're all striving towards, free of obstruction"?[48] Scale critically accentuates the qualitative spatiality such painting appears to induce as well. As Krauss's various emphases make clear, *that much* texturized, dimensional color precipitates intense spatial ambiguity: the question 'where?' comes to matter specially because points and nebulous concretions of variably colored paint *range*, not only in measure, value, and intensity but in apparent nearness and farness as well as over the canvas's entire lateral expanse. If scale could make that world seem a continuation of the miniature viewer's own space, now projected into painted terrains of color ramified as a kind of space, it would also heighten the reality effects of that projection. The sensation that the gap between oneself and a work has narrowed or is narrowing, in fact, invests that color with a mobile feeling complementary to that of one's body at rest—which explains the ever-present evocation in so many accounts of this work of breath and vapor. (In Olitski's own phrase, "Painting is keeping a surface alive.")[49] To be oneself local to color in this way—or more accurately, to experience the picture as a *colored medium*: habitable but internally inconsistent, a surging terrain of changing densities, varying hues, and textures, in which one feels suspended—is to know color as sensibility. Such a presence would realize the ambition Walter Darby Bannard expressed: "I was after a presenting quality rather than a space-relating quality. I wanted the intense feeling I had for a particular color to come right across, unhindered, undifferentiated, unalloyed."[50]

48. From a slightly greater height, Cavell speaks of a space "you can walk in." Cavell, *The World Viewed*, 118. Here I take "walk" to mean moving about unencumbered, rather than entering as such.

49. Jules Olitski, artist's statement included in *Jules Olitski: Recent Paintings, October 21 to November 9, 1967* (New York: André Emmerich Gallery, 1967), unpaginated.

50. *Walter Darby Bannard*, exh. cat. (Baltimore: Baltimore Museum of Art, 1973), 31.

Many of the works Bradley brought together to form *DeLuxe* showed effects of spatial extension linked to the self-disclosing color sensibility Krauss discerned in Olitski's first spray paintings. Not surprisingly, the included works of Olitski, Poons, and Bradley were the most faithful representatives of phenomenologically extensive color painting. Olitski showed *Loosha One* (1970, acrylic on canvas, 114 × 66½ in), a characteristic spray painting made more characteristic by the way in which the internal quasi-framing bands at lower left function. On close inspection, the purple and green edging doesn't arrest the painting's lateral extension so much as, by appearing to be surpassed by two areas of yellow that are close in value but nonidentical, it supports the illusion of a dynamically hued cloud extending in depth both toward and away from the viewer.

Poons's *Firstwild* (1971, acrylic on canvas, 96 ½ × 79 ½ in; fig. 3.7)[51] employs similarly subtle changes in hue, rather than value, to a comparably affecting end. At above-center right appear four ellipses—one large, two medium, one small—each at an independent angle of incidence to the horizontal normal and evocative of buoyant bodies in a zero-gravity environment. The largest, which conjoins the principal area of orange paint to the light-bluish underpainting, is drawn in clear gel medium, so it has the effect of smoothing and appearing to "wet" the drier color areas below and around it. While this device intensifies the dominant orange (as it does along the canvas's right edge), its lenslike transparency offsets any luridness. Its see-through quality declares that the four ellipses are not objects in this field but indexes of its spatial depth. By virtue of this "clarity," the large ellipse (both like and unlike a middle-ground figure set against the field, from which it differs in shape, texture, and value) needs a spatial volume in which to hang. We supply one projectively, thereby suturing the picture's space with our own. Thus the large ellipse does not appear to hang directly in front of the canvas but at some point in a mottled orange space coextensive with our own—not as near as our vantage point and not as distant as the three smaller, opaque ellipses at the corner's extremity.

51. Listed as untitled in the *DeLuxe* exhibition catalogue, the painting illustrates Michael Fried, "Larry Poons' New Paintings," *Artforum* 10 (March 1972): 50–52.

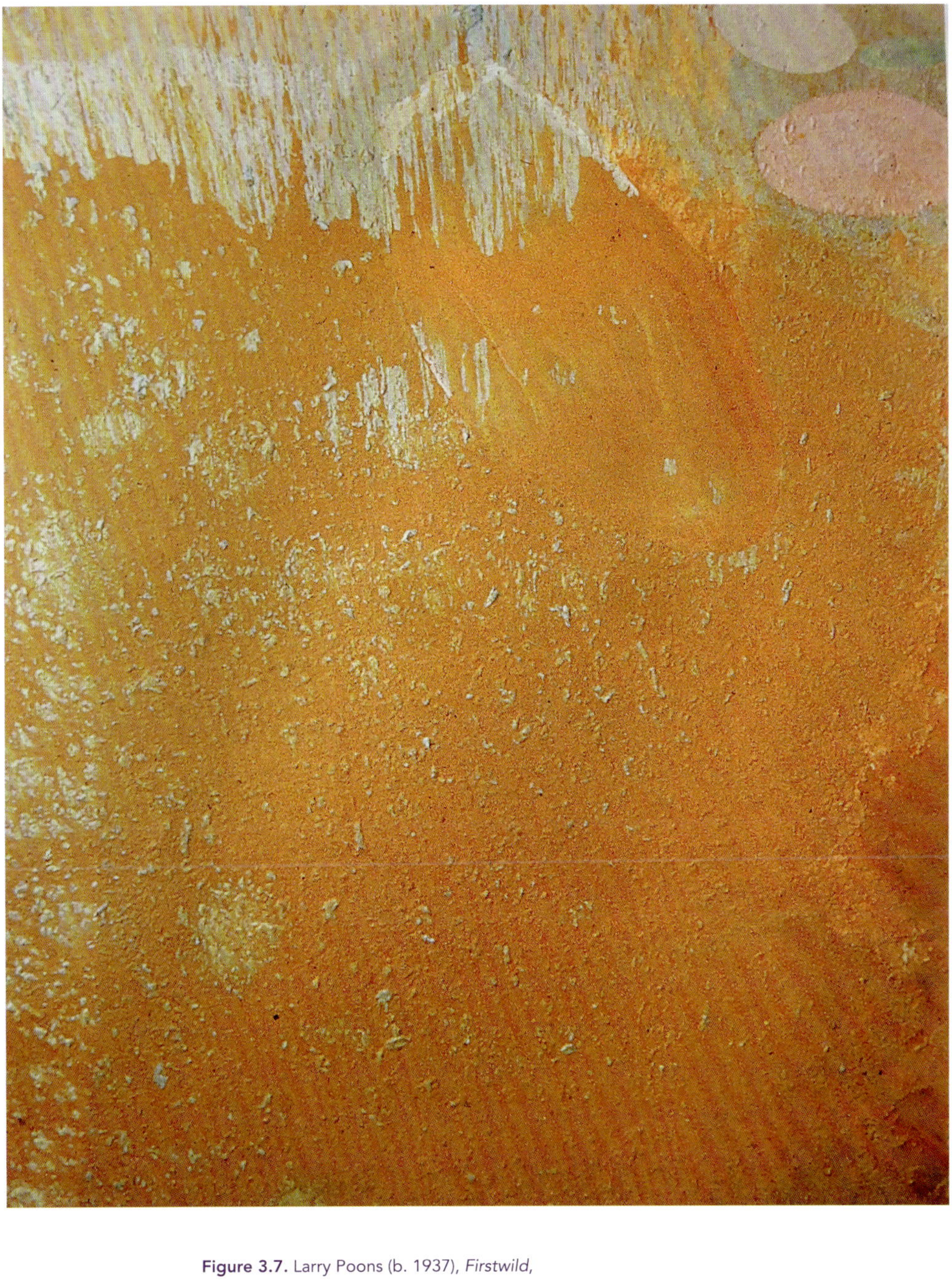

Figure 3.7. Larry Poons (b. 1937), *Firstwild*, 1971. Acrylic on canvas, 96½ × 79½ in. (245.1 × 201.9 cm). Art © Larry Poons/ Licensed by VAGA, New York, NY.

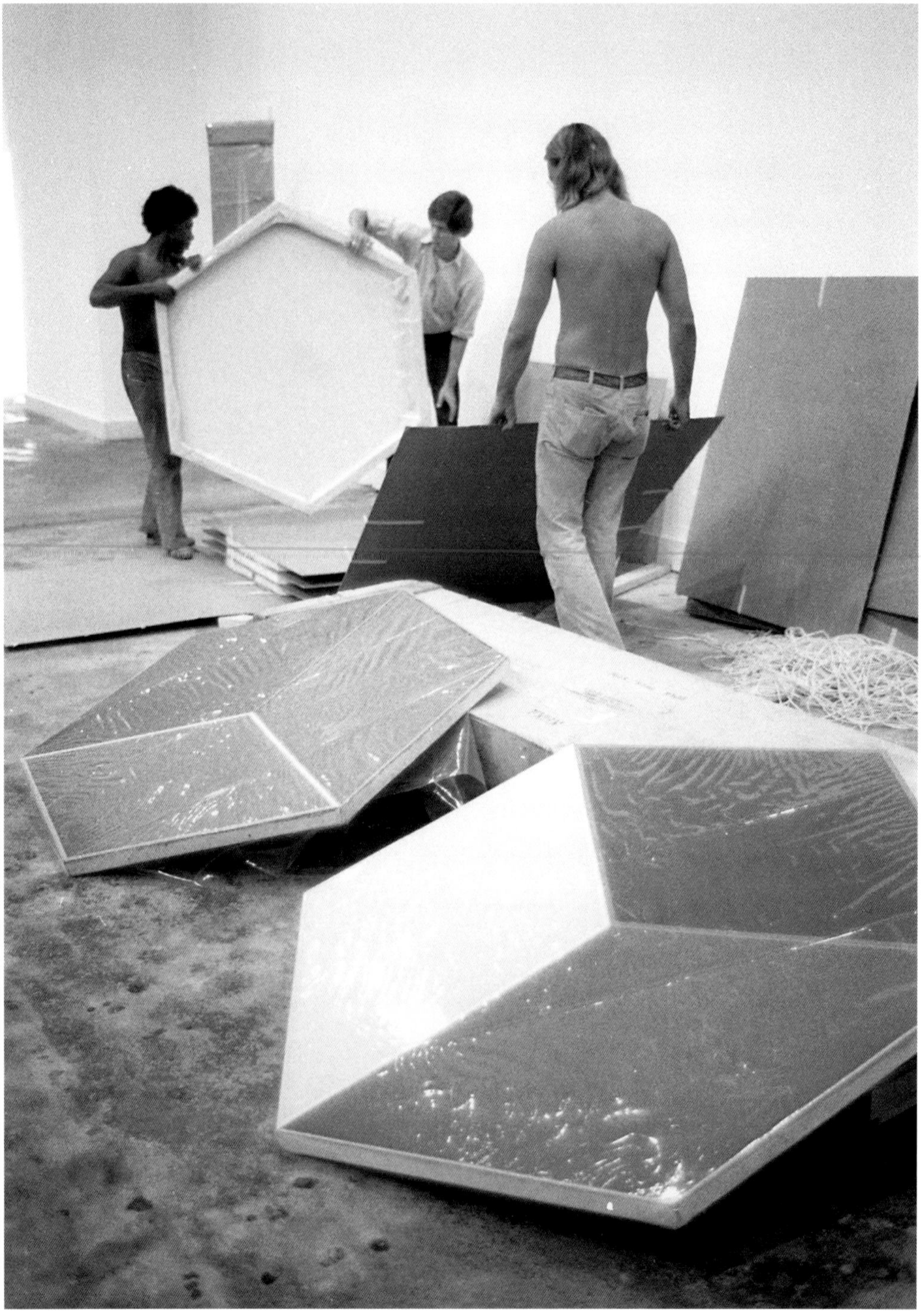

Figure 3.8. Installing components of Loving's work for *The DeLuxe Show*. Menil Archives, The Menil Collection, Houston. Photo: Hickey-Robertson, Houston.

Of the works in the exhibition, among the least obvious representatives of this idea were Loving's, a reversioning of the work that had headlined *Contemporary Black Artists in America* just months earlier (fig. 3.8), and two oval-shaped paintings by Ed Clark, which hung next to each other on the opposite wall, flanked by one painting each by Virginia Jaramillo and Sam Gilliam. At first Clark's, Loving's, and Jaramillo's paintings will seem to be out of sync with the evocations described above, but they are not. To the extent that they accentuate how much "more color" there is to see in painted color—or what happens when color becomes the *subject* of an art—the dim, low-keyed colors inhabiting Clark's ovals schematically represented the problem that the other pictures shared. The distracting format to which Clark conjoins his color makes it more suggestive than actually immersive, yet Clark's monumental strokes conveyed the *madeness* of this art in a way that little else did.

Loving's construction spatializes color by geometric rather than dynamic means. Despite its enormous lateral expanse, the picture embeds its multiple hexagonal units in a distressing axonometry, which compels us to experience the construction via a body-picture axis, along which its color areas advance and recede still more dramatically than color theory would predict. One receives the simultaneously thrilling and objectionable experience of being drawn into an impossible crystallographic architecture of cubes interrelated by alignment, stepping, and torsion—a treacherous stair from no place to nowhere. While one does not negotiate the structure physically but rather imaginatively, one digests the piece in cubic units, not one distinct hexagonal member at a time. Thus one experiences the work's stridently independent color areas as reciprocally defining each other, through forced and literally constructive interactions of color. "Cubes" cannot even form before our eyes without our prior unconscious consent to this relationality. It is through such a color-charged interaction that we "realize" the wall construction as a negotiable structure, a kind of parakinetic picture whose constitutive elements are built, partially unbuilt, compounded together (as at the six borders where matching hues nearly touch), and reoriented in space.

Virginia Jaramillo showed two pictures, including *Green Dawn* (1971, acrylic on canvas, 84 × 72 in; fig. 3.9).[52] *Green Dawn* is a flatly painted bright-green field with a whiplike rope of lurid yellow paint drawn across its upper right corner. Frank Bowling, who saw the painting in Jaramillo's studio, describes the yellow line as a kind of fault or fracture in the palpably solid field, its solidity given not only by the even paint application but by the ground color reaching unbroken around the stretcher to the back of the painting, which becomes thereby a monolithic squarish green tablet. To Bowling the "*acrid* lemon yellow line" has "no apparent purpose other than dynamite": the line lets Jaramillo "bring back inside the painting much of what was being forced off in order to control the objectness of this slab."[53] Which is a way of making room not so much for representation as for space, though not in the obvious way. The yellow passage, a continuous territory of impasto, neither performs the joining function of Barnett Newman's zips (which the whole arrangement seems jocularly to engage) nor floats freely in colored space. As texture charges the serpentine yellow line with the force of an exertion, *dynamite* seems the proper term: it breaks the green field into two independent units, which one experiences as farther away and possibly receding. The line distresses the spatial unity of *Green Dawn* by compelling one to anticipate the forward charge of yellow as a kind of eruption—that is, to see the color not as a line at all but as a magmatic field toward which the massive shards of the cracked green "slab" now appear to fall.[54]

Figure 3.9. Virginia Jaramillo (b. 1939), *Green Dawn*, 1970. Acrylic on canvas, 84 × 72 in. (213.4 × 182.9 cm). Courtesy of the artist. Photography by Daniel Gonzalez.

Thinking about *DeLuxe*, for me, has meant returning again and again to its organizers' confidence that children *might have had something to say* about the unexpected and possibly unintelligible effects of this art on them. That this might produce in one of them a desire

52. The other picture was untitled but shared *Green Dawn*'s dimensions. A reproduction of *Green Dawn*, printed sideways, accompanies a November 1970 *Arts Magazine* article by Frank Bowling ("Outside the Galleries: Four Young Artists," *Arts Magazine* 45, no. 2 [November 1970]: 30–31). The reproduction rotates the painting 90 degrees clockwise.

53. Bowling, "Outside the Galleries," 31.

54. Cf. the more literally immersive experience of Bruce Nauman's light-filled, para-architectural constructions, especially *Yellow Room (Triangular)* of 1993, a monumental, suspended triangular 'room' (in fact it is a freestanding plywood construction, one of whose sides ought to be set flush against a gallery, so that its two exposed sides jut out and terminate at a sharp point somewhere else in the space into which Nauman's room then becomes an *insertion*), which invites viewers to step up and through a doorway, whereupon they enter a white-painted interior suffused with yellow light.

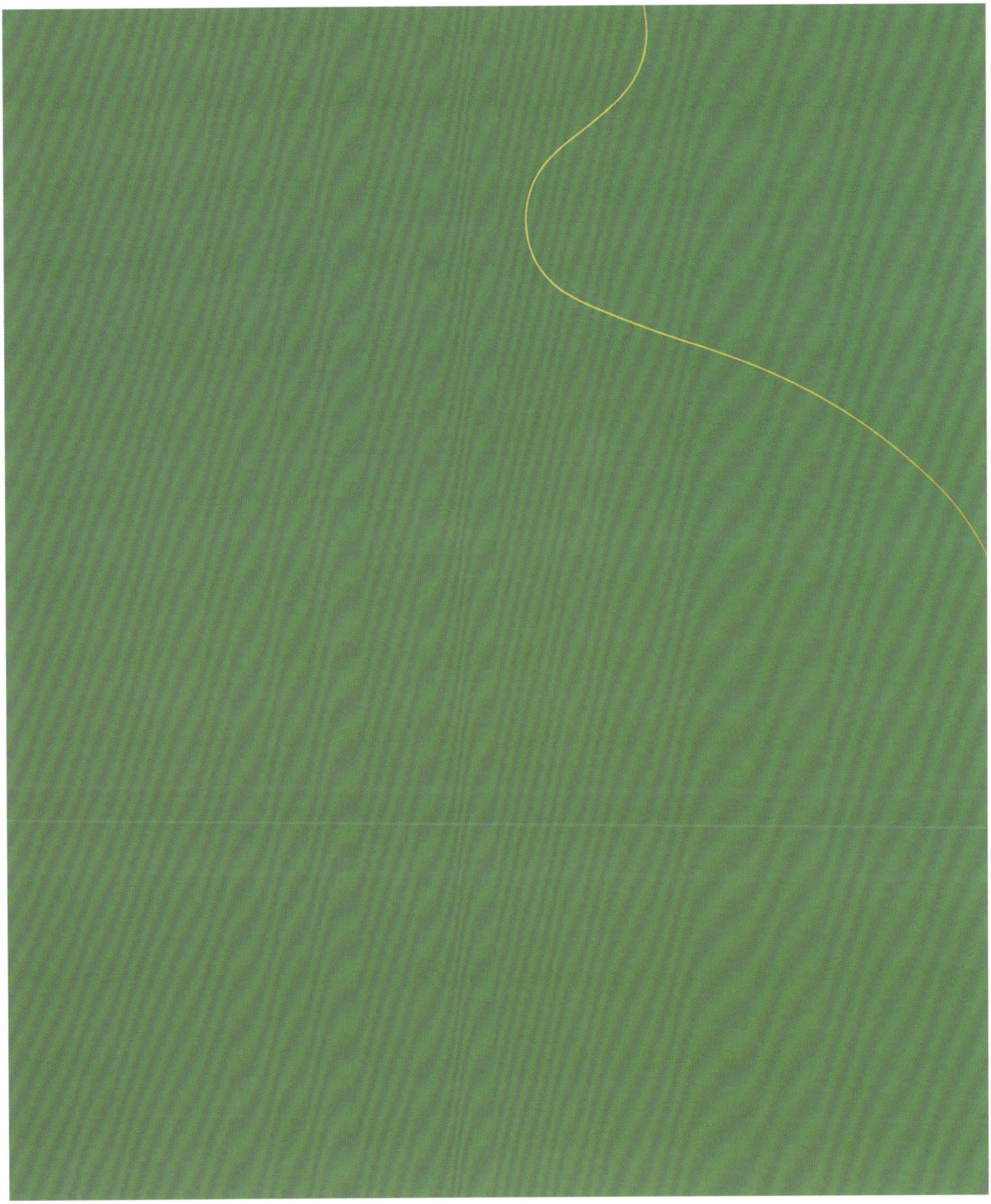

to seek after those effects, or what they revealed to her. That the response of pleasure or interest in fleeting connection with the indeterminate might become a thing of value. That she might feel there was more to know of experiences that remove and then return us to our intact selves, experiences in which one's tolerance for disorientation to one's proper place grows discernibly.

Because *DeLuxe* provided no helpful hand to guide viewers to any particular understanding of *this* art, it promoted an inkling of the aesthetic in children, thus complicating whatever might already be set up in them to deny how essential radically different things are to existence. The aesthetic was the vehicle of a strategic skepticism: the experience of something that one knows but cannot make intelligible can heighten attention to the ordinary and, of course, is foundational for critical consciousness. Emerson's "Self-Reliance" is instructive here:

> "A man should learn to detect and watch that gleam of light which flashes across his mind from within. . . . Else to-morrow a stranger will say with masterly good sense precisely what we have thought and felt all the time, and we shall be forced to take with shame our own opinion from another." . . . Language does not help us at this point; rather the habits of our vocabulary betray us. . . . To know what the words mean we have to forget the words and become aware of the occasions when some idea truly our own is stirring within us and striving to come to birth.[55]

"To know what the words mean we have to forget the words." In what strikes me as the same spirit, *DeLuxe* cast art in its most assiduously creative, individuating function by presenting color at a remove from its localizing usages in art. Color generalization and color subservient to representation—the most conventionalized forms that color takes in art—were present only as the body of norms set aside in favor of exploration.

The adventure of *The DeLuxe Show*, then, was to articulate Houston's Fifth Ward, a real space that explored color's identities *apart* from meaning or color propriety; rather than defining and separating points in space, color decisively dedifferentiates them. *DeLuxe*'s

55. Ralph Waldo Emerson quoted by John Dewey, in turn quoted in Stanley Cavell, "Something Out of the Ordinary," *Proceedings and Addresses of the American Philosophical Association* 71, no. 2 (November 1997): 22.

project, if realized, would set up in the viewer's mind a touchstone for the rewards of being alive to what is temporal, transitory, incomplete, momentary, and processual in color—as if doing so would better establish conditions for "a more imaginative chromatic architecture" (Stokes) than the one called for in ubiquitous, color-insistent cultural-discursive forms. As Lawrence Alloway wrote in 1970, "Vaporous color painting [is] aimed at the spectator's capacity for reverie rather than about his remembered knowledge."[56] Very much in this vein, *DeLuxe* presented color as *sensibility*. Entirely lacking the monomorphism and conclusivity of cultural color, *DeLuxe* color—superabundant, yes, but invested with dynamics that cause any one color to be seen as persistently *multiple*—provisionally formed an "area of endless potential events."[57] *DeLuxe* therefore identified color with the trenchant investigation of its microstructure, not only as if enlarged by a projector but as if brought into line with the multifarious quotidian identities we assign color in ordinary language. It was as though the "-ishes" pervading Wittgenstein's *Remarks on Color* (1950/53) were blown up and translated into the scale and facture not merely of painting but of exhibition. *DeLuxe* color was rather more colloquial than cultural.[58]

56. Lawrence Alloway, "The Spectrum of Monochrome," *Arts Magazine* 45, no. 3 (December 1970 / January 1971): 32.

57. Ibid.

58. Cf. Ludwig Wittgenstein: "Ask this question: Do you know what 'reddish' means? And how do you show that you know it? Language games: 'Point to a reddish yellow (white, blue, brown)'—'Point to an even more reddish one'—'A less reddish one' etc. Now that you've mastered this game you will be told 'Point to a somewhat reddish green[.]' Assume there are two cases: Either you do point to a color (and always the same one), perhaps to an olive green—or you say, 'I don't know what that means,' or 'There's no such thing.' We might be inclined to say that the one person had a different colour concept from the other; or a different concept of '. . . ish.'" Wittgenstein, *Remarks on Color*, ed. G. E. M. Anscombe, trans. Linda L. McAlister and Margarete Shättle (1950/53; repr. Berkeley: University of California, 1977, 20–21/20–21e, §30. And "My feeling is that blue obliterates yellow,—but why shouldn't I call a somewhat greenish yellow a 'bluish yellow' and green an intermediary color between blue and yellow, and a strongly bluish green a somewhat yellowish blue? 40. In a greenish yellow I don't yet notice *anything* blue.—For me, green is one special way-station on the colored path from blue to yellow, and red is another. 41. What advantage would someone have over me who knew a direct route from blue to yellow? And what shows that I don't know such a path?—Does everything depend on my range of possible language-games with the form '. . . ish [Liegt alles an den mir möglichen Sprach-spielen mit der Form '. . . lich']'?" Wittgenstein, *Remarks on Color*, 22/22e, §39, 40, 41. Emphasis in original.

These arguments reflect my convictions that (1) these works, arrayed in that space and time, made it possible to think about color in such terms, and (2) if such thinking fails to describe Bradley's intention, it still suggests a reliable interpretation of his statements and actions. It needs emphasizing that whatever revelations about color *DeLuxe* held in store, they would have been available only to a gaze adapted to the field of an object, contracted to the moment of one's attending. At this level *DeLuxe* was "about" what color reveals *only* through attention to divergences between its fixed conceptual identity and its protean manifestations. Wittgenstein found the same to be true about linguistic emplacements of color. The idea of the present discussion is only by degrees more complex than Bradley's statement that "the colors and shapes of the paintings and sculptures are seen in our daily lives."[59] Bradley may have found the following claim congenial in 1971: in this art, colors undergo a transfiguration that bears comparison with their intangibility in ordinary language. So disposed, color captured the involutions of experience that make up black life far better than the positivism informing so many contemporary accounts of black experience. Color painting revealed the condition of color as it inhabits our actual language games.

As Wittgenstein's landmark meditation had shown, our ordinary language game has very little use for the notion of "uniform color" upon which objectivist accounts of color center. Instead, because we employ our words to describe a world where actual objects and surfaces seldom display uniform flat color, our descriptions follow extremely imprecise, protean rules for the ordinary usage of color terms.[60] "It is an overriding concern of Wittgenstein's philosophy," writes Marie McGinn, to achieve a "resolution of the tension between our ordinary attitude and what philosophical reflection reveals that

59. Bradley, quoted in "Art Goes to the People," 14.

60. My reading of *Remarks on Color* owes much to Marie McGinn, "Wittgenstein's 'Remarks on Colour'" (*Philosophy* 66, no. 258 [October 1991]: 435–53), which differs from other accounts of its subject in understanding the contours of Wittgenstein's relationship to conventional treatments of color by reference to the *Remarks*' place in the philosopher's thought, a tenet of which the *Remarks* state forthrightly: "43. In philosophy it is not enough to learn in every case *what* is to be said about a subject, but also *how* one must speak about it. We are always having to begin by learning the method of tackling it. 44. Or again: In any serious question uncertainty extends to the very roots of the problem." *Remarks on Color*, 23/23e, §43, 44.

does not force us to qualify or compromise either." Such would honor both "the reflective discovery that the world I confront is the world as it exists for me and . . . our ordinary attitude that the world is wholly outside and wholly independent of my subjectivity."[61] Yet this means havoc for our conventional understanding of color. *Remarks on Color* yields no statements setting out what color is or any principle with which to decide the intrinsic color of an object.[62] Rather, Wittgenstein illustrates how "our tendency to think of our ordinary language-game of describing the color of natural objects in terms of two-dimensional, monochrome patches of determinate color" differs profoundly from the actual means we employ in describing color phenomena in visual space.

Through language Wittgenstein explored *the form of the uncertainty* that color discourse expunged in order to clear the way for monochromy—for a spectrum organized with clear dividing lines. The tradition, for Wittgenstein exemplified by Goethe and Runge, excluded from any objective conception these descriptions of color (the language game through which we actually *place* color in accounts of the visual world) because of their inherent indeterminateness.[63] As McGinn observes, for Wittgenstein "color is anything but the appropriate object of a theory," and rather a "spur . . . to philosophize."[64] Wittgenstein's speculative and fragmentary observations of the actual language used to account for color showed that "our preoccupation with a preconceived, idealized image of how our ordinary color concepts must work . . . owes more to the abstract 'geometry of color.'"[65] Through these observations he concludes *against* the determinism exemplified by the monochromatic patches of color we know from the color wheel or hardware counter—we show in too many ways that color is obscure to us. In direct contradistinction to the theoretician,

61. McGinn, "Wittgenstein's 'Remarks on Colour,'" 449.

62. Ibid., 441–42.

63. Popular studies of color continue to presume the rightfulness of domesticating color to an indexable order. For instance, Maitland Graves's classic *Color Fundamentals*, first published in 1952, opens on this epigraph from John Livingston Loews's *Road to Xanadu*: "The imagination voyaging through chaos and reducing it to clarity and order is the symbol of all the quests which lend glory to our dust." Graves, *Color Fundamentals, with 100 Color Schemes* (New York: McGraw-Hill, 1952), front matter.

64. Ludwig Wittgenstein, *Culture and Value*, 66e, quoted in McGinn, "Wittgenstein's 'Remarks on Colour,'" 442.

65. McGinn, "Wittgenstein's 'Remarks on Colour,'" 443.

"Wittgenstein finds that the problem of color has the form '*I don't know my way about*.'"[66]

This much anyone would grant: the geometry of color presents a determinate system, an ideal. Wittgenstein's insight discloses our desire to find that our ordinary language and this ideal, abstract system conform.[67] What justifies the system is not its native correctness but rather the conversion of its native inevitabilities into convention and habit: one not only "finds" its patterns, orderings, and relations everywhere but also uses them to decide what it means "to calculate, or to use, color terms correctly."[68] Thus even when we readily acknowledge that the ordinary language game in which we "capture" colors is hasty and imperfect, we remain "inclined to believe" (the words are Wittgenstein's) that behind it must lie some unitary, utterly world-adequate description.[69] As opposed to recognizing in our language game something *related to but distinct from* the geometry of color.

McGinn relates incisively Wittgenstein's technique for illuminating this thinking and the error it involves.

> The idea seems to be that by focusing on aspects of our ordinary language-game that either conflict with or escape capture within the restricted conception of grammar that our preoccupation with the geometry of color has given us, we shall gradually come to a more adequate picture of the grammar of our ordinary language, one that preserves, rather than legislates away, the indeterminateness and lack of precision inherent in our ordinary color descriptions. The

66. Ibid., 442. See also Wittgenstein, *Remarks on Color*, 21/21e, §32 and §33. Emphasis added.

67. Wittgenstein: "Lichtenberg says that very few people have ever seen pure white. Do most people use the word wrongly, then? And how did *he* learn the correct use?—On the contrary: he constructed an ideal use from an actual one. The way we construct a geometry. And 'ideal' does not mean something specially good, but only something carried to extremes." *Remarks on Color*, 21/21e, §35.

68. McGinn continues helpfully: "The result is a pressure both towards thinking of our ordinary description of, say, a brick house as red, or of a road as straight, as imprecise, and towards insisting that a correct description of what we see will be one that meets the standards of these idealized geometries. So . . . we are sent in search of the unique, absolutely determinate, correct description of the color or shape of an object." McGinn, "Wittgenstein's 'Remarks on Colour,'" 444.

69. Wittgenstein: "We are inclined to believe the analysis of our color concepts would lead ultimately to the colors of places in our visual field, which are independent of any spatial or physical interpretation." *Remarks on Color*, 10/10e, §61.

> picture of our color-language that Wittgenstein builds up by degrees reveals that our ordinary color concepts have little or nothing to do with the idea of a monochrome patch of color, or with the ideas of pure or saturated color.[70]

Instead of color patches, our ordinary language for color describes surfaces and objects with varying textures, degrees of transparency, opacity, cloudiness, et cetera. Put another way, we experience color plurally rather than locally, only by reference to interaction and, it must be said, discomposure. That our color *concepts* mingle constantly and complexly with destabilizers such as reflection and transparency —both forces of three-dimensionality and depth—allows Wittgenstein to show that ordinary color concepts depend crucially upon spatial and temporal ones.[71] "The whole idea of a unique, determinate color description is shown to be an illusion created by our tendency to idealize the grammar of our ordinary language-game."[72]

Wittgenstein's study shows that "we can get along very well without [geometrically precise] distinctions *and* without knowing our way about here."[73] That is, the surprising richness of the "ordinary language game" compels us to acknowledge the indeterminateness that already embeds our everyday concepts.[74] To do so is to acknowl-

70. McGinn, "Wittgenstein's 'Remarks on Colour,'" 446.

71. "Thus, without further specification of a method by which the description of color is to be determined, it simply makes no sense to ask, within our ordinary language-game, 'What is this color, here, at this spot?' Do we mean what color would we use to represent this spot in a painting? But what color is that? Is it the color of the pigment used, or the color we would describe it as in this context? Or is the color of the spot the color of a sample that it matches? And again, how should we allow for the effect of the surrounding context? And how do we allow for the fact that the mattness or shininess of a surface is an integral part of the overall color impression that we have of it? Is matt black the same color as shiny black? And can a transparent green glass match an opaque color sample? Can the red of a sunset or the blackness of a dark night match a color sample?" Ibid., 447.

72. Ibid.

73. "Here I would like to make a general observation concerning the nature of philosophical problems. Lack of clarity in philosophy is tormenting. It is felt as shameful. We feel: we do not know our way about where we *should* know our way about. And nevertheless it *isn't* so. We can get along very well without these distinctions *and* without knowing our way about here." *Remarks on Color*, 21/21e, §33. Emphasis in original.

74. McGinn writes: "The point here is not that color terms are vague, in the sense that the boundary between two colors, say red and orange, is not a sharp one. Rather, the point is that there is a complexity or richness in our ordinary language-game that is itself a source of indeterminateness." That our color terms accommodate a superabundance of effects and sorts of things that manifest them ("flat colored surfaces, surfaces of natural

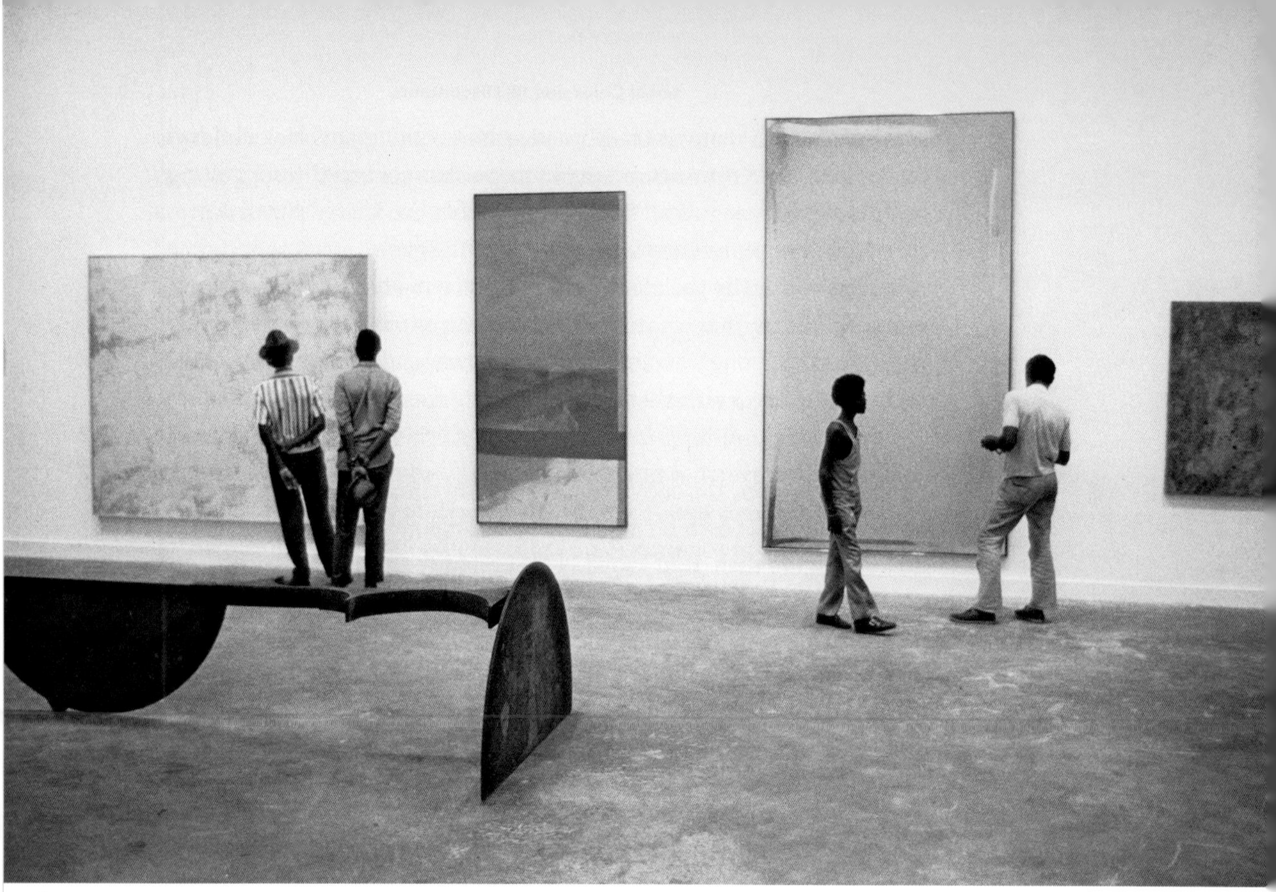

Black Power strategies sidestepped by *DeLuxe*'s organizers,[80] pervades the review—the last word of which, fittingly, belongs to a spokesperson for the Harris County Community Action Association, a black group. Member Vivian Ayers had these reactions:

> "Nobody I knew who went to the show was even able to describe what was there. To me it showed a curious absence of a sense of cultural relevance. Everybody knows the ghetto mood has changed over the last few years. The people know now why they wouldn't necessarily have a feel for all the white man's art they've been seeing. . . . Such a show taken directly to the people," Mrs. Ayers said, should have come from their own artists,

Figure 3.10. Visitors in *The DeLuxe Show.* Menil Archives, The Menil Collection, Houston. Photo: Hickey-Robertson, Houston.

80. Cf. this statement by Shawn A. Ginwright that the Black Power "concept rested on the premise that before a group could enter the open society, it must establish power through solidarity and sovereignty." Ginwright, *Black in School: Afrocentric Reform, Urban Youth, and the Promise of Hip-Hop Culture* (New York: Teachers College Press, 2004), 11. Ginwright is paraphrasing Carmichael and Charles V. Hamilton, *Black Power: The Politics of Liberation in America* (New York: Vintage, 1967).

"who are just now taking off on the aesthetics of black art. It just seemed to me that the way it was programmed it made a lot of hungry black kids standing outside with looks of perplexity on their faces a part of the show—they probably didn't mean it that way, but that is the way it came out. It was just not cool."[81]

Ayers's familiars play a critical role here: they are *all* the members of the community, for whom she speaks not only as caretaker of the young but as arbiter of relevance and even "feeling." The influence of racialism, moreover, backs Ayers's claims consummately: "The people *know now* why they wouldn't necessarily have a feel for all the white man's art they've been seeing." Ayers's assessment depends on the notion that modernist art is a proxy for white culture, and therefore as naturally repellent, and antipathetic, to blacks as to white people. Anything less than the total alienation of these parties (or their inanimate representatives) is unthinkable: thus "nobody I knew who went to the show was even able to describe what was there." But the polarizing action is her own: the image of "hungry black kids" outside looking perplexed is central to Ayers's portrayal. Even so, the photo accompanying Freed's article in the *Houston Post* (its caption reads, "Painting by Ed Clark captures attention of youngsters") and many other documents of the exhibition undo the chain (fig. 3.11).

No matter what their configuration, such projects raise questions —"Are they ready?" "Will they get it?" "Who thought that could ever work?"—that inevitably take shape around the same impassable gulf. Putting the question (and the question is put incessantly) tethers the viewer to that which she exemplifies, that category she most perfectly fits, and of which she is but "a specimen or representative"[82] —and separates her from what she is, herself. In this way the question writes the unique, perceiving subject out of the situation, enfolds her in a cycloptic horde—the community that sees from one experience, with one eye. And yet this viewer, over whom these questions supposedly worry, is an essential, perhaps *the* essential, means by which racialism claims to capture all reality in its concepts. In fact

81. Vivian Ayers, quoted in Hobdy, "DeLuxe Art Show in Ghetto Met with Mixture of Reactions."

82. Theodor Adorno, quoted in Gillian Rose, "How Is Critical Theory Possible? Theodor W. Adorno and Concept Formation in Sociology," in *Theodor Adorno*, ed. James Schmidt (London: Ashgate, 2007), 97.

art

Study in contrasts: Lyons Avenue and lyrical abstraction

By ELEANOR FREED

In a part of the city better known for urban decay than for aesthetics, the Menil Foundation is currently sponsoring a challenging social and visual experiment, the staging of a first-rate exhibition of contemporary abstract painting and sculpture.

The "DeLuxe Show" in the recently renovated De Luxe Theater on Lyons Avenue is attracting a somewhat skeptical but usually enthusiastic audience. While it is too soon to evaluate the degree of impact, opening week has already demonstrated that there is a vast untapped reservoir of curiosity and human potential for new experiences that is rarely piqued or reached by the conventional museum format.

The fact that something fresh from the outside has been brought in and superimposed into the heart of a downhill neighborhood has unleashed a tremendous surge of interest and some confusion among the community's citizens. All that can be said with certainty is that until Sept. 25 when these works are returned to New York many, many people who have never crossed the threshold of a museum are being confronted with art. Whether they are really being reached is something else again as this particular exhibition is pretty esoteric.

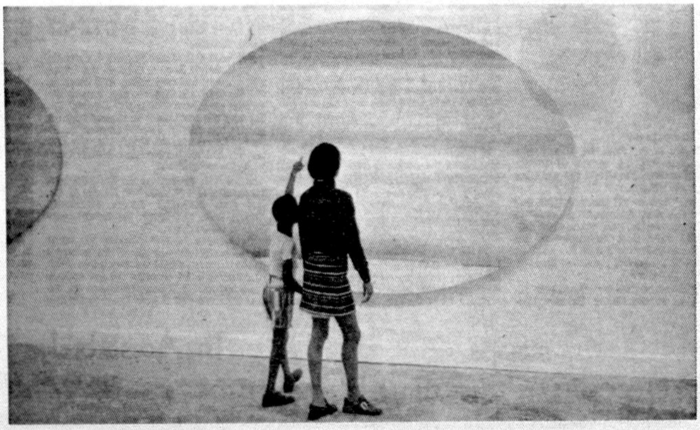

Painting by Ed Clark captures attention of youngsters

The abandoned theater has been converted in the space of three weeks into a sparkling white hall with lofty 20-foot ceilings. With its excellent lighting and great scale, and with the advanced art collection contained therein, it provides the equivalent of a museum experience. Since it is all seen in the context of Lyons Avenue there is a quality of surrealism which has been heightened by leaving the facade and marquee in its previous derelict state. Walking from the steaming heat of the street into a gleaming air-conditioned arena, from an area without visible signs of beauty into an extravaganza of pure color, form, shape and substance is bound to be an eye-opener.

Black painter Peter Bradley, associate director of Perls Galleries in New York, was given the green light and full financial backing to select an exhibition whose sole criterion was that it would contain the sort of art that he liked. Although he has assembled a first-rate collection by mostly well known artists (plus a few emerging ones), both black and white, who have already won recognition in museums and prestigious galleries, it is the environment that is newsmaking. Bradley likes to talk of his exhibit as "an elitist show" and this sort of painting has usually remained pre-empted by the art initiate.

Daniel Johnson, William Williams and the present guest curator, Peter Bradley, were three of the black painters whom Larry Rivers invited to particpate in "Some American History" for Rice University's Institute for the Arts. At that time they exhibited work with figurative and historical content in projecting some phase of black history. I recall quite a lot of static voiced during a tape session about their dissatisfaction with their role in this exhibit and how much they would rather have been exhibiting one of their own approaches to abstraction.

Bradley is disinterested and in fact disapproving of art with ethnic, social or political overtones so the collection that he has formed is a purist one made up mostly of lyrical color field painting. His own painting "Hemming", one of the most beautiful in the exhibit, is a misty atmospheric haze of blue and violet with a splattering of rose. Another that I liked especially was Olitski's tawny yellow canvas with slim streaks of minor key colors paralleling the corners.

The pair of elliptical paintings by Ed Clark contains subtle mutations that give the shaded and slubbed effect of Thai silks. Kenneth Noland's horizontal slivered paintings move quietly through different color ranges. Virginia Jaramillio's bold color field has a single serpentine stroke of contrasting hue. Al Loving's bright vibrant composition of 11 hard-edged cubes dominates the hall as most of the other work is in a lower key. Sam Gilliam stains drapes and swags his gigantic canvases with theatrical elan. (Richard Mock, who recently showed at Jones Hall, handles fabric in somewhat the manner of Gilliam.)

British sculptor Anthony Card is represented by a powerful curving yoke of rusted steel stretched between two halves of a corrugated disc set at right angles. Richard Hunt, black sculptor honored this spring at the Museum of Modern Art, continues to show the influence and inspiration of Julio Gonzales, the great pioneer in welded metals. The example here is a bit of space calligraphy that resembles a bird. Michael Steiner stacks planes of cor-ten steel.

Steve Cannon, black poet and anthologist, is writing the catalogue. The exhibition is being photographed practically around the clock and many of these prints are already hanging in the lobby of the theater. Mickey Leland who teaches pharmacy at Texas Southern is the community coordinator. Troops of volunteers are placing posters throughout the dis-advantaged areas. Perhaps the greatest excitement of all is being generated by the free movies in the balcony. Since desegregation all of the neighborhood movie houses have closed and the introduction of short films in the DeLuxe's upstairs balcony is a real boon.

Perhaps the next exhibition, if there is to be one, could be an assemblage of first-rate figurative art with names like Romare Bearden, Jacob Lawrence, Ben Shahn and leading examples of younger artists being represented. Galleries have already shown a willingness to cooperate.

The Black Arts Center sponsored by Hope Development in lower Lyons Avenue is still trying to complete its fund drive to remodel an old theater for a program geared mainly to the performing arts and creative workshops. When this is in operation and with an ongoing program in the DeLuxe Theater on upper Lyons Avenue the strip between the two, the main artery of Fifth Ward, could be the setting of an entire renaissance in the community. Interfaith Housing and HUB, Houston Urban Bunch, are already at work in Chapman Third Addition.

Maybe there could be a coordinated pilot project to design and provide good looking street furniture . . . benches, waste receptacles, signs, kiosk for posters . . . so that there could be inviting gathering places for the community.

Page 10 — Spotlight

Sunday, August 29, 1971, THE HOUSTON POST

Figure 3.11. Eleanor Freed, "Study in Contrasts: Lyons Avenue and Lyrical Abstraction," *Houston Post*, August 28, 1971, 10. Menil Archives, The Menil Collection, Houston. © Houston Chronicle. Used with permission.

Figure 3.12. Houston-area schoolchildren on a bus going to *The DeLuxe Show*. Menil Archives, The Menil Collection, Houston. Photo: Splash Goodie.

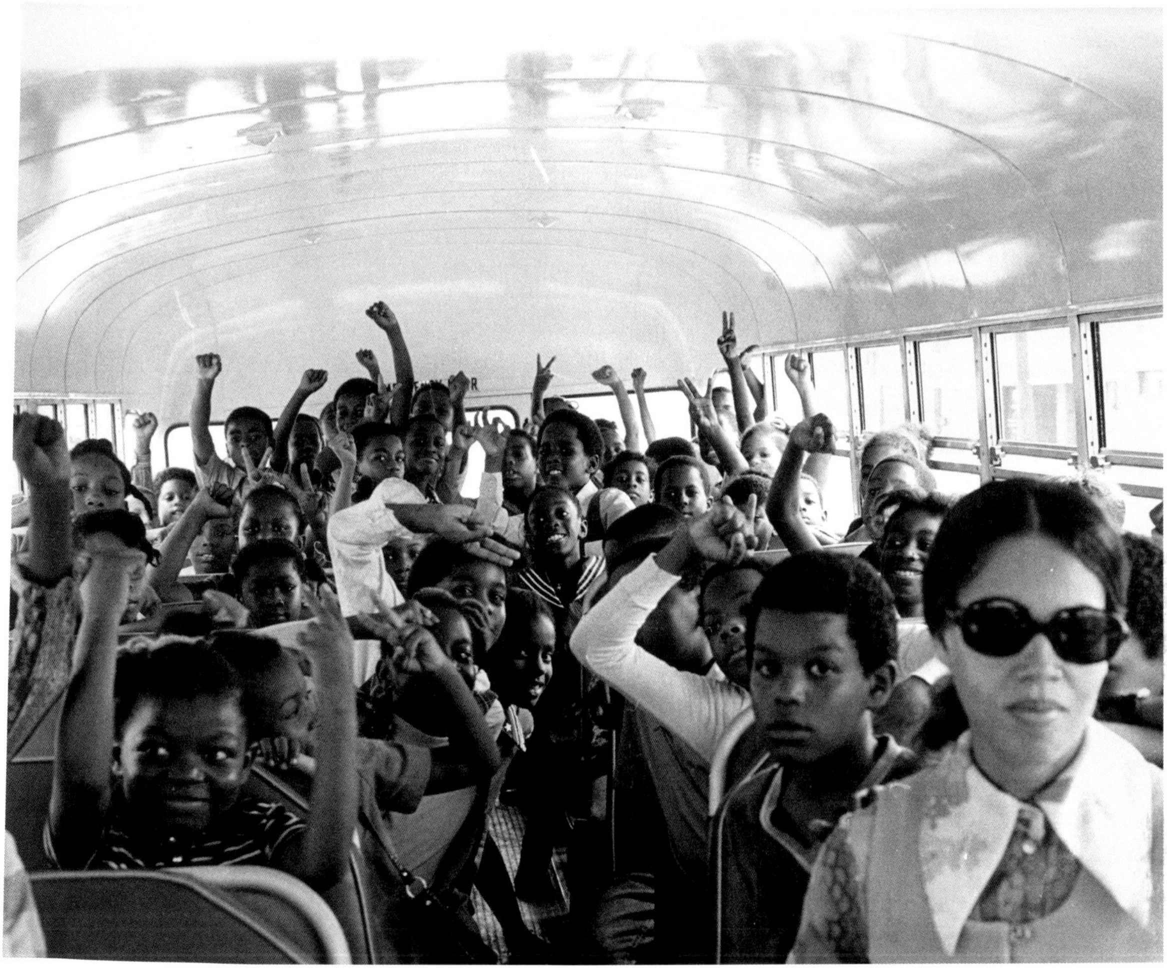

such questions extend identity thinking of the most inflexible kind: beholden to totalities, it shows an inexorable tendency to characterize the viewer as a community. So positioned as a proof of identity, Ayers forgoes all the frustrating and ecstatic *possibilities of nonidentity* in the relation between herself (as object) and the race concept that positions her socially. But in fact there can be no identity without nonidentity. Such denials, as we have seen, hardly exhaust all ways of thinking about black encounters with modernism. They merely conceal these other ways of thinking in order to imagine and represent modernism in their own, specifically performative ways.

Bradley and his cohort did not merely court but rather invited such condemnations by launching their experiment where and when they

name, though hardly adequate to styles of conceptual or actual movement across a range of persons. The ghetto was structurally essential to the new politics of race because in form it anticipated the projected outcome of revolutionary politics: "Two major steps in the solution of the major problems facing black America are economic independence and control of the vital institutions that serve black people. . . . The ultimate success of the black man's efforts to control his institutions is to be found in a larger structure that brings unity. . . . The foundation for developing the kinds of attitudes and structures mentioned above has existed for a long time in the black community."[114] An indispensable mechanism with which contemporary definitions of race—colored by the pressing need of structure and administration—brought to a halt the movements intrinsic to the social, the ghetto became a unifying paradigm for a range of projects seeking to bring black individuals into line with a determinative cultural location and a shared sense of place.

The sociological picture of ghetto experience, then, shows striking

---

not *simply* dominated by mainstream white consumer culture, but rather, in an effort to make place, black popular culture reappropriates the dominant racialized and essentializes meanings of the urban. Such reappropriations are attempts by blacks to create an urban culture of resistance" (23, emphasis added).

My objection to such theorizations centers on the nakedness of the extent to which in them the ghetto is nothing more than one needs it to be, and furthermore, the presupposition that what one needs from the ghetto is precisely its unique power to evoke, contain, and thus reify blackness. The ghetto authorizes the relentless pursuit of black meaning and offers seemingly unlimited resources for masking black complexity. Thus what passes for (what Haymes describes as) an antiessentialist cultural politics nevertheless links up with "the creation of new meanings for blackness and black identity" (135) and the production of a catalog of supposedly "new ways of experiencing and identifying blackness" (138). In Haymes's example, as in many others dating to the late 1960s, the ghetto serves to ground and delimit the operations of a population who happily *construct* the racialization of their spaces of habitat; these operations are inherently representational and relentlessly construed (that is, by Haymes, who nevertheless writes as though without exception his subjects share his construals) as "a threat to [white] tradition" (xiii).

How is it that in such accounts individual subjects never manage to fall away, or separate, from these populations? Because to this conception the whole population has already encompassed each of the subjects of whose falling away one might otherwise have occasion to speak. How is it that threat to tradition never goes further, never mingles with nontradition, never blurs the line? Because this scholarship avoids compulsively any horizon of thought on which a salutary devalorization of difference might occur or appear—or for that matter, any cultural situation offering no occasion to affiliate one's object, completely without remainder, to an in some way comforting preexisting *population* of objects.

114. Davis and Donaldson, *Blacks in the United States*, 244.

parallels with racialist knowledge structures pumped with black content and stalwartly shored up from within. Some contemporary accounts suggest that racialism's symbolic enclosures only exacerbated actual conditions in the ghetto. An influential 1961 study of the spatial organization of behavior hypothesized that the urban slum would bear out the truism that "the critical significance of belonging in or to an area has been one of the most consistent findings in working-class communities."[115] Marc Fried and Peggy Gleicher described how local spatial identity lent the urban slum a peculiar feeling of home that would intensify the foreignness of whatever lay or originated beyond it. The pair considered more "impressive how frequently such familiarity [born of this freedom of movement] seems to stop at the boundaries"[116] of the ghetto, usually drawn by salient topographical features.

In Houston, Highway 59 drew the line between the city proper and "Pearl Harbor," another nickname for the Fifth Ward, which lies to the west of 59 and was known for "mass and indiscriminate killings," as a notice about the exhibition put it.[117] Highway 59 drew the line between home and the world beyond. Between the inner space of the ghetto and the outer space surrounding it, "the former is generally well explored and essentially familiar, even though it may not be considered the area of commitment. The latter is either relatively unknown by many people or, if known, it is categorized in a completely different way."[118]

Fried and Gleicher felt that "the importance of localism . . . can hardly be emphasized enough,"[119] going further to describe the ghetto as encompassed by "a widely experienced subjective boundary surrounding the large local area and some of its immediate extensions which is virtually impermeable."[120] They describe a situation in which

115. Marc Fried and Peggy Gleicher, "Some Sources of Residential Satisfaction in an Urban Slum [West End, Boston, MA]," in *Environment and the Social Sciences: Perspectives and Applications*, ed. Joachim F. Wohlwill and Daniel H. Carson (Washington, DC: American Psychological Association, 1972), 143.

116. Ibid., 150.

117. "Open Art-Movie Show Sunday," *Houston Defender*, August 21, 1971, 8.

118. Fried and Gleicher, "Some Sources of Residential Satisfaction," 150.

119. Ibid., 143.

120. Ibid., 150. Putting a similar view to different ends, Gerald Suttles in 1972 observed "white ethnic" occupants of urban spaces developing and following rigid "cognitive maps to provide for themselves "a set of social categories of differentiating

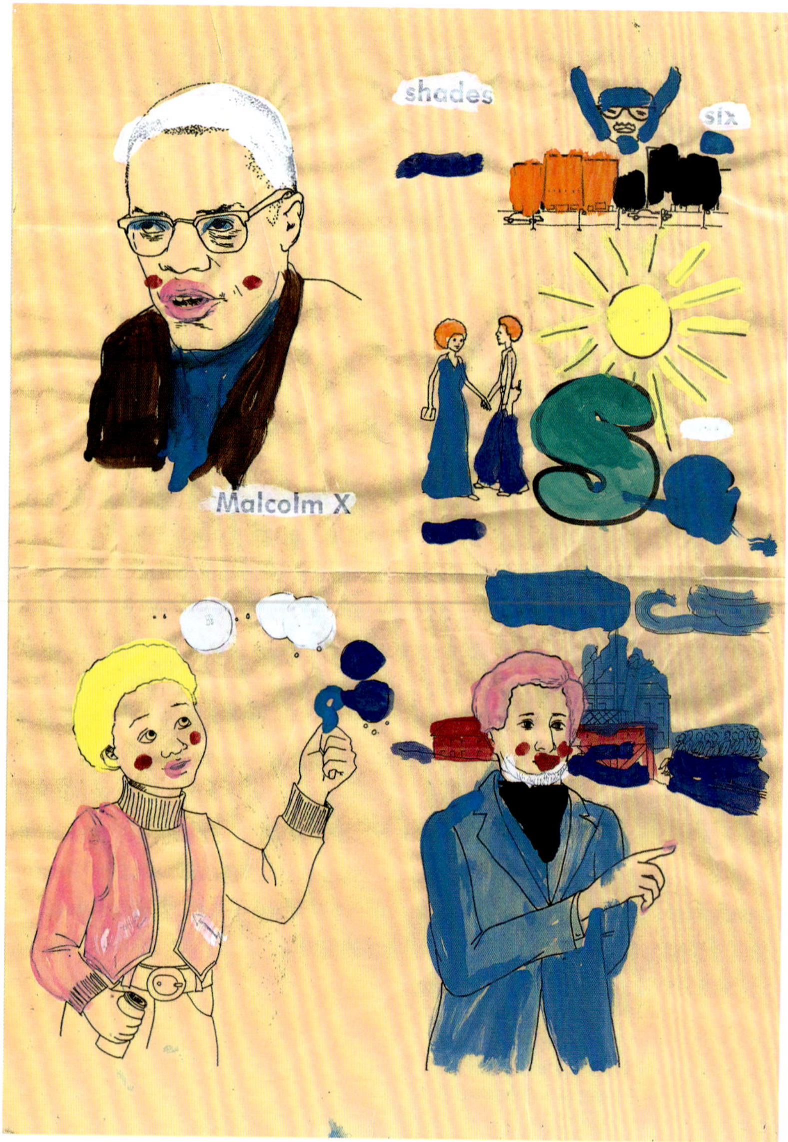

Figure 3.13a–b. Drawings by children created during workshops with Glenn Ligon at the Walker Art Center, 2000. Crayon, oil pastels, and tempera on paper, 22 × 16 in. (55.9 × 40.7 cm). Photograph: Tom Powel Imaging. Courtesy of Glenn Ligon.

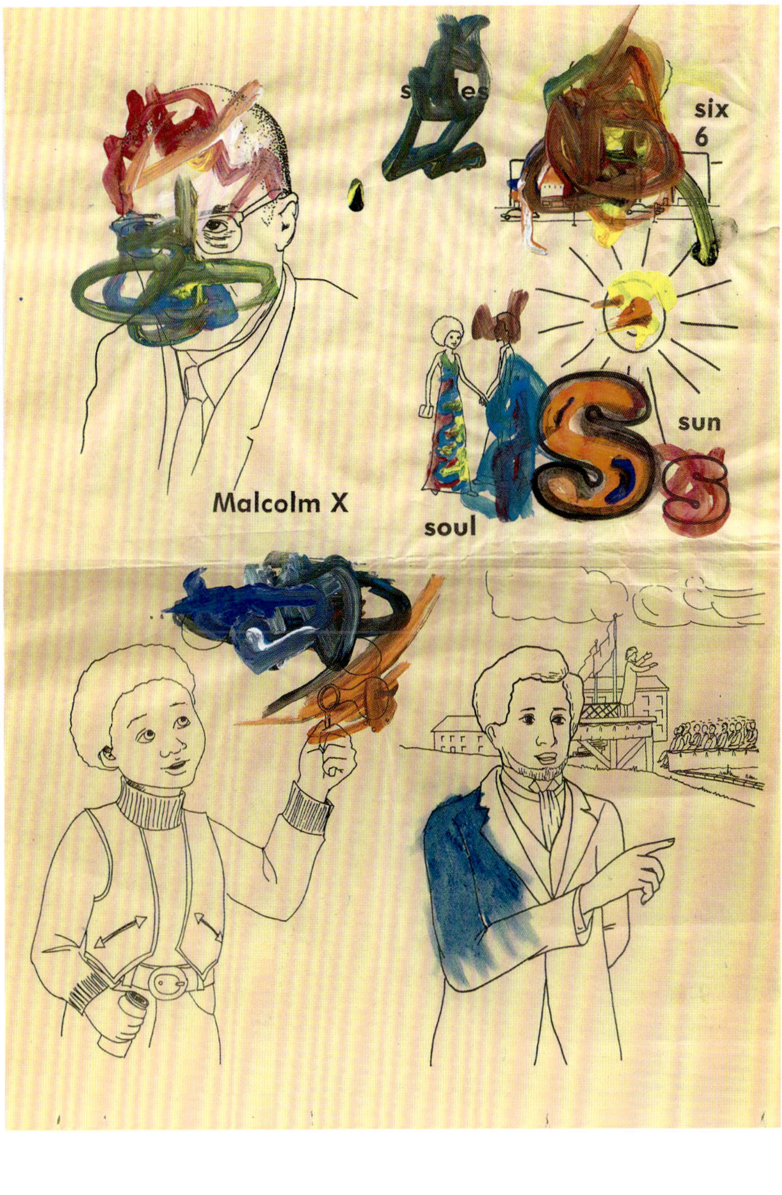
six
6
sun
Malcolm X
soul
Ss

Appendix

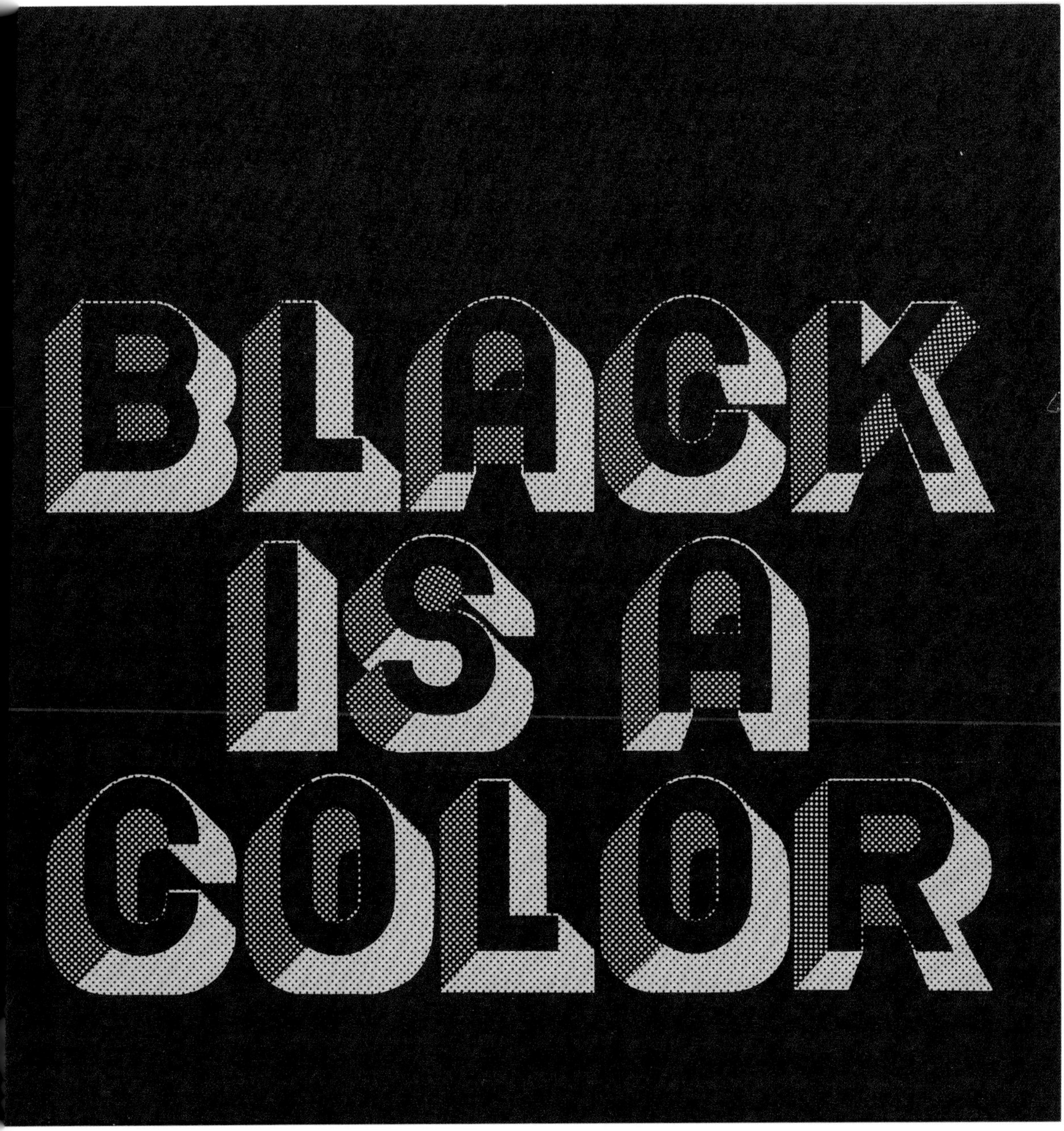

Figures A1–12. Raymond Saunders (b. 1934), *Black Is a Color*, 1967. Photos: Peter Butler. Courtesy of the artist.

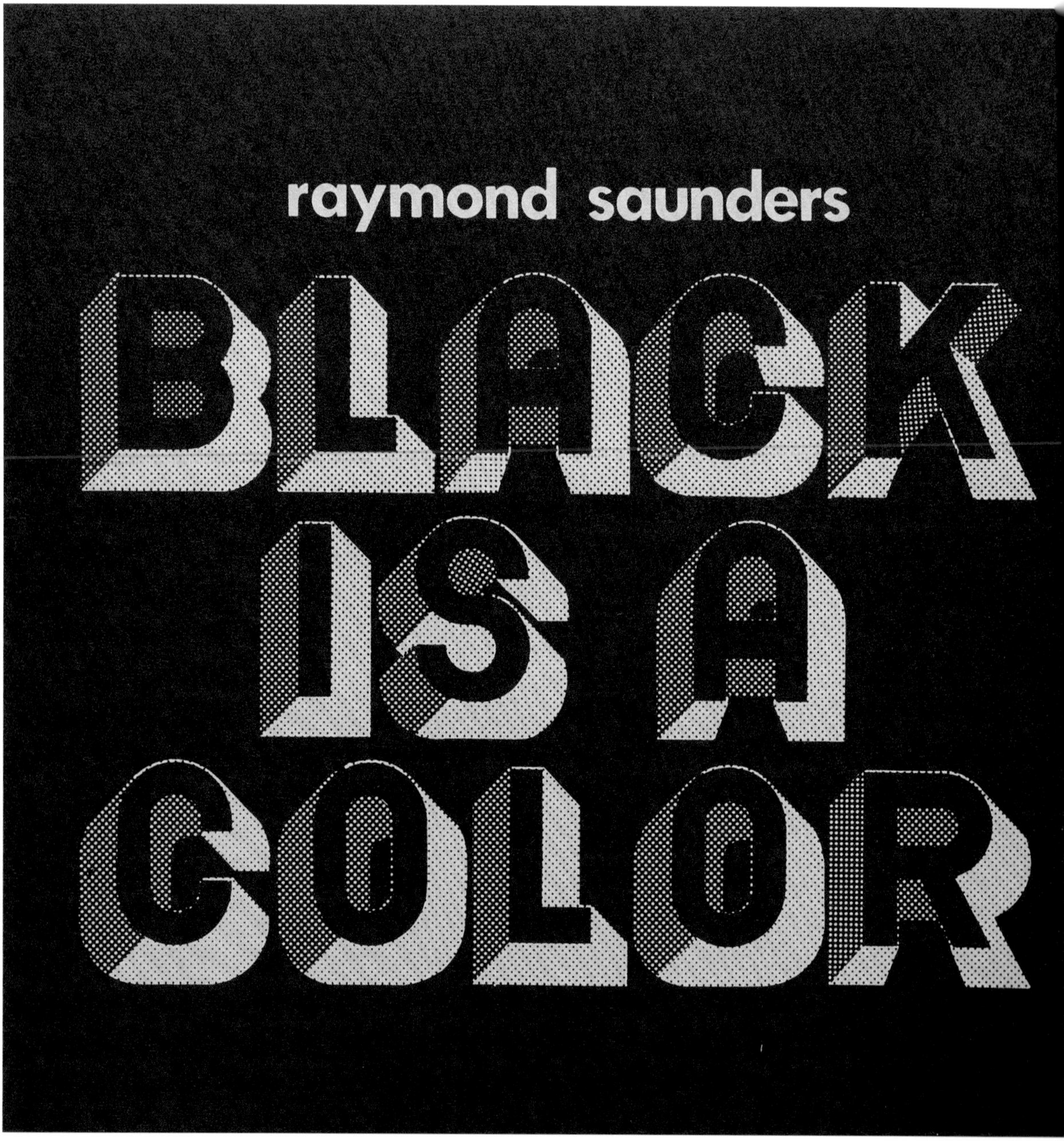
raymond saunders
BLACK
IS A
COLOR

arts magazine published an article (may, 1967) in which it claims that poet-novelist ishmael reed has "documented" the "explosive black arts movement." mr. reed himself, if the title he chose denotes his aim, assumed the heroic role of black artist's champion, hipping it through the musty debris of hypocrisy and lies, into the clear light of newly-daring truth, where a spade can at last be called a spade.

yet, after this one man takes it upon himself to call it a fucking shovel, we know nothing more about the spade at the end of his tirade than we did at the outset.

what's he trying to prove? all he says has been said before, with the same pitiful and dangerous inadequacy. on the one hand, he seems to be trying to support the black artist's cause, while on the other he lumps black artists, of which he names a mere handful, into one bag and throttles them with a string of almost incoherent hippishness.

more flip than hip, his diatribe may have been meant to give the black artist a lift, but glib and shallow as it is, the net result is far more degrading of the black man and artist than any mute rejection by a museum selection board (one of mr. reed's bones of contention).

using hip-talk as a kind of tribal mumbo-jumbo, he sets the black arts outside the current of art as a whole, and in so doing he does the black artist a grave injustice.

hip-talk is a language, effective when it illustrates something of human substance, but where is the substance of this subjective, emotional outburst, it all seems as futile and paradoxical as the demonstrations of those "half-way" young hippies who advance on their opponents shouting: "love, love, love!" while pelting them with rotten eggs.

who's supposed to be saving who? mr. reed appears to propose that the black arts should save america, as though the act of salvation were a function of some rarefied preservation hall, and the black artist a species of new orleans entertainer, who can "make america swing again." but let's face it — when has america ever swung? and why should it be the black man's responsibility?

this is a psuedo-messianic concept that mr. reed is free to subscribe to, but what makes him think he qualifies as a spokesman for black artists? is it because he's black — or because he's an artist? he doesn't seem at all sure in what measure the two are one, and the ambivalence of his approach renders his spade-calling curiously unconvincing.

apart from a disproportionate quotation from leroi jones, mr. reed's "documentation" of black arts is famishingly sparse. black music is harnessed to archie shepp, albert ayler and sun ra, latching on to examples of a certain discernible success, but what of the countless unsung but brilliant black musicians whom mr. reed blithely ignores? and, though he uses an interesting photograph of sun ra to illustrate his article, mr. reed gives mere caption-mention to the photographer himself, and focuses no attention whatever on the growing band of vital black photographic artists in america, of whom charles shabacon is just one member, albeit a highly creative one.

in approaching so vast a subject as the black arts, whose scope far outreaches the limits imposed upon him by the editorial requirements of arts magazine, it would appear that mr. reed bit off more than he could chew. but this is no excuse for launching into so sadly haphazard and scrappy an exposition, while still retaining an ambitious title-promise beyond his capacity to fulfill.

what is more disturbing, however, is mr. reed's assumption that success must be equated with material gain; that uptown and money spell success for all. uptown is no "open-sesame" to artistic fulfillment, nor is money, as mr. reed appears to believe. uptown is the art marketplace, but who says it's the art scene? what are we dealing with here, anyway — art or a popularity contest?

material success is extremely desirable, but it's a dangerous criterion by which to measure artistic achievement. mr. reed seems to have fallen into the trap, adding insult to injury by dragging art through the mud of socio-political antagonism. the 'we is all'mericans' bit, to which he so strongly objects, is beside the point. 'we is all artists' seems more akin to the subject.

i am an artist; examples of my work can be seen in american museums; i have been the recipient of national awards; i have just enjoyed the 'priviledge' of my fourth one-man show at an uptown gallery (reviewed p.60 of arts magazine, may, 1967); and i also happen to be black. i fail to see any profound significance in the mere conjunction of these circumstances. yet, if one is to take mr. reed's sweeping statements as criteria, it must be assumed that i am a phenomenal success. bullshit!

what are the true criteria for success, in terms of the individual artist's aspirations? is he committed merely to the realization of a stereotyped image of the artist who's "arrived," crowned with the laurels of popular acclaim; assured of a constantly re-plumped bankroll and entree into the inner sanctums of madison avenue (which seems to be mr. reed's contention), or is it rather that the artist is committed to respond to the unending challenge of his very nature as a creative person, and to discover the depth, width, range of his own unique vision as an artist, and, hopefully, as a human being?

i'm not here to play to the gallery. i am not responsible for anyone's entertainment. i am responsible for being as fully myself, as man and artist, as i possibly can be, while allowing myself to hope that in the effort some light, some love, some beauty may be shed upon the world, and perhaps some inequities put right.

every creative person is subject to periods of profound discouragement, when denied recognition of the vision he embodies in his work. the denial seems to constitute a rejection not only of his work but of all he is striving to be. in his angry rebellion, he may well lash out at the first apparent obstacle —which can easily take the form of some highly publicized social or political defect in his environment. it's a plausible explanation for some deadlock in his progress. it can be a very real one too, in which case his anger is perfectly valid. but when anger, a human reaction, gets syphoned off into serving merely as a political expedient, it is robbed of genuine humanity, and is useless as inspiration to the artist as a man.

some angry artists are using their arts as political tools, instead of vehicles of free expression. using his art and his anger in such a way, the artist makes himself a mere peddler, when he might be a prophet.

every artist, regardless of his skin color, may suffer from the vagaries of museum selection boards. confusing this age-old problem with questions of race is just casting about for a scapegoat, when the real culprit — the dragging, grinding mechanism of american social and cultural awareness gets clean away, unchallenged. all americans are culturally deprived, not just black americans.

the prevailing system repeats its sterile terms of reference for success (to which mr. reed himself, oddly enough, seems to subscribe). the image that fits into those terms may not easily be stretched to include the black artist, particularly if he claims his blackness as the reason for his achievement. but the basic question is, does the black artist, or any other artist for that matter, want to mold himself to this prescribed, but worn and shabby image in any case?

the image itself is the result of distortions in human society, stemming from deprivation, but this is the plight of every man. the underdog, the low man on the totem pole in this society, will continue to suffer because of the blindness and selfishness of society's leaders. this is nothing new, and what has this got to do with art itself, or the real quality of the artist?

art projects beyond race and color; beyond america. it is universal, and americans — black, white or whatever — have no exclusive rights on it.

when are americans going to wake up to the fact that america is not the world, nor the cultural center of it. there's a big, big world out there, where people of all colors are living; yearning, competing, suffering, reaching out (and some succeeding) with every turn of the earth.

no one can honestly deny the existence of discrimination and oppression against black people (and black artist, by extention) in america, but the black man is not the only human being ever to have suffered these ills. counter-racism, hyper-awareness of difference or separateness arising within the black artist himself, is just as destructive to his work — and his life — as the threat of white prejudice coming at him from outside.

pessimism is fatal to artistic development. perpetual anger deprives it of movement. an artist who is always harping upon resistance, discrimination, opposition, besides being a drag, eventually plays right into the hands of the politicians he claims to despise — and is held there, unwittingly (and witlessly) reviving slavery in another form. For the artist this is aesthetic atrophy.

certainly the american black artist is in a unique position to express certain aspects of the current american scene, both negative and positive, but if he restricts himself to these alone, he may risk becoming a mere cypher, a walking protest, a politically prescribed stereotype, negating his own mystery, and allowing himself to be shuffled off into an arid overall mystique. the indiscriminate association of race with art, on any level — social or imaginative — is destructive.

isolationism: us-against-the-world, is stultifying. it undermines the very emancipation the black man so deeply desires, and to which he is entitled. us-coming-out-into and becoming-a-part-of a wider reality — becoming what we really are — is what will truly free us.

in america, black is bound to black not so much by color or racial characteristics, as by shared experience, social and cultural. this is the same in any rarefied social (or racial) enclave, but "no man is an island, entire of itself." the artist deals with the human condition. he is "involved in mankind." this is as valid for the black artist as any other. he uses his heart, his eyes, his mind as interpreters of his own deep vision of himself, and the world as it is reflected in those depths.

if he wants to get out there; if he really wants to know, there is nothing that can stop him. a hell of a lot depends upon his curiosity and his own determination. the artist can only realize himself through active effort to be what he really is.

both as artist and as human being he can learn to channel his energy, rather than expend it in futile protest. he has to learn the lie of the land around him, and where he can cut through. he has to send his mind, his emotions, his eyes ranging across the whole field of vision open to him, probing its boundaries to find where he can push them further and further out.

the creative imagination is his channel, but it has to be dug (painfully slowly sometimes, as it has been throughout history) through the resisting barriers of established convention; then it can bring its new, irrigating force to the parched and thirsting desert of cultural and spiritual backwardness.

but the artist doesn't exist for the sole purpose of changing the world.

each artist has to do for himself what is necessary for his own development, fulfilling himself as an individual, not as one of a herd. he has to enter into the total experience of himself and his vision, which transcends the cramped boundaries of any stereotype—angry or otherwise. it is a risk, but life is full of risks, if you're going to live at all. living is being hurt, happy, sad.

humility is frowned upon these days, yet the very immensity, complexity and universality of art should be a reminder to the artist that he cannot be the be-all-and-end-all. the pressures and oppressions the black man has so triumphantly endured could be translated into positive strength that will persist in the teeth of rejection, refusing to be eliminated. this goes for the black artist too.

in order to be recognized and accepted, does the black artist have to depend upon the uptown critic or the politico-sociologist to define the meaning of his own experience? it is high time that the black artist make his own rejection of misguided, inadequate — if not out-and-out dishonest — interpreters of his condition. from the depths of his own integrity he has to believe in his capacity to distinguish the real from the false — and to recognize manipulators when they try to use him.

racial hang-ups are extraneous to art. no artist can afford to let them obscure what runs through all art — the living root and the ever-growing aesthetic record of human spiritual and intellectual experience. can't we get clear of these degrading limitations, and recognize the wider reality of art, where color is the means and not the end?

raymond saunders

exhibiting artist,
terry dintenfass gallery, new york city

professor,
california state college at hayward

part of this article was previously published
in arts magazine, june, 1967

design: e. marc treib

Acknowledgments

For their inestimably helpful counsel and readings of the manuscript, I wish to thank Julia Bryan-Wilson, Kris Cohen, Douglas Crimp, Rachel Haidu, Anna Lee, Glenn Ligon, Carmen Merport, Fred Moten, and Hamza Walker. Particular conversations about this book's subjects constituted major events in the improvement of the ideas and formulations presented here; for these, I thank Elizabeth Alexander, Geri Aramanda, Lauren Berlant, Yve Alain-Bois, Peter Bradley, David Breslin, Malcolm Bull, Steve Cannon, Tom Crow, Lisa Corrine Davis, Lisa Dorin, Anita Duquette, Mel Edwards, Fred Eversley, Jonathan Fine, Helen Fosdick, Hal Foster, Michael Fried, Christopher Heuer, Melissa Horn, Jonathan Katz, Jacqueline Lichtenstein, Mara Kearney Loving, Rosalind Krauss, Jeremy Melius, Eric Michaud, Julian Myers, Senga Nengudi, Molly Nesbit, Howardena Pindell, Mark Reinhardt, Lowery Stokes Sims, Howard Singerman, Richard Taws, Anne Wagner, Amy Whitaker, Jack Whitten, William T. Williams, and Sebastian Zeidler. Dan Cohen, Art Evans, Deb Fehr, Julia Silverman, Katie Steiner, Cody Mejeur, and Cy Weisman provided research and image procurement assistance and made all the difference thereby. Many artists, collectors, galleries, and museums—too many to list here—were responsive and generous in providing images. Raymond Saunders was exceedingly gracious to permit the reproduction in full of *Black Is a Color*. Throughout the production of this book, Susan Bielstein's editing was sympathetic and exacting, while Anthony Burton, Ruth Goring, and James Toftness provided critical and perceptive support. Long before it became a production, this book was as projects in gestation tend to be: an inchoate cluster of responses and intentions. What stopped me abandoning the project at a couple of singularly low points were the momentum and exhilaration continually regenerated in ongoing dialogue with Matthew Jesse Jackson. Matthew's is always a strong nearness, irrespective of location.

Index

Darby English is the Carl Darling Buck Professor of Art History at the University of Chicago.

The University of Chicago Press, Chicago 60637
The University of Chicago Press, Ltd., London

Printed in China

25 24 23 22 21 20 19 18 17 16 1 2 3 4 5

ISBN-13: 978-0-226-13105-4 (cloth)
ISBN-13: 978-0-226-27473-7 (e-book)
DOI: 10.7208/chicago/9780226274737.001.0001

This publication is made possible in part by support from the National Endowment for the Humanities and the Creative Capital | Andy Warhol Foundation Arts Writers Grant Program. Any views, findings, conclusions, or recommendations expressed in this publication do not necessarily reflect those of the National Endowment for the Humanities.

Library of Congress Cataloging-in-Publication Data

Names: English, Darby, 1974– author.
Title: 1971: a year in the life of color / Darby English.
Description: Chicago ; London : The University of Chicago Press, 2016. | Includes bibliographical references and index.
Identifiers: LCCN 2016012924 | ISBN 9780226131054 (cloth : alk. paper) | ISBN 9780226274737 (e-book)
Subjects: LCSH: African American art—United States—Exhibitions—History. | Art, Abstract—United States—Exhibitions—History. | Art, American—20th century—Exhibitions—History. | Contemporary Black Artists in America (Exhibition) (1971 : New York, N.Y.) | De Luxe Show (Exhibition) (1971 : Houston, Tex.) | Art and race. | Art and society—United States. | Modernism (Art)—Social aspects—United States. | Nineteen seventy-one, A.D.
Classification: LCC N6538.N5 E538 2016 | DDC 700.89/96073—dc23 LC record available at http://lccn.loc.gov/2016012924

♾ This paper meets the requirements of ANSI/NISO Z39.48-1992 (Permanence of Paper).